THE ENCYCLOPEDIA OF
MODEL
RAILWAY

THE ENCYCLOPEDIA OF
MODEL
RAILWAYS

OCTOPUS

First published 1979 by
Octopus Books Limited
59 Grosvenor Street
London W1

ISBN 0 7064 0989 2

Produced by Mandarin Publishers Limited
22a Westlands Road,
Quarry Bay, Hong Kong

Printed in Italy by New Interlitho S.p.A. - Milan

Contents

Contributors

Lyn D. Brooks

Bruce A. Chubb

The Rev. Peter Denny

Harry Drummond

Norman Eagles

Rolf Ertmer

Bob Essery

Cyril J. Freezer

Ray Hamilton

Robert D. Hegge

Michael R. Hoar

David Jenkinson

Don Jones

Martin Levy

John Paske

Geoff Pember

John Porter

Frank Roomes

Paul Stapleton

Edward Templeton

Vivien Thompson

Bill Vaughn

Jerry Veit

Cliff Young

Edited and Designed by
Terry Allen Designs Limited

Endpapers: The North American Lines, part of a magnificent layout designed and built by John E. Porter.

Half title page: A Maffei Pacific from a live steam garden layout by J. Van Reimsdyjk.

Title page: A superb model by Guy Williams of the *King George V* No. 6000. It is finished in the livery of 1935, when it was repainted for the new Centenary Cornish Riviera Limited.

Contents: Union Pacific's aptly-named 'Big Boy', the largest steam locomotive built, reproduced in Japanese brass.

Contributors: Donald Santel's Ohio, Michigan & South Shore Railroad model captures the atmosphere of the area, and its rugged terrain, with startling realism.

This page: Another view of the Japanese brass model of Union Pacific's 'Big Boy', reproduced in exquisite detail and fitted with mechanical stoker.

Foreword

That men should make models of anything is nothing new.
That men should wish to model transport objects is equally
unremarkable; for applied technology is a subject which has
always been found fascinating by many people. But that men
should wish to model one aspect of transport – namely
railways – in such numbers as to make the hobby second only
to angling in the United Kingdom (if statistics are to be
believed) is a phenomenon worthy of investigation – hence
this encyclopaedia.

Over the years, model railways have evolved into an
immensely complex subject embracing a great variety of sub-
specialisations. Controversy between adherents of different
systems and standards is not unknown – indeed it can be said
to have been the beneficial life blood in those many cases
where progress has evolved from conflict. This book, by
drawing on the talents of many eminent exponents of the art,
draws the essential threads together.

As a modeller myself I have long felt the need for a general
guide to model railways which explains, especially to those
less familiar with the subject, the broad spectrum of the
hobby in a concise yet adult and readable way.

D. Jenkinson B.Sc.
Head of Education & Research
National Railway Museum
May 1979

REVIEW
OF THE HOBBY

At a level crossing late at night, a coach halted to await the passing of a train. Out of the dark and drizzling rain loomed the massive bulk of a steam locomotive, working steadily and noisily upgrade with a heavy coal train, and for a few moments the fierce red glow from the firebox gave the passengers in the coach a lurid glimpse of the crew as they toiled on the footplate. As the locomotive passed out of sight around the curve, its steady exhaust beat faded, giving way to the rhythmic thudding of steel wheels on steel rail as the wagons filed by.

Silent and unannounced, a single banking engine came drifting swiftly down the gradient and over the crossing, while the solid shadows of the wagons kept rolling slowly by. At last the seemingly endless procession of coal wagons was brought to a close as another banking engine appeared, struggling manfully in the rear amid clouds of steam and smoke. As it too passed away into the night, the crossing bells rang, the barriers lifted and the coach continued on its way.

To most of the passengers in the coach, this interlude was simply an unforseen and unwelcome interruption in their journey, but to the author it was pure magic. This is atmosphere – all railways have it, even those which abandoned steam years ago – and it is this which many modellers strive to capture in their models.

The lure of the full-size railway is what in the first place draws many people to the model railway hobby. It is at the intangible level of the emotions that the railway makes its strongest appeal, although the technological and historical aspects are undeniably full of interest.

A Millie class 15a 4-8-2- of the South African
Railways circa 1975 at De Aar.

The Earliest Models

The story of railway modelling is a long and curious one, going back as far as the history of railways themselves.

Technical modelling began long before the railway age. In the days of the wooden-walled navy, making an accurate model was often the only way that a ship designer could indicate to the board of admiralty exactly how a new design of vessel would appear – since his exalted customers frequently had no great ability to read technical drawings.

It is more than likely that railway modelling started in just such a fashion. In the early days of Britain's railways, one of the pioneer engineers, Timothy Hackworth, certainly made models of his proposed locomotives, and as time went by, the most beautiful and elaborate models were created, based on various locomotive designs – of which some were successful and some abortive. Happily, many of these early models survive in museums and private collections. As the railway networks spread, both in scope and geographical extent, there gradually grew up a desire to possess miniature representations of existing locomotives; and thus began a tradition which has lasted until the present day.

Craftsmen and Toymakers

One basic law is as true now as it has always been – there are always more potential buyers for finished models than there are craftsmen who can make their own. From the early days of the hobby there has been a strong commercial manufacturing element ready to satisfy this demand.

By the late 19th century, a number of firms had begun catering for what can loosely be called the 'ready-to-run' purchaser – the person who wants to be able to go into a shop, buy his model, and use it. First in the field were the toymakers of Germany – firms like Märklin and Bing, who developed the art of tinplate modelling to such a high degree that their early examples now command astronomical prices in the world of the auction salesrooms. Other names from this period are Ives of North America and Carette – a Frenchman who set up business in Nüremberg because of the availability of skilled German craftsmen. In Britain, early in the 20th century, W.J. Bassett-Lowke and, later, Frank Hornby, became household names.

Today, some of these names still survive – after a multiplicity of takeovers – while there have also been later arrivals such as Fleischmann and Rivarossi, Lima and Arnold. Complementary to the major manufac-

An 'Ives Toys' catalogue circa mid 1920s.

turers of complete model railway systems, there are now hundreds of smaller firms which cater for more specialized requirements.

As a result of these developments, railway modellers are in the fortunate position of having thriving trade support for almost every imaginable aspect of their hobby. Starting with the overt commercial manufacturer, whose output can be measured in thousands of finished units and whose work force may be lavish, there is at the other end of the scale the individual craftsman, working purely on a commission basis. His models will be limited in number, he may only accept work which appeals to him, and he may virtually command his own price if he is so minded. Many of these people stumbled into commercial model making almost by accident, as a by-product of their own private modelling activities.

The craftsman/modeller is one of the most significant elements in the model railway business, yet his place is difficult to categorize. At one extreme one finds him as the pattern maker for one of the commercial organizations while at the other he will be found creating exquisite miniatures purely for his own satisfaction. Throughout the history of the hobby he has set the standards which others have tried to emulate. On many occasions the commercial world has been only too happy to learn from these skilled individuals, incorporating some of their ideas in the next generation of

ready-to-run models and thereby bringing about an improvement of standards.

In the early days, that part of the hobby which now forms the mainstream of railway modelling, namely the attempt to model the railway scene as a whole, hardly existed at all. With the exception of high quality, expensive models, the choice of equipment was virtually confined to the toy trade. Although there were many good things, there were many crudities as well. It took time for the concept of accurate modelling of the total scene to develop and for a long time the trade was unwilling to espouse this cause.

In consequence, many purchasers of ready-to-run equipment began to turn their minds to the idea of supplementing commercial models with their own handiwork, be it extra coaches and wagons or additions to scenery. Thus gradually the middle ground between purely *making* on the one hand and purely *acquiring* on the other, was invaded by an increasing number of people who did a bit of both – the forerunners of today's railway modellers.

Strange as it may seem, there is no such person as the typical railway modeller. The only common bond which modellers share is simply a desire to own some kind of miniature replica of some chosen part of the world of railways. Since that world is in itself so varied, it is not surprising to find that model railway devotees display a similar degree of diversity.

It took Geoff Pember 700 hours to scratch-build this Great Eastern Railways 4-2-2 with full rivet detail.

First Principles

As with all worthwhile pursuits, the model railway hobby repays thought, consideration and planning. Assuming that an interest in full-size railways is the likely first step to becoming involved with model railways, the initial inspiration may ultimately determine the type of layout the modeller builds. So a good way for him to start would be to ask himself what exactly it is about prototype railways that appeals most strongly to him. Are, for example, his interests mainly mechanical or aesthetic? Does his enthusiasm embrace the whole field of railways or does it focus on such things as locomotives and coaches? It may be that he likes the railways at a particular period in their development, of a certain part of the world, or even a specific railway company.

From these and other similar considerations, the modeller should be able to narrow the choice down to an achievable object. But once having decided what his priorities are as far as the prototype, there are three further questions of importance to consider: what scale of model is wanted, what standard of model is desired, and how much money is available? No-one but the modeller himself can provide the answers to these questions; but the answers are probably easier for him to find if he is fully aware of the 'pros and cons' of the various options open to him.

Many newcomers to the model railway hobby are possessed by an understandable urge to get something running, in the hope that by some form of magic alchemy all will turn out well in the end. For the fortunate few it may, but if the truly outstanding examples of model railway building are examined, they tend to reflect a singleminded determination on the part of the builder to pursue particular objectives. In a curious sort of way, the apparent straitjackets into which many modellers willingly fasten themselves turn out to be a wide frame of reference when actually developed.

The move towards more coherently planned model railways dates back to the 1930s and 1940s, when railway modelling, as opposed to merely assembling train sets, began to take form. One of the real pioneers in this field was a British clergyman, Edward Beal. He, perhaps more than anyone else, began to encourage a greater pursuit of realism in the total scene. His output of books, articles and good advice was formidable, and his influence profound. To the modern enthusiast, some of his ideas may now seem a little strange or, possibly, out of tune with present circumstances. But one quotation from a book he wrote in 1955 should be writ large above every modeller's work table: 'Railway modelling is a pleasure rather than a fad, and should be free from the pedantry which dictates. Yet our aim in this writing is to indicate a consistent course of action'.

The pursuing of a consistent course of action without descending into pedantry is perhaps the key to successful modelling, and therefore it is sound advice to make an early decision regarding the approach to be adopted. The choice is bewildering, but in the pages that follow, an attempt is made to classify the various options.

From the Leeds Model Co., the LNER 0-6-2- Tank Class N No. 31672 with die-cast body.

Scale and Gauge

In the whole vocabulary of model railways there are no two more misunderstood and wrongly used words than 'scale' and 'gauge'. Essentially, the word 'scale' relates to the ratio in size between model and prototype, expressed as some form of direct comparison. It can be stated as a common fraction (e.g. 1/30), a ratio (e.g. 76:1), or a written statement (e.g. one quarter inch equals one foot). It does not matter how it is expressed, its purpose is to convey an exact dimensional relationship.

'Gauge' is the word which relates to the distance between the running rails on the railway track itself. There are many different gauges to be found on the world's railways but they all fall into one of three basic categories: broad gauge, standard gauge, and narrow gauge. Historically, the prefix 'standard' became associated with George Stephenson's original track width of four feet eight and a half inches (1,435mm), which was then first used by the Romans for horse-drawn carts and chariots. Railways with wider gauges than this – e.g. the many Indian railways with five foot six inch guage (1,676mm) – became known as 'broad gauge', while track widths below 4′8½″ such as those of the many metre gauge systems of the world were 'narrow gauge'. Most of the world's major railway systems have adopted the standard gauge, but there are many broad and narrow gauge systems too.

So far the story, while not exactly simple, is at least unambiguous. It is when translating it into model terms that scale and gauge become intermixed, because so

Fullsize comparisons can be made from this diagram, which shows sizes, gauge/scale and track gauge equivalents.

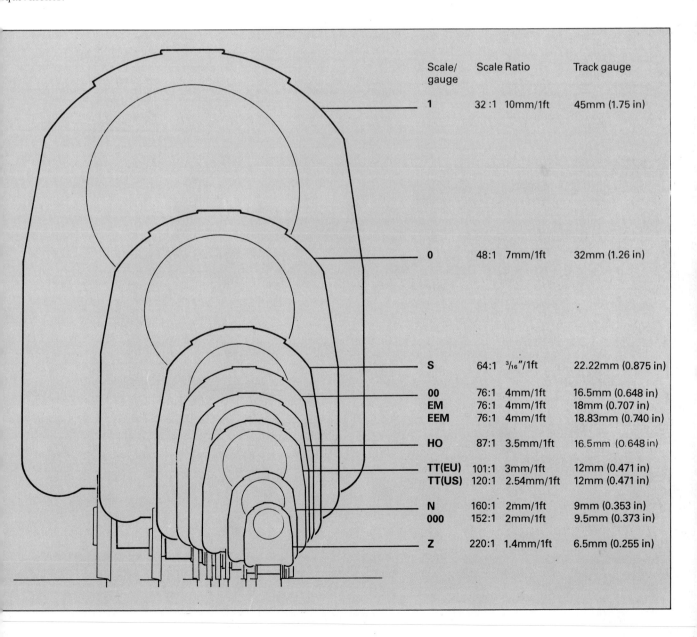

Scale/ gauge	Scale Ratio		Track gauge
1	32 :1	10mm/1ft	45mm (1.75 in)
0	48:1	7mm/1ft	32mm (1.26 in)
S	64:1	³/₁₆″/1ft	22.22mm (0.875 in)
00	76:1	4mm/1ft	16.5mm (0.648 in)
EM	76:1	4mm/1ft	18mm (0.707 in)
EEM	76:1	4mm/1ft	18.83mm (0.740 in)
HO	87:1	3.5mm/1ft	16.5mm (0.648 in)
TT(EU)	101:1	3mm/1ft	12mm (0.471 in)
TT(US)	120:1	2.54mm/1ft	12mm (0.471 in)
N	160:1	2mm/1ft	9mm (0.353 in)
000	152:1	2mm/1ft	9.5mm (0.373 in)
Z	220:1	1.4mm/1ft	6.5mm (0.255 in)

many different miniature gauges have been adopted by the modellers themselves. In model terms these are used not so much to define the form of prototype railway being modelled, but more to fix the scale in which the model will be made.

A man with a lot of space at his disposal might choose a gauge of $1\frac{3}{4}''$ (45mm) in order to make models in a scale of $\frac{3}{8}''$ to one foot. Another may adopt a gauge of 9mm ($\frac{1}{3}''$) between rails on which he could operate models of precisely the same prototype trains, but on a much reduced scale in order to fit a smaller site. Thus, in modelling terms, the gauge adopted by the modeller frequently hints at the scale dimensions of his models.

Complications may arise in view of the fact that gauge can vary in both the model and the prototype. For example, in model terms it is possible to run both a standard and a narrow gauge locomotive on a track of say 9mm gauge, but the narrow gauge locomotive would have to be modelled to a noticeably larger scale.

A second curiosity, particularly common in Britain, is the odd habit of mixing up imperial and metric measurements, often throwing in a few ratios for good measure! Thus we find that two of the most popular

scales adopted in Britain are 4mm to one foot, and 7mm to one foot. A further complication is the compatibility of gauge and scale.

When George Stephenson adopted $4'\ 8\frac{1}{2}''$ as the standard gauge for railway construction, he chose just about the most awkward dimension possible as far as future railway modellers were concerned. Exact scale reduction of this track gauge usually produces a quite unworkable figure, and so it is small wonder that almost from the start modellers have rounded up, or rounded down, the correct value for the gauge. Usually the difference is only marginal, but in some instances the discrepancy can be wide enough to be significant.

From this divergence has stemmed the phrases 'fine scale' and 'coarse scale'. For example, if a model is an exact miniature replica of the prototype in all its aspects, then it is often referred to as being fine scale. A somewhat crude representation on the other hand, although possibly still recognizable as a model of a particular prototype, would be categorized as coarse scale if the departures from accurate scale values were too great.

Reverting to the essential issue of scale and gauge, it

A gauge 1 version of the class 80 0-6-0 locomotive, from Märklin, used for shunting and branch line work.

is important that the modeller has a reasonably clear idea of the different options, because if he is to own or make anything at all resembling a working model railway he must eventually choose one of the many scale/gauge combinations available. In theory, of course, he could choose to model in any scale he liked, and a few modellers do just this; but over the years particular ratios have achieved a measure of both national and global standardization and the commercial makers, large and small, tend to stick to these values. It would be far too long a story to recount the detailed history and evolution of each standard, but it is useful to enumerate them for the sake of clarity. Each has acquired a popular name, and these names will be used here. In the first instance it should be assumed that a standard gauge prototype is being modelled – the variation of non-standard gauges will be covered afterwards.

Gauge 1

With but a few exceptions, gauge 1 is the largest size adopted by modellers who wish to make a complete model railway as opposed to an individual model. It can be taken to mark the dividing line between model railways and miniature railway engineering. The gauge 1 track gauge is $1\frac{3}{4}''$ (45mm) and the accurate linear scale of models is $\frac{3}{8}''$ equals one foot (ratio 32:1), or, more commonly in recent years, 10mm to one foot. This latter gives a scale ratio of approximately 30:1, a less correct value.

Gauge O

This gauge started as $1\frac{1}{4}''$ (31.75mm) but, more recently, has been standardized at 32mm. The linear scale is 7mm to one foot (ratio 43:1). Mathematical readers will at once realize both the hybrid nature of these values and, possibly, their inaccuracies too. An alternative scale of $\frac{1}{4}''$ to one foot (ratio 48:1) is fairly common for gauge O, and is widely used in North America. To be strictly accurate, when working in the 7mm to one foot scale a more correct gauge would be 33mm, and several British workers have adopted this value – often referred to as 'Scaleseven' to distinguish it from traditional gauge O. It is the smallest practical gauge for live steam operation, although it has been done experimentally in the smaller gauges.

Only 1,000 models were made of Pocher's Bayard 2-2-2 which served the Italian Napoli–Portico route from 1839.

S Gauge

This gauge is exactly half the size of gauge I and has possibly the most perfectly logical and accurate set of standards in the hobby. It is an entirely non-metric size: the track gauge is $\frac{7}{8}''$, the linear scale $\frac{3}{16}''$ to one foot, and the scale ratio 64:1. Apart from North America, where S gauge has a reasonable following, there is no real trade support for this scale, and models, perforce, are predominantly hand-made. 'S' stands for 'seven', 'sixteenths' and 'sixty-fourths', all important dimensions in this gauge.

HO Gauge

Literally 'half O', this gauge dates from the 1920s and the early attempts to produce smaller size commercial model railways. In most countries other than Britain, which paradoxically was the country of origin, HO has become the most popular model gauge. The gauge itself is 16.5mm (0.65''), the scale 3.5mm to one foot, and the scale ratio 87:1. These are very accurate values, although some manufacturers have, over the years, deviated a little from the strict 87:1 value.

OO Gauge

This, the most popular British standard, is also the most hybrid and illogical. The track gauge is 16.5mm – exactly the same as HO – but the scale is different, being 4mm to one foot (ratio 76:1). This ratio makes the model track gauge of 16.5mm proportionally seven inches narrower than the correct prototype gauge of 4' 8½''.

The origins of OO are older than HO and it is an easier linear dimension in which to work. Moreover, when commercial models were first produced for HO gauge, it was found difficult to fit the comparatively bulky electric motors in use at that time into models of British outline and still retain the 87:1 scale ratio. This was because British full-size rolling stock was rather small compared to its American and European counterparts, being built to a more restricted loading gauge. In consequence, many manufacturers elected to increase their linear scale for British models to the older established 4mm to one foot standard, while also retaining 16.5mm gauge to ensure running compatibility with HO. The age of miniaturization had not yet dawned, and by the time it was possible to make British outline models to correct HO proportions, 4mm to one foot scale had established too strong a foothold to be ousted from popularity. One consolation is that at least OO and HO models will run on the same track.

EM Gauge

Stemming from this confusion, three derivatives of standard OO gauge have evolved in Britain and North America, all embodying an increase in track gauge to achieve a correct scale value for the 76:1 linear ratio. In North America the term 'OO' is applied uniquely to 76:1 ratio models running on 19mm gauge track. This scale/gauge combination has only a minority following, but some fine models exist.

In Britain the move to widen the gauge has taken two stages. Shortly after the Second World War, some modellers adopted the simple expedient of moving the

18

existing wheels of OO models out on their axles as far as they would go, and making new track to suit this revised dimension. This resulted in a track gauge of 18mm (18.25mm in its more developed form), known as EM. In time this developed and it still enjoys a wide following. However, during the 1960s the search for still better wheel and track standards led to the adoption of a virtually accurate 18.83mm gauge for 4mm scale models. This is known in Britain as either Protofour or Scalefour depending on the precise system followed. For the moment this is where the vexed question of 4mm to the foot scale rests!

TT Gauge

Literally 'table-top' – this standard is again a little variable. The 12mm (0.47″) gauge is American inspired and uses a fairly accurate scale ratio of 120:1. However, in Britain – for much the same reasons as with OO/HO – the few manufacturers who offered items in this scale adopted 3mm to one foot as the linear scale (a ratio of 100:1 and even more distorted than OO). The British side has suffered something of an eclipse compared to America, where TT gauge is still quite widely used. In Britain, a similar modification of TT was carried out in order to retain the 3mm to one foot scale and this resulted in a wider gauge which is used by a small number of devotees.

N Gauge

N stands for nine – referring to the 9mm (0.35″) track gauge of this increasingly important modern standard which rocketed into prominence during the 1960s. After HO/OO it is unquestionably the most popular model railway gauge. The scale ratio is 160:1 for European and North American prototypes, but once again the British are different, favouring a 2mm equals one foot scale (actually about 148:1) for commercial models. There is also in Britain a small but flourishing following for 2mm equals one foot scale utilizing 9.5mm gauge track. As with the variants of OO and TT gauges, this more accurate ratio is the prerogative of the more dedicated fine-scale modellers.

Z Gauge

This micro/miniature size with its tiny 6mm (0.24″) track gauge has been established commercially by Marklin, using mainly German prototypes.

Opposite: OO gauge GWR 'Hall' class 4-6-0 from Hornby in imaginery livery and named 'Lord Westwood'.

Below: Märklin's Z gauge model of the Deutsche Bundesbahn 0-6-0 shunter locomotive which was in service for 40 years until 1968.

Broad and Narrow Gauge

It is now necessary to clarify the situation for the modellers of broad and narrow gauges. One common solution is to take an existing gauge and evolve a correct linear ratio to suit it. For example, a linear scale of 6mm equals one foot would produce a scale exactly compatible with TT gauge track (12mm) for a model of a two foot gauge railway, thus avoiding the need for the modeller to make his own track.

Even more convenient is the situation in which a common linear scale can be combined with an equally common gauge. Thus, 4mm scale models on TT gauge track are exactly correct for 3′ gauge prototypes; while a 7mm scale model on HO gauge track is a not too unreasonable compromise for a 2′ 6″ gauge prototype.

Some intriguing new titles have been coined for some of the more successful narrow gauge systems. If taken a step at a time, the seemingly complex nomenclature makes itself clear, viz: 'HOn3'. This should be read as HO size (the HO now referring to the scale ratio 87:1) followed by 'n' denoting narrow gauge, while the '3'

refers to the three foot gauge of the prototype. In model form this results in 87:1 scale models running on 10.5mm gauge track – a very popular combination among North American modellers since the USA had at one time a considerable mileage of 3′ gauge railroads.

The above example shows how time and usage have imparted scale connotations to the names originally devised purely for gauges. It is quite common to hear phrases like 'HO scale' and the like. Strictly speaking, these are nonsense phrases but, amazingly, they rarely seem to cause any confusion – even though they may irritate the linguistic purists!

The choice of scale/ratio adopted by the modeller will, to a considerable extent, be influenced by the space at his disposal, the sort of layout he wants to build and other practical considerations which are covered in the next chapter. So at this point we will leave the matter. However, following on from a consideration of scale and gauge, it is equally necessary now to give thought to the question of modelling standards and the problems that can arise.

A 3012 Sante Fe 2-10-2 manufactured by Westside, passing a Heisler Pacific Fast Mail model on the North. American Lines layout.

Modelling Standards

Let it be said from the outset that it is quite impossible to make a railway model which is totally perfect, in the sense that every single working part is reduced to a constant scale. Certain things cannot be scaled down, a point which some less tolerant souls tend to forget in their pursuit of absolute fidelity to prototype.

Even on the full-size railway, working tolerances are often extremely precise, and the physical separation between individual components can sometimes be very small indeed. There are, at the British National Railway Museum, two preserved 4-4-2 express locomotives from the old Great Northern Railway, whose main driving axles are set so close together that it is almost impossible to insert a finger between the flanges of the leading and trailing wheels. This dimension of only 12.5mm ($\frac{1}{2}''$) would reduce to an impossibly small working tolerance of less than 0.01mm (0.005″) in 4mm scale. What chance does the modeller have when the true working tolerance itself is measured in less than one millimetre? The answer is compromise.

Another area in which the modeller must almost always compromise is that of curvature. Stretches of main line railway are characterized on the whole by quite gentle curves. This enables the axles of rolling stock to traverse them with a relatively small amount of lateral movement on the fixed wheels. Unfortunately, when it comes to the model railway it is rarely possible to maintain an identical geometry. For example, the smallest possible radius round which it is normal to permit a main line train to travel – and then only dead slow – is approximately 120m (400′). This gives an approximate 2.75m (9′) radius reduced to gauge O terms and about 1.5m (5′) radius in OO or HO. Yet because of considerations of space, many model main lines have curves that are very much sharper still. For such radii a larger amount of lateral tolerance needs to be given to the wheels of the model, involving a departure from exactly scale dimensions.

Over the years, pioneer workers have worked hard to reduce the degree of compromise. A better understanding of wheel and track relationships has gradually developed, and certain modellers such as the late W.S. Norris, who had the necessary resources as far as skill and workshop facilities were concerned, have been able to achieve models that were nearly perfect.

Similar considerations applied to the modelling of locomotive superstructures. Early models tended to be very basic in this respect – and at times, boiler, chimney, dome and cab were all that were thought necessary to represent a steam locomotive. To paint it in the approximate colours of the real thing and not worry too much about even the most basic aspects such as the wheel arrangements was a common course of procedure. Once again, the models were not bad but they were simply not accurate.

During the inter-war years the move to finer standards was initiated by individuals who, dissatisfied with the crudeness of commercial products, began to make their own models. The appearance of these hand-built examples showed the potential modeller just what could be achieved and in turn persuaded him to urge the commercial manufacturers to do better. And so, standards gradually improved.

One of the most important steps along this road was the establishment both in Europe and America of agreed standard dimensions for the more popular gauges. In Britain the British Railway Modelling Standards Bureau did some fine pioneer work in agreeing track gauges, clearances, wheel characteristics and so forth. But the pity was that the BRMSB had relatively few 'teeth', and so the main commercial firms, interested more in the toy trade, were not successfully persuaded to follow the recommended standards. This was less true in the USA, where the National Model Railroad Association established such a high degree of acceptable standards for the various gauges that it is nowadays hardly worthwhile for a manufacturer of American outline models to depart from the recommended NMRA standards. If so, the models will either be ignored or poorly reviewed by the contemporary model railroad journals, and there is no question of them selling at all.

With time there has been a gradual closing of the gap, so that in the present day some of the best products of the trade are superior to even the better handbuilt models. Although some dedicated handbuilders (or scratchbuilders, to use the favourite modelling term) tend to feel that the commercial model is always second best, this development has been widely welcomed, since its effect has been to improve the general standard tremendously.

Nevertheless, there will always be a place for the scratchbuilder; and no matter how high the standards of commercial products, there will always be some modellers who try to improve upon them. It is, for example, still a widespread practice for modellers to obtain commercial products of acceptable quality, and add to them those extra details (the process is referred to usually as super-detailing') which cost considerations have perhaps caused the manufacturer to omit, in order to get his product to the customer at a realistic price.

An L&NWR 4-4-2 made in Germany by Bing Brothers, who also made O gauge British outline models for Bassett Lowke.

To Buy or To Build?

No matter how many aids to better modelling are provided in the way of tools, kits, components, descriptive articles and so forth, the inescapable fact remains that we all have our limitations, which, in the model railway context, will sooner or later cause us to purchase that which we cannot make ourselves. At what point in the process this decision takes place is for the individual to decide, for there is no particular virtue, *per se*, in making everything oneself. It can give cause for deep and lasting satisfaction, but it can equally give rise to a deep degree of frustration – especially if, after many hours of work, expectation exceeds fulfilment.

In the last analysis therefore, there are probably two over-riding reasons why a modeller will resort to purchase. The first is the simple, inescapable fact that he could not make as good a model with his own two hands. At one time, as we have seen, it was not too difficult to make better models than the commercial offerings; but increasingly, with the use of modern injection-moulding techniques, photo-engraving methods, miniaturization of components and so on, it is becoming more and more difficult for the average man to improve on the commercial product. It is therefore of doubtful value for him to spend a great deal of time making something which can be purchased in superior form.

Secondly, time itself is of great value to the modeller, and 'off the shelf' models save time, thus allowing the modeller greater scope for developing other aspects of his scheme which cannot readily be purchased. These may be in the area of scenic work, complex control mechanisms, or whatever his particular interest happens to be.

Unique Models

Since it is now possible to purchase such a tremendous variety of locomotives, coaches, wagons, signals, buildings, structures, control units and other components, it is tempting to imagine that the art of the scratchbuilder is obsolete. But this simply is not so. There is still a very real desire on the part of many people to make things for themselves, to create something personal and unique. The range of subjects that can be modelled in each different scale is endless, and so the scratchbuilder will always have the opportunity to create and own a model which is not available commercially.

The modeller interested in the railway scene as a whole, and who does not see himself essentially as a scratchbuilder, is perhaps best advised to adopt one of the popular scales. Here the availability of completed models, kits and components is so comprehensive that possibly 90 per cent or more of his needs can be met. On the other hand, the modeller who really likes making things and, perhaps, does not want to be upstaged by the ever improving standards of commercial models, may prefer to adopt a more esoteric standard. Perhaps the best way to sum it all up is to recommend that the potential modeller should always exercise discrimination – remembering that the art of discrimination is not to let the other person do all the discriminating for you!

The Cost Factor

As with most hobbies, railway modelling can be as cheap or expensive as one chooses to make it. On the side of economy is the fact that with the tremendous advances that have been made in production techniques it is possible to buy a relatively sophisticated commercial model at low cost, the only possible drawback being the knowledge that thousands of other people may acquire exactly similar models.

Nowadays an increase in price means not so much an increase in quality as an increase in exclusiveness. In the case of a limited run, handbuilt Japanese brass model for example,, the price may reflect its rarity, in other words its investment value to the collector. This state of affairs can best be compared to the difference in price between a photographically reproduced print sold in a department store and a signed, limited edition lithograph on sale in a gallery. Both, fortunately, can give equal pleasure to the owner.

The successful railway modeller is not necessarily he who has the deepest pocket. This trend can only be commendable, for the model railway hobby, above all things, is essentially a democratic pursuit. It is true that there are rich private patrons at whose fingersnap models of superb quality can be commissioned – but at the other extreme there are some highly skilled 'kitchen table' craftsmen. With almost non-existent workshop facilities, they can, by utilizing little more than discarded tin cans or cardboard boxes, fashion such exquisite and authentic miniatures as to make their richer brethren green with envy.

It is interesting to speculate why this should be, for in many fields success is often directly proportionate to financial investment. In model railways this is rarely, if ever, the case, and this fact can only be of encouragement to most of us. Success however can be related to investment in time and thought. The mark of a successful model is that it evokes the character of the prototype, and that it gives, if only for a moment, the illusion of being real.

Below left: 'OO' gauge GWR Dean 'single' locomotive, *Lord of the Isles.*

Below: From the mid-1930s period, a Brill gas electric made by E. Suydam Co. These locomotives were used for branch line work and were brought into service when the steam locomotive proved to be unprofitable. The gas electric was fitted with a General Motors V16 diesel which drove a generator to power the bogies. It was named 'doodle bug' long before the same name was used for the V2 rockets produced by Germany in World War II.

The Search for Atmosphere

Even people who do not necessarily consider themselves railway enthusiasts would agree that railways have an undeniable atmosphere of their own. A few would perhaps argue that with the passing of the steam locomotive much of the magic disappeared, but for most people the lure of the train is still powerful.

For the railway modeller, however, if he admits the possibility of recreating atmosphere in miniature, he is entering the realm of the intangible, in which facts and figures cannot help him. For this reason alone, the subject defies logical analysis. Yet there can be no doubt that many modellers have successfully encapsulated the essential character of the real railway in their models. Although there is no foolproof recipe for success, there are various guidelines which can usefully be followed.

Perhaps the best place to start is with geographical location – all railways have a setting, and the relationship of a railway to a landscape through which it passes is by no means random. The modeller, therefore, must first study his chosen setting to determine its most distinctive characteristics. It may have a specific style of architecture or particular types of building materials. It may have a distinctive climate or geology, and it may be characterized by a particular form of agriculture. The permutations are endless, but the modeller must try to establish as far as possible the nature of these key elements that give his chosen location its peculiar character.

Having defined the sense of place, the next step is to establish a railway identity. Once again, history will help, because individual railways began to develop their own visual trademarks long before phrases like 'corporate identity' or 'house style' had entered the vocabulary. Such features as station buildings, signalling methods and track layouts show considerable variation from railway to railway, even within the same country. In many instances it is possible to identify the railway company concerned before even a train appears – the modeller should seek out these hallmarks and reproduce them if he can.

Naturally, the modeller is on safer ground once a train appears, since the locomotive and rolling stock will probably carry the colours and lettering of the relevant railway company or system. But the test of a good model railway is that it suggests the correct region and railway even before a train has appeared. If a train of a different railway should appear on the scene, it would immediately seem out of place.

Of course, the historical period, be it past or present, is most clearly defined by the actual rolling stock operated and the liveries in which it appears. But other useful clues can be provided by ensuring that such things as road vehicles are also in keeping, and that if miniature figures are used, they are dressed in correct costume. Even the type face on posters, or the design of street lamps, can be indicative of place and period.

If one regards the building of a model railway as somewhat akin to painting a picture, then one can learn

The charm of the English countryside is brilliantly captured in the Rev. Peter Denny's Buckingham Branch railway.

from the artist, even though the model picture is neither two dimensional nor static. Obviously, the more accurate the individual models are, the more convincing they will be to the onlooker; but as in picture making, it is not wise to rationalize everything into precise dimensional terms. Good pictures should have points of emphasis – so too should a model railway. Good pictures will have dominant and subordinate features – so too will good model railways. Although precisely accurate modelling can be very effective, so equally can the more impressionistic approach. Essentially the modeller is trying to appeal to the emotions, not just to the intellect.

The way in which a model is operated can have an effect upon its realism just as much as the way in which it is built. Railways run to a precise set of rules, and if the rule book is applied in model form the model railway can be operated as punctiliously as the prototype. In this respect, even a relatively unsophisticated model railway can be totally convincing if it is correctly operated. An incident observed at a particular model railway exhibition bears this out.

One of the layouts at the exhibition was being operated to a working timetable, and a particular sequence in the timetable called for a locomotive to perform a series of routine movements in the freight yard and station, prior to clearing the main line so that a passing non-stop freight should come through. As luck would have it, this operation was not quite completed before the main line train was due – a situation very

much in tune with the prototype, one might add! In consequence the freight train approached the signals very slowly indeed, apparently in case it had to stop.

Now in reality, drivers of loose-coupled freight trains do not like to stop, except where booked to do so. They prefer to keep moving, even if only very slowly, to avoid the wagons buffering against each other and this model railway attempted to reproduce this feature. It must have been effective, because one genuine railwayman watching closely said out loud: 'He's a cautious so-and-so, isn't he?'

One other area which often attracts attention, is the state of cleanliness of the railway. Real railways are sometimes very dirty; and even in the leisured days of the Victorian period, things were not as universally spick and span as some would have us believe. For this reason many modellers choose to weather their models, and there is no doubt that, properly done, this can do much to reduce the 'toy train' feeling. American modellers are particularly adept in this field. However, weathering is a somewhat controversial subject – many modellers prefer to keep their trains spotlessly clean and run them in a landscape where it is forever spring!

It should not be assumed that faithful representation of a specific section of railway at a specific period is the only way to achieve atmosphere. Just as the landscape painter has the choice between representing what he sees and creating a totally imaginary composition, so too has the modeller. This brings the term 'freelance' into the vocabulary.

An area around the Rio Grande is depicted in John Porter's North American Lines layout. A Class B Climax No. 4 of the Red Spot Mining and Logging Corporation crosses the main line.

Railways in the Imagination

Broadly speaking, there are two forms of freelance modelling. One approach is to put models of real locomotives, coaches and so on into imaginary settings. This can best be done by building a model railway through a stretch of countryside where in fact no railway ever existed. All that is needed is to bend railway history a little, as in the case of Peter Denny's Buckingham branch line or Norman Eagles' Sherwood section of the LMS.

The other option is to create a complete imaginary world, through which the lines of make-believe railway companies run. At first this idea may seem implausible, but if the modeller really understands how railways work, the results can be totally convincing. Witness, for example, the late John Allen's 'Gorre and Daphetid' system in California; or, on a smaller scale, the late John Ahern's pioneering 'Madder Valley' railway, still happily to be seen at the Pendon Museum near Oxford. The best of the freelance systems have been just as well thought out in terms of 'where', 'which' and 'when' as those layouts which purport to represent real railways in actual locations.

Regardless of his technical skill, the modeller cannot hope to achieve realism and atmosphere by mere pursuit of detail. But if he is somehow able to convey in model form the elusive but unmistakable character of the full-size railway as it is known and loved, then he will have succeeded.

So we return to the original assumption that the key to the subject is the appeal of the full-size railway. We make our own models because there is some aspect of the real railway which we wish to encapsulate in miniature – what precisely that aspect is will be different for each and every modeller. Over the years, ideas have come and gone, points of emphasis have changed, scales and gauges have had their ups and downs; but throughout the history of model railways this underlying motivation has remained constant. There is no best way to approach the hobby – there are simply different ways. The rest of this book tries to describe and explain some of them.

Below: GWR 'King George V' 4-6-0 pulls a Plymouth express across a temporary timber viaduct at the Pendon Museum layout.

Right: From Norman Eagles' Sherwood Section, an LMS 2-6-2 Tank on a local train from Nottingham Castle to Oxton.

THE

RIGHT CHOICE

By now the potential modeller will have realized that successful railway modelling involves something more than going into the nearest shop, purchasing a boxed set and plugging the whole thing into the nearest electric supply point. Of course, many of us start this way; but experience suggests that unless the modeller fairly quickly develops this concept into something more challenging, his interest in the subject begins to wane. Nevertheless, before starting to build a 'proper' model railway, it is wise to formulate a definite plan of action. The previous chapter outlined some of the general considerations which the modeller should bear in mind, but from this point onwards it is time to take a practical view.

The planning of a model railway can itself be a fascinating and rewarding occupation. Indeed, some enthusiasts – generally referred to as armchair modellers – rarely get much further than this stage! The object of planning the model railway is to ensure as far as possible that the completed system will satisfy the owner in terms of the objectives he set himself at the beginning. The extent to which the finished model fulfils these objectives is often directly proportional to the amount of effort devoted to the planning phase.

It is likely that choosing a prototype will be the first major step taken by many railway modellers; but this decision is not always totally clear cut. While there are a happy few modellers who know precisely what they want to model and can subordinate their whole planning to this predetermined goal, most modellers probably start with a variety of conflicting objectives.

Detail from the magnificent North American Lines layout built by John E. Porter in England. Canadian Pacific K1a 4-8-4 No. 3100 leaves Highfield on a Time Freight whilst H1a 4-6-4 No. 2816 rides the turntable. Both are brass models produced for Van Hobbies of Canada.

Choice of Prototype

What are the factors which have to be assessed by the majority of modellers when choosing a prototype? Consider first the modeller whose aim is to model one specific railway company. He is faced with two further decisions: which part of the network should the model attempt to represent and during what period in the company's history? A precise-minded person might decide to model location X on Wednesday 28 July in the year Y. This is fine, but what if his favourite locomotive class never visited location X, or was scrapped before the year Y? Perhaps an alternative place and date should have been chosen. But then the modeller liked location X – perhaps because it was a favourite holiday area, of which he had sufficient local knowledge to enable him to make accurate models of the buildings – and he may have chosen year Y because he had a series of contemporary photographs which enabled him to verify a whole range of ancillary detail.

This dilemma is particularly relevant to the keen historical modeller whose aim is to recreate a specific historical scene. In order to take advantage of all such considerations he may have to settle for a period of two or more years rather than a specific day, week or month.

A different problem faces the modeller who is torn between two incompatible prototypes but who only has the space or time to model one of them. For example, it is not unlikely that a modeller may have an equal interest in two different railways, widely separated geographically. Unless they had a jointly owned stretch of line, or their trains met at a certain station, then he has a problem.

A similar situation affects the modeller whose interests span a considerable time scale. He may like mid-Victorian steam locomotives on one hand, and modern diesel and electric motive power on the other; but to operate both on the same layout would at once destroy the illusion of reality.

Understandably, many enthusiasts are unconcerned by the possibility of such anachronisms. They may argue that their principle aim is to have models of things they like, regardless of whether this is geographically or historically feasible; and their modelling schemes are devised accordingly. Their intention is to create, in model form, their personal version of the ideal railway.

Below: A coal train stands in a siding at Dawson Spring on W. Allen McClelland's Virginia & Ohio Railroad as an EMD SD-24 passes through.

Opposite: 'N' gauge layouts, such as Gerry Veits' Hohenburg model, enable modellers to accommodate longer trains.

How Long is a Train?

Most railway modellers accept that one of the most intractable difficulties – regardless of scale – is the matter of train length. As soon as one decides to model an express passenger train or a main line freight, the constraint of train length becomes critical. Even a relatively modest train of ten coaches can take up as much length of track as 1.5 metres (5′) even in N gauge, while a mile-long North American freight would occupy 10 metres (11 yards). Not surprisingly, many modellers find themselves obliged to run trains which have less than the correct number of vehicles, but if taken too far, this situation can become unsatisfactory. The easiest way out, if this factor is of paramount importance, is to opt for a smaller scale and to look for the longest site available for the layout.

Another solution is to make a virtue out of necessity, and model the kind of prototype operation which utilized short trains. In America the short-line system has many adherents for similar reasons, while in Britain, this has led to a sub-culture of branch-line modelling.

At first sight the concept of the branch line appears to have almost everything in its favour. It allows the possibility of a very accurate model capable of realistic operation. But the very compactness and simplicity of the branch can be a drawback – one or two locomotives, a couple of coaches and a handful of freight vehicles often served to operate the whole line – and few modellers are, in the long run, satisfied with such limited scope. In consequence it is by no means uncommon to find a layout which started as a simple country scene eventually becoming so over-stocked with models that it begins to look like a main line junction at rush

hour . . . and the illusion of reality vanishes. Furthermore, for the most part, branch-line modelling is not compatible with the widespread desire to own and operate glamorous and impressive main line rolling stock. So it is possible that in opting for this tidy solution to the problem of train length, the modeller may restrict the choices open to him in other respects.

If the branch line does not appear attractive, there are other types of railway which have short train lengths. In narrow gauge, for example, there is tremendous scope for fitting a lot into a small space. Narrow gauge railways often seem to bend the rules. Curves are often impossibly sharp and signalling non-existent. If you invent your own narrow gauge railway there is no-one to say what is and what is not prototypical, providing the atmosphere you convey is convincing.

The other possibility is to go further back in time. In general, the earlier the period, the shorter were train lengths. It is worth remembering that a scale model of Stephenson's 'Rocket', together with a suitable train of four-wheelers in gauge I, may well occupy considerably less length than an N gauge representation of a Union Pacific 'Big Boy' and freight train.

Once he has chosen his prototype, no modeller can ever know too much about it, whether it be in such obvious respects as the colour of the rolling stock or more obscure details such as the design of station notice boards and the style of staff uniforms. Fortunately, for anyone who is sufficiently interested, there is a very wide literature indeed about the prototype railway – much of it written either by modellers, or with modellers in mind. One of the most useful steps a modeller can take is to steep himself in as much literature as he can find relating to his chosen subject.

Choice of Site

If the aim is a working layout, as opposed to a collection of static models, then the question of siting is clearly going to be of prime importance and may well prove to be the most crucial factor in determining the type of layout, mode of propulsion and so forth.

It has to be accepted that railway modelling can be a very space consuming hobby; and the tolerance of what are generally referred to as 'the domestic authorities' can at times be stretched to the limit. It has been truly said that the railway modeller who is about to enter the state of wedlock is well advised to be totally honest about his hobby before it is too late! Of course, model railways need not necessarily take up vast amounts of space. There are many possible locations for a model railway – some less space-saving than others.

The Spare Room

If the modeller can obtain the exclusive use of a spare room in his home, this is perhaps the ideal situation. He can close the door on the rest of the household and, for the most part, confine the inevitable chaos of the construction phase to one area. But in being 'spare' it may well also be, by definition, the smallest available room in the house. This in turn may involve the use of a smaller scale than would otherwise have been preferred. Nevertheless most modellers would, if pressed, agree that the exclusive possession of one room is a very strong plus factor in the decision to build a model railway at all.

The Attic or Loft

In older houses, built with solid rafters, roof purlins and joists across the bedroom ceilings, there is often a considerable void area in the main roof. In terms of usable floor area (i.e. that which can be reached without having to bend double), the space will not be as great as the overall area occupied by the house. Nevertheless, the attic is usually about as big as the largest room in the house, which makes it ideal for modellers.

The conversion of the loft space can be an expensive and time consuming project. Extra strengthening supports may be needed to take the additional load, and it is wise to consult a builder or architect if it is proposed to convert the loft into a permanent layout site. Floor and ceiling will need to be added and possibly a skylight or some form of ventilation, and power and light must be laid on as well; but if the modeller is prepared to devote time and thought to the problem, the loft may well prove to be an ideal choice for the layout.

Unfortunately, much modern building makes use of pre-formed roof trusses to support the rafters and roof. The loft space is still available; but may well be interrupted at intervals by diagonal timbers, thus making the conversion either difficult or impossible.

The Basement or Cellar

Older houses often have cellars or basements, and in some countries, notably the USA, this feature is still widely incorporated in house building. At one time cellars were used for food storage, but since the use of modern refrigerators and deep freezes the cellar is now redundant in this respect. Provided it is dry and can be given both heat and light, the cellar can be a fine choice for a layout site. Like the attic, it frequently extends over a larger area than any single room in the house.

The Garage

Many houses have garages. But the trouble is that most of these garages are filled with motor cars! Nevertheless, the garage does offer some scope. It may be possible to construct a railway round the walls in such a way that there is still room for the car to occupy the central floor area. Alternatively the layout could be built on hinges and fold up against the wall when the car was in the garage. A more drastic possibility would be to leave the car outside all the time. Many modellers have concluded that, since the modern motor car is designed to fall apart in about eight years, and is a depreciating asset anyway, there is no real need to cocoon the wretched thing in a nice dry garage. It is a point worth considering – especially since there is very little evidence that cars which are kept in garages depreciate any less rapidly than those left outside.

The House Extension

It is a relatively simple matter to obtain attractive yet moderately priced extensions to the main dwelling. These are often advertised as conservatories, sun lounges and so on. In terms of the resale value of the property they are positive assets in this role; but there is no reason why they should not be used in the first instance as a model railway room. They achieve all the advantages of the spare room site without depriving the household of existing living space.

Modellers can save space by reducing the depth of buildings on their layout, as Frank Roomes' Lutton Branch.

The Garden Shed

Portable buildings come in many shapes and sizes. Provided the garden can accommodate such a structure, and the local regulations permit of its installation, this may well prove an attractive solution. The size, within limits, can be chosen to suit the type of layout required, and like the spare room, the garden shed can become the exclusive den of the modeller. It will need insulation, power, light and heat, and must be rendered proof against break-in. One obvious snag is the separation from the main dwelling. This may be particularly irksome when the telephone rings, or if the modeller likes to keep up a conversation with the rest of the family while he is working. But if the shed has been properly chosen, it has the advantage that it can be dismantled and moved to a new location elsewhere.

The Garden

Depending on the climate, the size of the garden, and the levelness of the ground, the garden railway has much to commend it. Space is usually no problem – and the trains really do seem to be going somewhere. It is, however, rather difficult to integrate in scenic terms since the background obstinately remains 12″ to the foot scale! Nevertheless, the garden railway is a popular choice for some modellers, especially in the larger scales, and can be combined with the garden shed site to produce a very effective compromise. In this situation, the shed itself could well house the stations and sidings, thus protecting the rolling stock from the weather, from which the main lines could be taken through the shed wall to circumnavigate the garden.

Permanent or Portable?

Having established a site for the layout, the modeller must then decide whether the layout itself is to be of a permanent or portable nature. The sites discussed so far all permit the modeller to install a permanent layout, but many people prefer to make their railways portable. An important consideration is that the portable layout is relatively immune from the problems of house moving – and is also handy for display at model railway exhibitions. In addition it is much simpler to modify, or to rebuild completely, than a permanent system. Yet another possibility is a portable layout made in modular form which can be erected in a variety of different configurations in a similar manner to NTRAK.

For these, and other, reasons many modellers deliberately make their systems portable, even when they have a permanent site available. However, there is one telling point in favour of the portable layout, which, for many people, turns out to be crucial – it does not need a permanent site at all. Space-starved modellers can, therefore, contemplate building a model railway even without permanent 'running rights'; for portable layouts can be and have been designed to meet an astonishing variety of criteria.

In the simplest form, a portable layout may be no more than two or three sections of baseboard hinged together that can be erected almost anywhere – even in the living room. Other more ingenious solutions have involved layouts which run along narrow shelves or even fold into the wall. Some layouts have actually been built as part of the furniture, with folding lids to cover them when not in use, while others are visually integrated into the decor of the room itself. The possibilities are endless, and some of the ingenious solutions adopted show a considerable measure of imagination. There have been layouts on coffee tables, book cases, old television sets and even musical instrument cases – so the man who claims he has no space for a model railway is not really trying!

Don Jones' garden layout in 'OO' gauge has 1,000 yards of track and is among the biggest garden layouts.

Which Scale?

At first glance, the most obvious factor determining choice of scale would seem to be that of space. It is true that where space is almost non-existent, certain gauges may be ruled out; but usually the site available will permit a certain measure of choice. Let us therefore consider the possibilities of the two extreme situations – the very large site and the very small.

The very large site may most conveniently be defined as that which will permit the installation of a reasonably satisfying system even in gauge I – something at least six metres by three (20′ × 10′). In this space any scale may be chosen according to preference. Some modellers are primarily interested in owning or building a relatively small number of top quality items to the highest degree of absolute fidelity to which they can aspire; in which case, they may see the large site as giving them a chance to fulfil their ideals in gauge O or gauge I. Other modellers, essentially more interested in the operation of a complex system than in the super-detailed quality of each and every component, may equally see in the large site a heaven-sent opportunity to create a vast railway empire in N gauge.

It is equally feasible to think in terms of more than one system – perhaps two layouts in different scales, or a combination of standard and narrow gauge. The choice can be exceedingly difficult. Paradoxically, the possession of a large site can be a highly frustrating experience, offering as it does opportunities for all scales and forcing the modeller to sort out his priorities.

On the other hand, in a situation where space is at a premium, most modellers automatically think of the small scales. It is, for example, perfectly possible to build a very worthwhile N gauge layout in a space of some 2m × 0.5m (6′ × 2′) and even in HO or OO gauges, this space can be made use of. It is, of course, virtually impossible to fit a comprehensive gauge O layout into a small site, but if the modeller is interested in modelling in gauge O at any cost, then it is possible to think in terms of a diorama type of presentation – perhaps a model locomotive depot, or a small goods yard scene. Much can be achieved in a space no more than 2.5m × 0.5m (8′ × 2′).

Clockwork, Electric or Steam?

If the model is to be working rather than static, then the source of power must be determined. Today most model railways adopt electric propulsion in one of a variety of forms, but there are other choices available, some of which may prove to be of great attraction. Essentially, the two prime alternatives to electrification are clockwork and live steam.

Ex-LNWR 0-8-4 Tank engine No. 7952, pictured on the Sherwood Section layout, spent much of its life shedded at Buxton.

Clockwork

Right from the outset, the modeller should be weaned from the idea that clockwork propulsion is the prerogative of the toy train set. It is true that from the earliest days of commercial model making, clockwork has been used as a simple and reliable means of making the wheels go round. It needs no wires, complex controls, nor any other infrastructure – just a key. But clockwork operation of a genuine model railway can be a most satisfying experience, and this form of power has much to recommend it.

Firstly, the source of power is within the locomotive itself – just as with the real thing. Secondly, the clockwork locomotive will only run a finite distance on one winding of the mechanism. This has an obvious similarity to the steam locomotive's need to take on water from time to time. Then, perhaps even more than its electrically powered equivalent, the clockwork locomotive is highly sensitive to load and gradient, while if it is fitted with a high quality mechanism it will accelerate and decelerate in a most realistic way.

Over the years, clockwork mechanisms have taken various forms. Originally it was a matter of winding the mechanism and letting the locomotive run until rewinding was needed. Then came reversible mechanisms, followed by controlled speed mechanisms and the achievement of longer lengths of run between rewindings.

The secret of success with clockwork is for the operator to understand his models so well that, with a given load to pull and given distance to travel, he can adjust the amount of winding and speed setting so that the train will come to a stop at exactly the desired spot. This can be a real art, particularly since every locomotive will perform slightly differently – again, just like the prototype. Properly executed, this form of propulsion can be uncannily realistic and very rewarding.

Live Steam

There are few more pleasing experiences than to see a miniature steam locomotive in full cry. For the most part, live steam models are usually built to a larger scale than the model railway gauges covered by this book, and are used for passenger haulage in parks, gardens and the like. However, it is perfectly possible to operate live steam models in gauge 1 and gauge O, and just as an exercise in achieving the impossible, it has even been done in N gauge.

Gauge 1 is perhaps the most likely choice for the live steam enthusiast, and many fine models exist in this scale – usually working on garden layouts. The most common method of raising steam is a spirit burner rather than coal firing, but even so, it is necessary for the operator to attend to his locomotive as would the driver of a full-size machine.

Once started, of course, a miniature live steamer can be left to run on its own for a while; but, sooner or later, it will be necessary to stop it to refill the boiler or to take on more fuel. Also, to alter its speed once it is in motion involves frantically chasing after it and adjusting the regulator.

In order to avoid this somewhat undignified situation, some ingenious modellers have experimented with electrical remote control. This technical achievement allows them to sit back and just enjoy the sight and sound of steam. However, electric control is confined to regulating the movement of the locomotive, and servicing must still be carried out manually.

It is now possible to obtain certain commercial products – including a growing range of top quality locomotive kits in gauge 1 – but live steam propulsion is pre-eminently the province of the scratchbuilder, and a fairly high degree of expertise is required. Nevertheless, this corner of the hobby commands a dedicated and enthusiastic following.

Aster Live Steam American outline locomotive, one of eight models available in kit form or ready assembled.

Electricity

Electric propulsion is the choice of the majority of modellers and for the smaller scales it is the almost universally adopted medium. For models of electric and diesel-electric locomotives, it is a logical choice, but most modellers of steam outline locomotives in any case prefer the convenience of electricity to the complications and expense of live steam. Historically, electric propulsion has been used in all the model railway gauges, although several different methods have been used to convey the current to the locomotive. All involve some form of physical contact between the electric motor and the conductor rail or conductor wire.

The oldest methods employed a third conductor rail from which the locomotive collected its current by means of a pickup shoe or bar. The third rail could be located either between or outside the running rails and, until well after the Second World War, this system was widely adopted in all scales. With one or two exceptions such as the Southern Electric lines in England, the appearance of a third rail was not in accordance with the prototype; and so pioneer modellers began to seek alternatives to improve the appearance of their track.

The simplest alternative, and one that is still widely used, was stud contact. In this system, the third rail is replaced by a continuous wire concealed below the track. At intervals, vertical screws or nails project upwards between the running rails. Current is collected from these studs by means of a skate below the locomotive, kept in contact by light spring pressure, and long enough to bridge the interval between any two adjacent studs. Since only the tops of the studs are visible, this system marked a great improvement in the appearance of model track and it is still in use to a limited extent, its most loyal manufacturer being Märklin.

From stud contact, the next step was to '2-rail'. Tracing its origins back to just before the Second World War, 2-rail did not become widespread until the 1950s, but is now used by almost every modeller in every scale. In this delightfully simple system, the locomotive draws current from one running rail and returns it via the other. The key to 2-rail is insulation. Apart from where it is fed to the motor, current must not be allowed to pass from left to right hand wheel of locomotives and rolling stock, nor from left to right hand running rails. The development of plastics made this simpler – it would have been extremely difficult to insulate the earlier, all metal components in this way.

Today it is difficult to conceive of the ferocious opposition which the introduction of 2-rail aroused in the hobby at the time. The 2-rail concept was thought by some to fly in the face of all reason, and many were the articles written to explain why it was either much too complicated or would not work anyway.

In the case where the prototype railway employs a real conductor rail or overhead wire, there are several ways of supplying power to the model electric locomotives. One is the old familiar 3-rail concept, using the conductor rail or overhead wire to get the current to the model. Another possibility is to adopt 2-rail, and install the conductor apparatus purely for appearance's sake. A third possibility is to have one locomotive picking up from the overhead wire and another from one of the running rails. Current will be returned from both locomotives via the second running rail. Since the outputs are totally separate, the two locomotives can be independently controlled. This system had its origin in the old commercial 'Trix-Twin' system, where an apparently 3-rail track was, in fact, a sort of 'double-2-rail' – all three rails being insulated from each other.

Top and Centre Hornby Dublo and Märklin three rail track, bottom Märklin track with centre Stud contact.

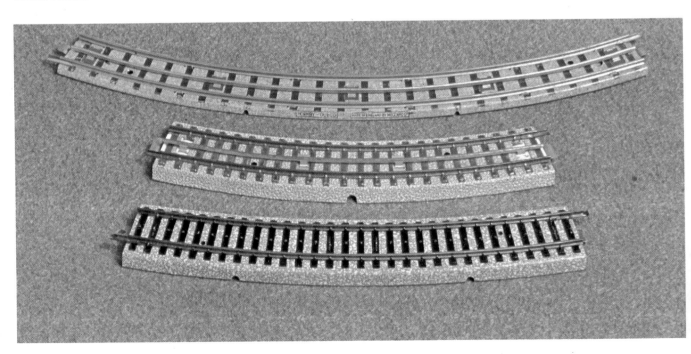

In order to safeguard life and limb, model railway electrification must, of course, employ low voltages. The most common modern standard is 12 volts, but 6 volts and 24 volts are quite widespread alternatives. All involve transformers and, in most cases, rectifiers, since most models operate on direct, rather than alternating, current.

To control speed, one of three basic methods is normal. Oldest is the variable resistance method – akin to a dimmer switch on a lighting circuit – whereby the control handle sweeps across a rheostat coil, thus varying the supply to the locomotive. Following this came the British-developed variable transformer which was rather more sensitive, and finally, in more recent years, transistorized control has become very widespread and very popular. The silicon chip has now made its appearance, opening up a range of exciting and hitherto unsuspected possibilities.

This is not the place to develop a long study of model railway electronics, for most of the systems which the modeller may wish to use are fully described, either by the relevant manufacturer, or in the specialist magazines and publications. With the exception of the new silicon chip systems, one common thread runs through them all – the importance of the track section, or 'block' as it is often called in North America.

In an electrified model railway, the track is normally divided into a number of sections, each electrically isolated from its neighbour. By means of his control panel the operator can send power from a control unit to one or more of these sections in order to make a train move. The most straightforward way of achieving this is to confine each control unit to a single section of the layout – it being necessary to ensure that the control units in adjacent sections are set in identical positions to avoid jerkiness when trains move from one to the next.

The alternative is to arrange that each track section can be switched to any one controller. Obviously this must be arranged so that it is not possible to have one section connected to more than one control unit at any one time. However, having achieved this aim, the operator simply connects his control unit to those sections of the layout which he wishes to use, and the train remains under the control of a single control unit throughout its journey. This method, by far the most popular today, is known as cab control and has been developed in many sophisticated ways.

Before embarking upon the building of a model railway, the would-be modeller is well advised to study in more detail the control options open to him – especially if he chooses electric propulsion. None of the available methods is particularly complex in itself but, depending on the individual, any one can be developed to a very high degree. Using the latest technology, an electronic specialist could have a field day. However, with or without the benefit of the silicon chip, it is possible to operate a model railway with no more than one wire to get the current there, and another one to bring it back!

The controls and transformer with which Cliff Young operates his Denver & Rio Grande layout.

The Art of Compromise

By now, it will be well appreciated that there are many considerations to be borne in mind before building a model railway. Faced with all the constraints thus far covered – not to mention many more which may be created by the individual modeller's own particular wishes – it may seem surprising that model railways get built at all; but they do, and in increasing numbers as the years go by. The reason is after all, that in one form or another, the typical modeller is prepared and willing to compromise in order to achieve his aims.

The art of compromise is fundamental to railway modelling, although the methods by which compromise is achieved are by no means universally agreed. In fact, some of the most useful compromises are not accepted at all by some modellers, and many are the heated debates which ensue in the correspondence columns of the model railway press. There are, for example, modellers who are prepared to go to a great deal of time and effort to ensure that there are no dimensional discrepancies at all in their models, or the track on which they run, but yet are forced to accept that to build to these standards may limit them to layouts of stark simplicity with somewhat short and simple trains. Nevertheless, they will strenuously argue the correctness of this approach over that of the man who contends that a better form of

The realism of this scene, photographed by Robert Hegge, was achieved by Glenn Davis, of St. Louis, using various kits and giving close attention to detail.

compromise might be to cut out some of the super detail in order to give time to build a layout on which longer trains can be run over greater distances.

Yet another form of compromise might be adopted by the modeller to whom operation is the keynote. Here, everything may well be subordinated to the creation of a model railway network allowing maximum scope for operation. This may involve over-sharp radii, coarse scale standards, suppression of much of the scenic background, the shortening of train lengths, or possibly all four together, in order that the most complex possible network can be fitted into the space available.

Whatever the degree or form of compromise adopted by the modeller, it is a rare man indeed who does not have to compromise somewhere. In fact, the extent to which a model railway succeeds in being convincing is perhaps a measure of the degree to which the chosen compromises materially assist the illusion which the modeller is trying to create.

In the final analysis, the biggest area of compromise is the landscape. Viewed rationally, it is a preposterous aim to try and encapsulate a stretch of countryside – be it real or imaginary – within the confines of a spare bedroom or garden shed. Nevertheless, this is what many modellers attempt to do, and in many cases succeed in doing.

Another superb example of the modeller's art at its best: a detail from the Golden Gate Model Railroad, San Francisco.

Layout Planning

It has been calculated that to build a scale model of London's Waterloo Station in 3.5mm or 4mm scale would occupy almost the whole of a tennis court – and even then the trains would not reach Vauxhall, only a mile down the line! Fortunately, few people have the ambition to reproduce this degree of complexity, even if they had the means to do so, but it does serve as a reminder of the problems of layout planning. Even a quiet country branch line 8 kilometres (5 miles) in length would occupy some 50 metres (55 yards) if modelled exactly to scale in N gauge.

In order to achieve a workable solution, most modellers tend to reduce markedly the scale distances between stations, thus reducing the overall length of the system, while at the same time simplifying the track arrangements and selectively shortening the actual length of the stations themselves. The particular site available, and the scale adopted, will influence the degree of compression. Much too will depend on whether the modeller wishes to represent a real station or whether he prefers to design an imaginary facility. The latter is more popular, since in the last analysis, no-one can say that a fictitious railway is wrongly scaled when there is no reality to compare it against.

Such a course is made easier by the fact that there is no hard and fast relationship between any particular track layout and the space it requires at a particular station. Most full-size station layouts use a lot of space, and in theory it would be possible for them to be laid out in a much smaller area without the complexity of the track plan being reduced in any way. In prototype terms this compression would probably not be acceptable – in model terms it may have to be, according to circumstances. It is for the modeller to decide whether he wants a sprawling layout or a tightly knit one.

Looking north from Highfield on the North American Lines layout, showing the main line and engine facilities.

The best alternative to faithfully modelling actual track layouts is to attempt to understand the principles underlying the laying out of track, and then to design a track arrangement to suit the operational possibilities envisaged on the finished layout. This exercise can be very rewarding and stimulating, since it puts the modeller in the same position as the real railway engineer, designing a station to fit parameters such as traffic requirements, site constraints, train lengths and so forth.

In order to understand the principles of layout planning, the modeller should appreciate what can and cannot be done in a given space. For example, where a turnout leads into a siding there will be a greater or lesser length of dead ground, as the tracks diverge, where two vehicles cannot stand side by side.

The need to understand track geometry is less essential if the modeller proposes to use one of the many systems of readymade track on the market, since he can juggle the actual components on the baseboard to achieve a satisfactory arrangement. However, the manufacturers of readymade track usually offer only a limited range of track sections and turnouts, and so to that extent the possibilities of layout planning may be limited. But if the modeller is able to build his own track, he can – like the real permanent way engineer – make special formations to fit specific locations.

One common mistake in track planning, made by most modellers at one stage or another, is to assume that they can get more into a given space than the track geometry will permit. It is a hard lesson and one sometimes not learned until too late. In general, the best advice is to allow more space for the desired point formations than seems likely to be needed. This way any errors will work to the modeller's advantage, rather than sending him back to the drawing board.

The complex track layout of Altenbeken Station built by Rolf Ertmer.

Layout Types

In designing the layout itself, there are two complementary objectives. One is to achieve a satisfactory plan, taking the whole system into account. The second is to ensure that within the overall plan, the individual elements (stations, goods yards, locomotive depots, etc.), are adequately designed to cope with the modeller's operating requirements.

Exactly how many such elements are present depends very much on what the modeller requires of his complete system. Some are quite happy to model a single but fairly complex station – others like to have several depots between which they can operate their trains. Fundamentally, layout planning relates not so much to the detail of the individual stations but to the overall type of layout to be built. There are several identifiable

variants, although one basic question transcends them all – whether the layout should form a continuous closed circuit or whether, like the prototype, it should start in one place and finish in another.

The Simple Oval

This type of circuit is a development of the familiar boxed trainset. It can be single or double track, and the trains inevitably traverse the same ground time and time again. The oval can have either one or several stations distributed round it, depending upon space.

The Modified Oval

This variant is no different in track plan from the simple oval, but part of the system is now concealed from the observer and thus the basically circular nature of the trackplan is disguised. In this type of layout – widely adopted for exhibition use – the concealed portion of the

This diagram shows the five main layout types in their simplest forms; the shapes and sizes can be varied to suit the location and space available, and additional running lines, branch lines and stations added as desired.

Right: A layout from an NTRAK Modular system modelled in N gauge.

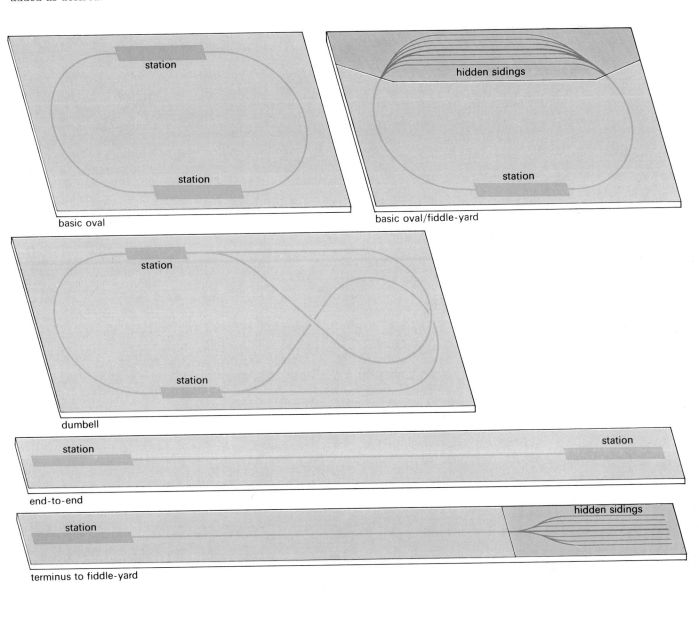

basic oval

basic oval/fiddle-yard

dumbell

end-to-end

terminus to fiddle-yard

system usually makes no attempt to be anything more than a storage area for the trains waiting to make a circuit through the visible portion. In theory the hidden area represents the rest of the railway system. Although continuous running is possible, the more usual operating procedure is for each train in the storage area to make a single circuit of the system, thus presenting to the observer the image of a series of trains passing the same point.

The Dumb-Bell

The problem with the plain oval is that running is one-directional, and so to reverse a train involves the transposition of the locomotive from one end of the train to the other. The dumb-bell layout overcomes this by incorporating a pair of reversing loops. Each serves as a form of terminus, where trains reverse direction simply by traversing the loop. Usually these systems are so arranged that the reversing loops are hidden from view, and each loop can form a separate hidden storage area if so desired.

Almost all continuous circuits can be reduced to either simple ovals or dumb-bells. Circuits can be doubled back over each other or twisted into figure-eight formations, while reversing loops can be disguised in a variety of ways. In general, it is best first to determine the form of continuous circuit desired and then adapt it to fit the site available.

End-to-End

In this type of scheme, the layout takes the form of a route from one terminus to another, via as many (or as few) intermediate locations as desired. It is crucial that the track capacity at each end is approximately the same, otherwise operational problems will ensue, but the track layouts need not be identical. This form of layout is a popular choice in the USA and lends itself very well to the modelling of a complete self-contained railway system.

Terminus to Fiddle-Yard

This basically British-inspired type of system accepts the fact that distance is an insuperable problem. The modeller, therefore, models but one terminus from which the trains proceed into a storage area representing the rest of the country. The storage area is christened 'fiddle yard', because behind the scenes no attempt at all is made to operate realistically. The sole object is to receive and dispatch trains from and to the scenic part of the layout. Locomotives can be turned simply by picking them off the track, and rolling stock can be similarly dealt with. This system has one advantage over the pure end-to-end layout in that there is a theoretical connection with a larger railway system, thus allowing for a greater variety of traffic.

The Modular Layout

In this portable system, the layout is built in a series of identical sized sections which can be connected together to form a bigger display. It can be planned so that the individual modules can be assembled in a variety of different ways. Modular layouts have reached their most widespread expression in the 'NTRAK' system in which groups of N gauge modellers build compatible modular sections.

The broad categories outlined above encompass the vast majority of model railway situations likely to be encountered. Of course, the individual is free to mix them up as he wishes – in general, long and narrow sites lend themselves to end-to-end systems, while a wider shape is essential for a continuous circuit.

The potential modeller would be well advised to invest in a drawing pad and sketch out as many varieties of scheme as his site will permit, and his own ingenuity can devise. It is much cheaper than making a series of abortive starts on the model itself, and it will teach the modeller a great deal about what is and is not possible in a given area with a given scale. This is one area above all where an ounce of practice is worth a pound of advice. The ideal layout plan is that which best suits the modeller in question, and once he understands the principles at work, he is the best person to devise it.

TRACK PLANS

The creation of a model railway, regardless of its size or simplicity, calls for careful planning, particularly of the track design. Time spent at the initial stage, checking that enough room has been provided to accommodate all the features that are planned, will be rewarded when construction begins.

Most modellers find that they soon have to compromise, for their ambitions are invariably greater than the space available. Even those who make small-scale drawings can easily under-estimate the size of various components. It is essential, therefore, to measure everything accurately, including train lengths and the room allocated for curves, and to ensure that gradients are not too steep when planning to take one track over another.

The object of track planning is to try to follow full-size railway practice. Railways have evolved over 150 years in a way that enables them to move traffic smoothly and efficiently. It makes sense, then, to copy the experts, adapting the track designs used in full-scale operations to the space available. Model railway design is one field where originality does not pay dividends.

The best approach for most modellers, once they have decided the type of railway they will operate and its geographical location, is to design a system that can be built in stages, based on conventional operating practice. A passing loop trackplan will satisfy most novices with limited space and experience, and many will, with time, go on to build more complex layouts, incorporating a terminus, sidings, 'fiddle-yard' and roundhouse.

The plans on these pages show how correctly designed track formations can be fitted into a variety of areas. They provide a comprehensive range of trackplans, from simple layouts to large, permanent room-size developments, to meet the needs of beginners and experienced modellers alike.

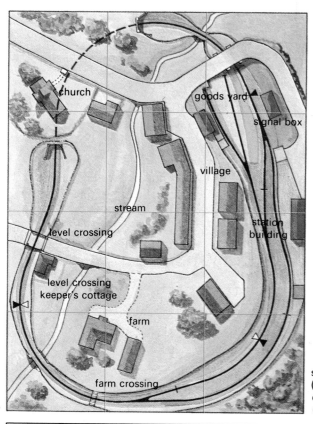

Left: This simple, small layout offers maximum opportunity for landscaping, whilst the inclusion of a passing loop in the station enables two trains to be run, or for the locomotive to run-round its train and reverse its direction around the circuit.

Below: A simple terminus-to-fiddle-yard layout suitable for siting at one end of a small room. The 'hidden sidings' or 'fiddle-yard' shown is of the magazine type which can be lifted out and reversed, or replaced by another magazine holding an alternative selection of trains.

church

goods yard

signal box

village

stream

level crossing

station building

level crossing keeper's cottage

farm

farm crossing

size 2m x 1.5m
(6 ft 6 in x 4 ft 10½ in)
each square equals
0.5m (1 ft 7½ in)

key

turnout

section power feed

section break

isolator

building

railway building

platform

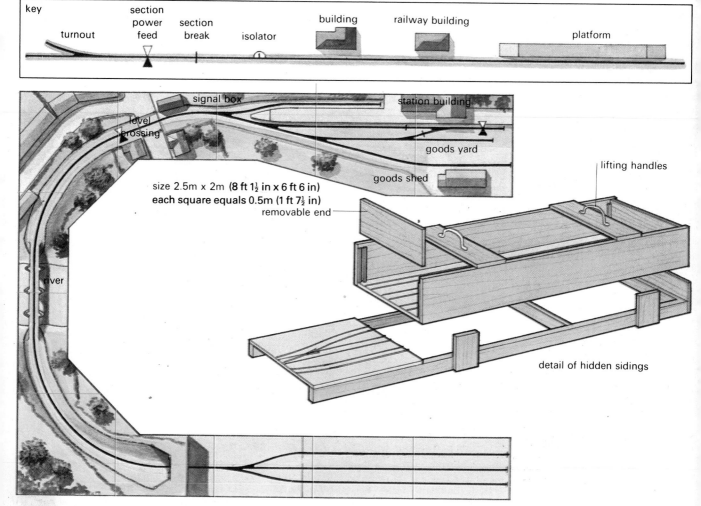

signal box

level crossing

station building

goods yard

goods shed

size 2.5m x 2m **(8 ft 1½ in x 6 ft 6 in)**
each square equals 0.5m (1 ft 7½ in)

removable end

river

lifting handles

detail of hidden sidings

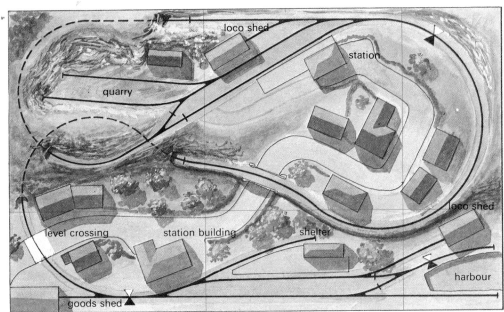

size 1.25m x 0.75m (**4 ft x 2 ft 6 in**) each square represents 0.5m (**1 ft 7½ in**)

Above: A narrow-gauge layout with plenty of scope for scenic development based on the Welsh slate-carrying railways, featuring a quarry or mine and a small harbour station. The reversing loop hidden in the tunnel enables 'point-to-point' or 'out and back' running of the trains.

Below: A layout based on European practice and suitable for those modellers with a bias towards collecting locomotives, featuring a large roundhouse and a three-track basic oval, with minimal waste of space.

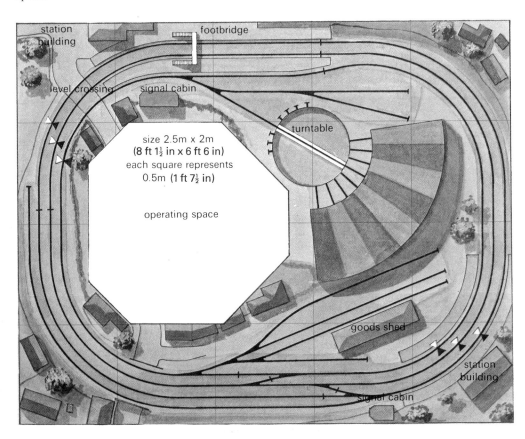

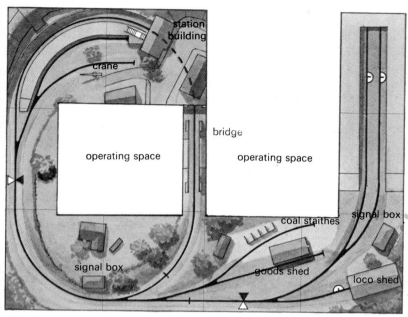

size 2m x 1.5m
(6 ft 6 in x 4 ft 10½ in)
each square represents
0.5m (1 ft 7½ in)

Above: A simple oval and terminus layout which can be developed in two stages; the oval section first, adding the terminus and locomotive shed at a later date. The bay platform of the passing station enables point-to-point running of trains with the terminus, and the bridge can be made as a lifting section for ease of access.

Below: A larger development of the layout above offering additional operational scope, and incorporating a triangular junction enabling trains to be reversed and locomotives to be turned. In OO/HO scales, and smaller, the operating space on the right is only of use for access, and could be covered with a removable scenic section.

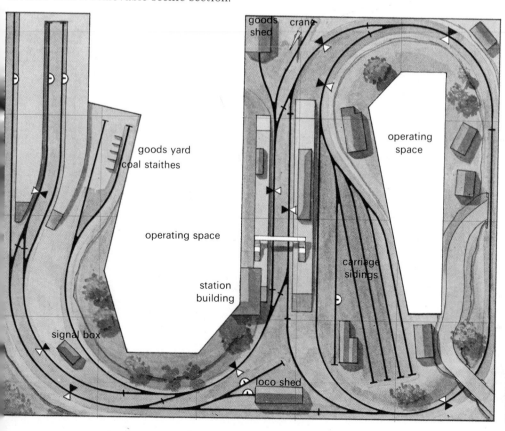

size 2.5m x 2m
(8 ft 1½ in x 6 ft 6 in)
each square represents
0.5m (1 ft 7½ in)

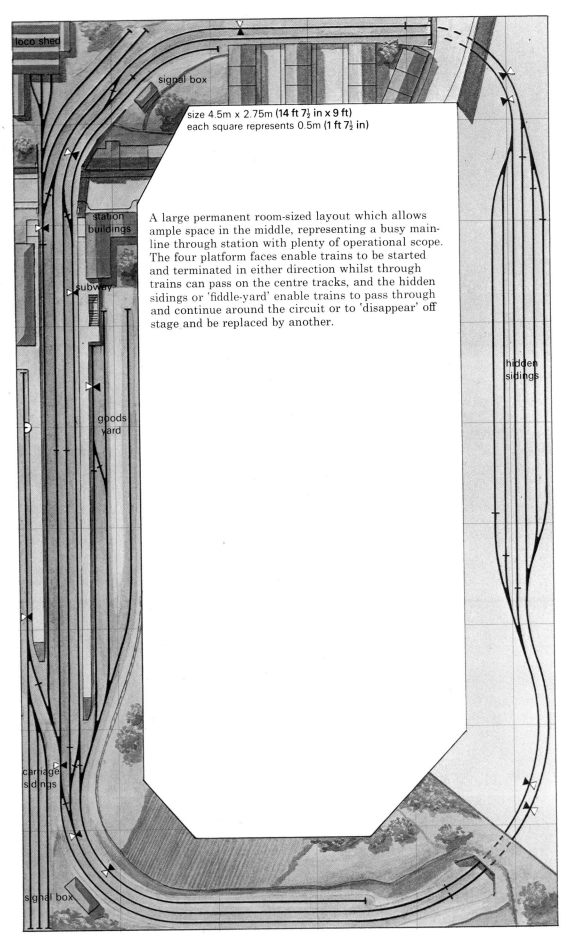

loco shed

signal box

size 4.5m x 2.75m (**14 ft 7½ in x 9 ft**)
each square represents 0.5m (**1 ft 7½ in**)

station
buildings

subway

A large permanent room-sized layout which allows
ample space in the middle, representing a busy mainline through station with plenty of operational scope.
The four platform faces enable trains to be started
and terminated in either direction whilst through
trains can pass on the centre tracks, and the hidden
sidings or 'fiddle-yard' enable trains to pass through
and continue around the circuit or to 'disappear' off
stage and be replaced by another.

hidden
sidings

goods
yard

carriage
sidings

signal box

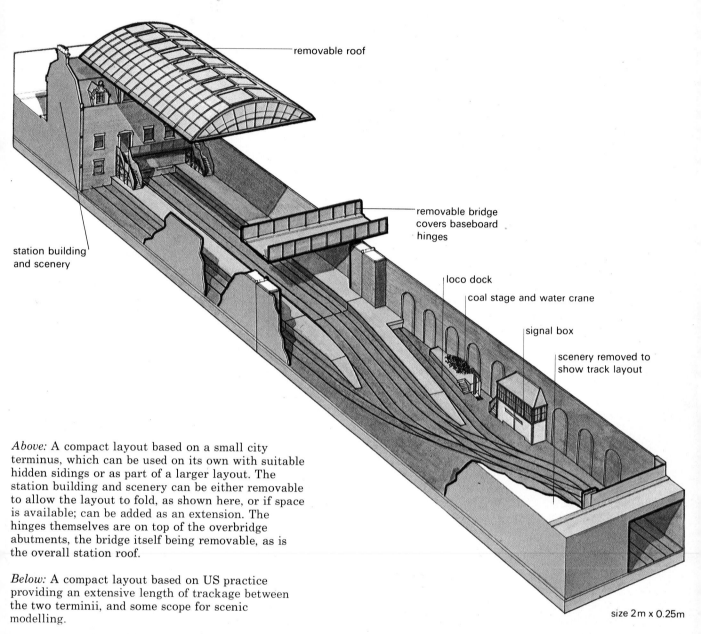

removable roof

removable bridge
covers baseboard
hinges

station building
and scenery

loco dock

coal stage and water crane

signal box

scenery removed to
show track layout

Above: A compact layout based on a small city terminus, which can be used on its own with suitable hidden sidings or as part of a larger layout. The station building and scenery can be either removable to allow the layout to fold, as shown here, or if space is available; can be added as an extension. The hinges themselves are on top of the overbridge abutments, the bridge itself being removable, as is the overall station roof.

Below: A compact layout based on US practice providing an extensive length of trackage between the two terminii, and some scope for scenic modelling.

size 2m x 0.25m

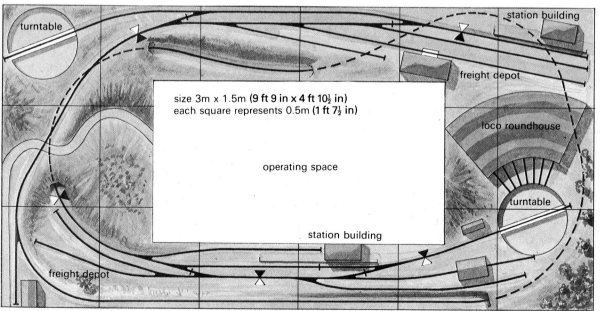

turntable

station building

freight depot

size 3m x 1.5m (**9 ft 9 in x 4 ft 10½ in**)
each square represents 0.5m (**1 ft 7½ in**)

operating space

loco roundhouse

turntable

station building

freight depot

NTRAK Modular System

A system of modular construction, in which the combined talents and equipment of many enthusiasts come together to produce a large layout, has added a new dimension to the hobby, particularly for those modellers with N gauge equipment. The concept – known as NTRAK – was first suggested in Spring 1973 by an American, Ben Davis, of the Belmont Shores Club. His idea was to produce a layout system consisting of small interchangeable modular units, each of which could be built by individuals or clubs, and for these to be assembled at any convenient location.

Within a year, the first layout was ready for public view in Las Vegas and measured 2.4m × 7.3m (8′ × 24′). By the time the NTRAK enthusiasts were celebrating their fifth anniversary in 1978 some 200 modules were known to have been assembled in America and other countries. Layouts as large as 7.3m × 29m (24′ × 96′) and containing 40 modules have been assembled. The individual components, in this particular case, came from places as far apart as 3,200 km (2,000 miles).

Each module is usually 61cm (2′) wide and can be either 1.22m (4′), 1.83m (6′) or 2.44m (8′) long. The modules are made with three through tracks to enable continuous lap running, designed in such a way that when the various modules come together they will each fit to produce a large and often complex layout. In addition to the mainline, each module will probably have its own special feature, such as a mountain route or a coal yard and mining track or other branch lines.

What makes NTRAK so attractive to modellers is its versatility. So long as they follow the simple and basic requirements for modular construction – set out in the NTRAK manual – they are free to use their own design and construction methods. So a large layout may be produced which incorporates a variety of modelling techniques. Another advantage is that modules from a home layout can be removed easily and taken to a club or a convention to be assembled with those of other modellers. This has proved to be a great asset for many clubs, for the advent of NTRAK has done away with the need to have a permanent club room, which can be expensive to hire. Instead, members bring their modules on club night to a suitable venue and a large and impressive layout can be constructed easily and quickly, then dismantled at the end of the evening.

Soon after NTRAK's first convention appearance enthusiasts organised themselves into a non-profit participation group with the aim of promoting model railroading in general, and N gauge in particular. Much of the credit for NTRAK's success goes to Jim Fitzgerald, one of its originators, who has edited and developed its newsletter from a single typewritten sheet to a lively, illustrated publication which appears six times a year.

It has a circulation of 1,500 and its news and photographic coverage of modular layouts and new N gauge equipment has greatly contributed to the rapid growth of interest, not only in the USA but in other countries. The newsletter goes out to Āustralia, New Zealand, Philippines, Japan, South Africa, Netherlands, Germany and the United Kingdom, as well as to US Navy ships.

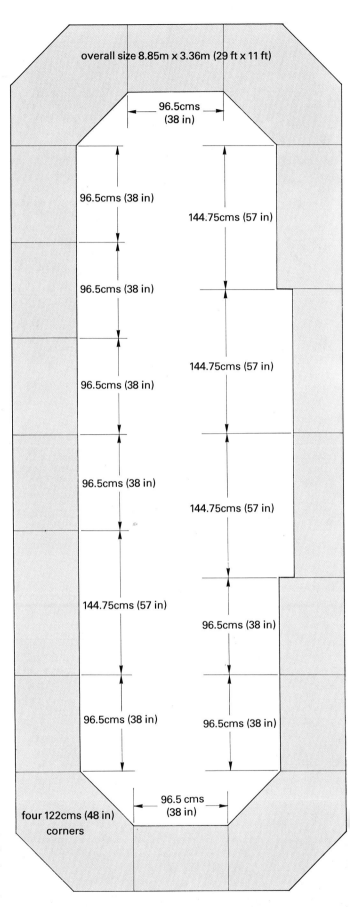

A diagram showing how several N-track modules can be combined to form a layout.

Above: Two examples of N-track modules, one (left) using foreground activity and a backdrop to create depth, the other utilising most of the modular area.

Below left: Three typical N-track modules, note the three common connecting tracks at each end.

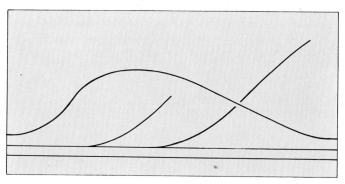

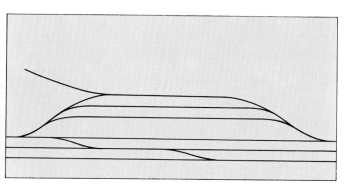

In England, a 4m × 4.25m (13′ × 14′) layout was assembled at High Wycombe, Buckinghamshire, in 1976, and by the end of 1978 more than a dozen such layouts had appeared in London and the Home Counties. The largest at that time was 3.3m × 8.8m (11′ × 29′) which contained 18 modules from eight different sources as far apart as Leicester, Oxford, Gloucester and High Wycombe.

Size and concept

The NTRAK concept, then, is enabling enthusiasts to demonstrate the advantages of N gauge by showing compact but beautifully detailed modular layouts linked together so that long prototypical trains can run on the mainlines around the layout. These long trains are a special feature of N gauge layouts and are often the envy of modellers who work with other scales. They are also a crowd puller at conventions and exhibitions, particularly when there is an attempt on the record. The normal train length for NTRAK layouts is 70–100 cars, but at Denver, Colorado, in 1977 a 355-car train was hauled by one N gauge locomotive on a very large layout. The train was over 30m (100′) long and there were times when both ends were out of sight at the same time.

The biggest NTRAK layout so far constructed appeared at the Dearborn, Michigan, convention in 1978. It was 3.6m × 29m (12′ × 96′) with a 16.5m (54′) yard area. This layout covered almost 16 scale kilometres (10 miles) from the tip of the yard, in and around the mainline, and back out to the end of the yard again, and a train running at 96 scale kilometres an hour (60 mph) took six minutes just to complete one circuit of the mainline.

The simple NTRAK concept has had such a rapid growth of interest that the N gauge manufacturers have been encouraged to produce a wider range of equipment, and that will undoubtedly attract many more modellers to modular systems in the future.

BUILDING LAYOUTS

Part of the fascination of the model railway hobby is its diversity. Modelling railways is a very personal business and everyone tends to go about it in his own way. Passionate debates arise over seemingly minor points of detail, and for any modeller who will tell you one way of doing something, there are ten who will tell you another.

So the information contained in this chapter is not intended to stand as the definitive statement of method – the only correct way of building a model railway – but is best seen as a distillation of experience and shared wisdom. The ideas are drawn from almost every conceivable source, and some from outside the hobby altogether, but all have been tried and tested.

From these pages it is hoped that the reader will obtain enough inspiration and confidence to try things out in practice. For the beginner, of course, everything is new, but even for the veteran there are always further aspects of the hobby to explore. There is much that the modeller has got to find out for himself – often by bitter experience – but there is at the same time a lot to be gained by taking advantage of the vast pool of knowledge and practical knowhow that exists in the hobby.

Success in railway modelling is not merely dependent upon skill and technique but is also a matter of approach. Far too many modellers build a layout, become dissatisfied with it and start again from scratch. This is often because in putting their ideas into practice they discover some underlying flaw in their approach. Time and trouble taken at the planning stage are always well rewarded later, and if the layout is well thought out to start with, in practical terms, then the modeller can devote his time to operating the layout and expanding it rather than consigning his creation to the scrapheap.

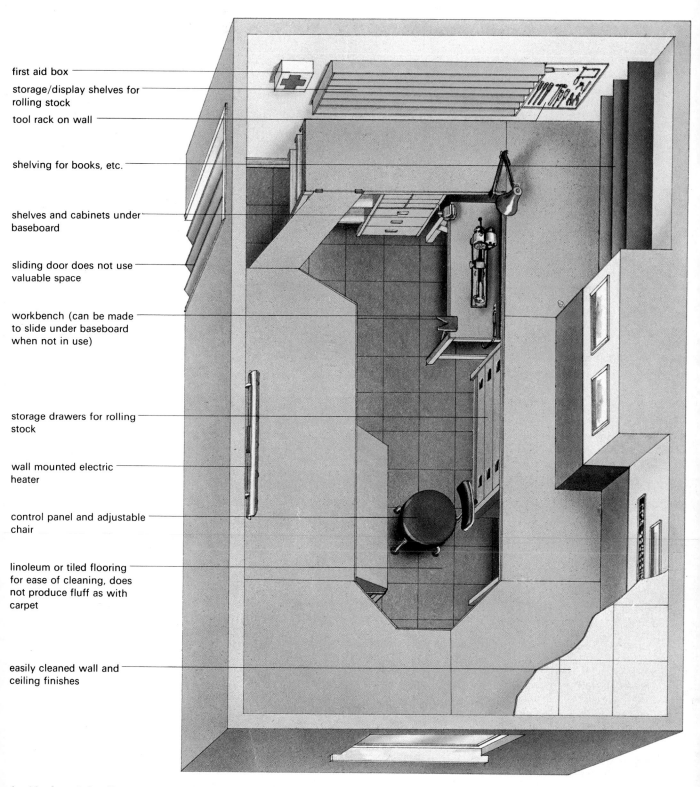

first aid box

storage/display shelves for rolling stock

tool rack on wall

shelving for books, etc.

shelves and cabinets under baseboard

sliding door does not use valuable space

workbench (can be made to slide under baseboard when not in use)

storage drawers for rolling stock

wall mounted electric heater

control panel and adjustable chair

linoleum or tiled flooring for ease of cleaning, does not produce fluff as with carpet

easily cleaned wall and ceiling finishes

An ideal model railway room and workshop for a permanent layout. Not all modellers have a room available to devote entirely to railway modelling, but some of the points shown here could be used to advantage for semi-permanent and temporary layout sites; of particular importance are easily-cleaned wall and ceiling surfaces which attract the minimum of dust and dirt, and the elimination of carpets which produce dust and fluff which quickly becomes entangled in model locomotive and rolling-stock mechanisms and wheels.

The Ergonomics of Model Railways

The science of ergonomics concerns the comfort, convenience and safety of man in relation to his surroundings, and is a discipline from which the railway modeller can derive much benefit. A layout that fulfils these criteria will be a lasting pleasure to work on and to operate.

Baseboard height and width have a great bearing on this matter. Generally the baseboard should be set slightly above waist height so that when seated, the operator can enjoy a lineside view, and standing up he can see the whole layout. In order to avoid damaging items at the front of the baseboard, no-one should be expected to stretch further than an arm's length to reach anything, and so all track should be laid within a metre or so (3' to 4') of the baseboard edge. Baseboards wider than this should be avoided unless access is possible from both sides, while high-level baseboards should be proportionally narrower.

Access

The business of getting in and out of a railway is sometimes overlooked until the last minute. Ideally, there should be no baseboards across the way to the control area, but this is only practicable in a fairly large room, or in lofts where the entrance is through the middle of the floor.

One answer is the lifting section – basically a hinged flap, as found in bar and shop counters. However, the hinges must be set above rail level or the flap will not lift properly. Never put a lifting flap too close to an inward opening door. Keep the baseboard far enough away to allow the door to open; otherwise re-hang the door to open outwards, or convert it to sliding operation.

If the baseboard is high enough, a simple duckunder can be used instead of a lifting flap. Leave a clear area under the baseboard, 750mm (2' 6") wide, preferably carpeted so that the visitor can crawl through in comfort. It is also sensible to strengthen the baseboard above the duckunder, and pad the underside, since someone is bound to bump into it sooner or later.

Lighting

Another important aid to comfort and convenience is good lighting. If standard domestic lighting is all that is available in the railway room, before beginning work on the layout it may be worthwhile installing spotlights or overhead fluorescent tubes.

Both for your own comfort and that of the models, it is important to keep the railway room well ventilated and at an even temperature. Severe variations in humidity and temperature can cause baseboards and trackwork to distort.

Safety

Tidiness is also a point to watch, as undue rubble can create a fire hazard as well as incurring the displeasure of the domestic authorities. In particular, electrical leads must be kept clear of walkways, and radiant fires adequately guarded. If you are at all unsure about mains wiring it is advisable to consult a qualified electrician. Providing a first-aid box is also a sensible precaution, but hopefully it will never be needed.

Ease of access to every point of a layout is an important factor in model railway design. The curtains conceal another point of access to parts of the Sherwood section.

Opposite: Two means of building permanent baseboards across doorways. *Above:* A lifting flap can be placed across the doorway, but sufficient room should be allowed behind the door to allow it to be opened in case of an emergency.

Below: Where space is at a premium, the door can be replaced by a sliding or folding door, enabling narrower baseboards to be used. This diagram also shows a duck-under solid baseboard in place of the lifting flap, a simpler arrangement more suitable for the younger and more agile enthusiast. Note the carpeting on the floor beneath, for comfort, and the strengthened battening and foam padding for safety.

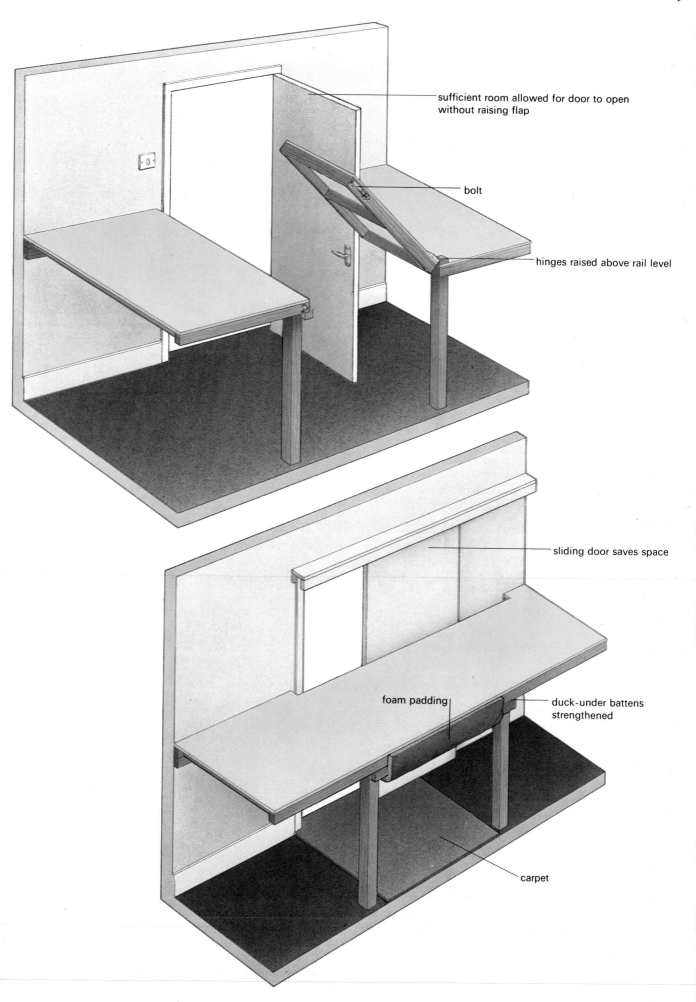

sufficient room allowed for door to open without raising flap

bolt

hinges raised above rail level

sliding door saves space

foam padding

duck-under battens strengthened

carpet

Baseboard Basics

Baseboards are without doubt the most important part of a model railway – the edifice can only survive if the foundation is sound. Whatever method of baseboard construction is employed, there are certain basic points to be observed.

Firstly, it is essential that the frame be strong enough to withstand knocks and bumps. These are bound to occur at some time, as for example when visitors may lean against the edge of the baseboard, even when discouraged from doing so.

Apart from such incidental stresses and strains, it is worth bearing in mind the permanent load the supports will have to bear. Electrical control equipment in particular can be quite heavy, and extra strength may have to be built in around the control panel.

Once a firm foundation has been provided, the modeller can consider the surface on which the track is to be laid. He has the choice between providing an overall baseboard top, or laying individual trackbeds for each section of railway on an open-topped framework. Materials recommended for baseboard tops include blockboard, plywood and hard insulation board: but especially chipboard or particle board, which is rigid and yet soft enough to accept pins and screws readily. A thickness of 12mm ($\frac{1}{2}''$) is usually adequate, provided that the board is laid upon a sufficiently sturdy frame. Material to be avoided at all costs are soft wallboard, which lacks strength and hardboard which, while being too hard to take pins, is far too pliable and will bend under stress of any kind.

Ironing Out the Bumps

The desire of all railway modellers is to achieve smooth running trains, and for this they will need well-laid track on a level baseboard. It goes without saying that the track can only be as level as the baseboard upon which it is laid.

Creating a plane surface is not difficult but demands a certain amount of care. A piece of chipboard or particle board, for example, flat to start with, may exhibit bumps as soon as it is laid on a frame however much care may have been taken in constructing the frame. The bigger bumps will be obvious immediately, while the smaller undulations can be discovered by running a straight edge or spirit level over the surface. The quickest method of eliminating these irregularities is to use a power drill fitted with a sanding disc. Hand tools such as planes will be slower, but a great deal less messy – a point worth bearing in mind if the work is being done indoors.

Undulations along the track do not necessarily cause derailments, but they can make the motion of a train resemble that of a roller coaster. Slopes which cross the track are altogether more serious since if one rail sags below the other derailments are almost inevitable.

Both when planning and when actually building a layout, avoid gradients and curves that are too abrupt. This will not only facilitate smoother running of trains, but it will also be following prototype practice. At the start of a gradient the line should climb gradually at first, while between straight and curved track there should always be a transition curve.

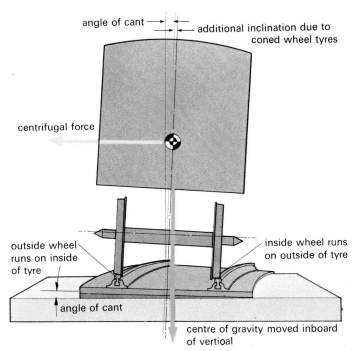

Above: In order to ease the passage of trains over curved track, prototype rolling stock is fitted with conical wheel-tyres, and the track itself is banked-up on the outside of the curve, or 'superelevated'. The speed of the train around the curve produces centrifugal force acting away from the centre of curvature, tending to move the centre of gravity towards the outside rail. This force also causes the wheels to bear against the outside rail and thus the larger, inner edges of the outside wheels are in contact with the rail, whilst the smaller outside edges of the inner wheels run on the inside rail, producing an additional tilt in the train towards the centre and restoring equilibrium. The difference in circumference of the inner and outer edges of the wheel tyres also compensate for the slightly greater length of the outside rail of the curve, thus minimising tyre and rail wear. Model railway vehicles are also provided with conical wheel-profiles, but superelevation should only be attempted if the vehicles are provided with some means of compensated suspension.

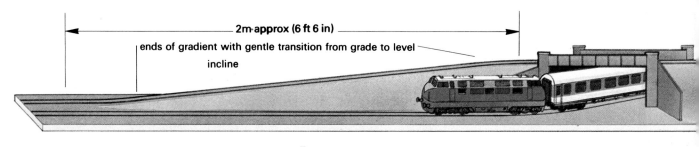

2m approx (6 ft 6 in)

ends of gradient with gentle transition from grade to level

incline

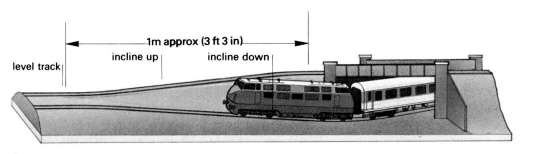

1m approx (3 ft 3 in)

incline up | incline down

level track

Above: When planning flying junctions, the length of the gradients involved can be halved if both tracks are given inclines up and down. The dimensions shown are for OO/HO gauges.

Below: When planning multiple-track curves, additional spacing of the track centres is required to provide adequate clearance for the overhangs of bogie vehicles on adjacent tracks. The sharper the radius used, the more clearance has to be allowed.

Below: The importance of strong baseboard construction can be appreciated from this view of the Northern American Lines.

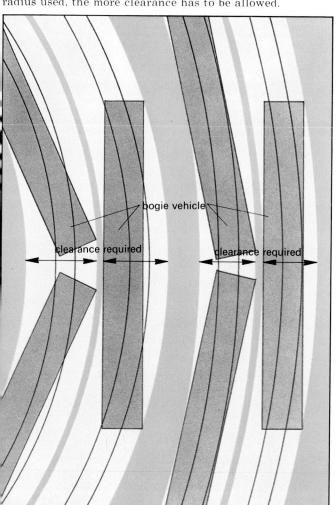

bogie vehicle

clearance required

clearance required

Portable Baseboards

Before taking the drastic step of building a permanent baseboard, think for a moment of the possible future of your railway. Are you likely to move house shortly? Would it be convenient to be able to move the layout into a different room? Might you perhaps want to show your railway at exhibitions? By taking the trouble to make your baseboards portable you could end up with an infinitely more flexible model railway, and one that will be able to survive most conceivable upheavals.

Another advantage of portable baseboards is that they can be used in places to which you do not have permanent access. This particular factor is of relevance to many model railway clubs who share their clubrooms with other organizations and have to dismantle everything at the end of each running session.

Baseboard Size

There is a widespread belief – firmly held despite evidence to the contrary – that a baseboard unit as large as 2m × 1.5m (7′ × 5′) is truly portable. This makes nonsense of the concept. 'Portable' in this sense means something that can easily be carried by one person without causing personal injury, or damage to the surroundings. Damage to property, possessions and to the model itself is bound to ensue if excessively large units are transported: it is best to keep the baseboard size below 1.5m × 0.75m (5′ × 2′ 6″). On club layouts, where there is generally more space and more willing hands are available, a larger module is feasible.

Of course a baseboard of the above size is too small for a complete layout in all except the smallest scales. A typical OO/HO portable layout would extend over four to eight such boards. There comes a point, however, when a layout simply becomes too large to be practicable in portable form. For example, if more than ten sections are involved then so much time will be taken up by assembling and dismantling the layout that little will be left for running the trains.

Principles of Construction

The construction of a straightforward portable baseboard is shown opposite. Lightweight but sturdy materials are used: 50mm × 25mm (2″ × 1″) timber covered with chipboard. While flat baseboards are much simpler to build, the construction of multi-level portable baseboards is perfectly feasible, but requires the use of stronger frames.

The success or failure of a portable model railway depends chiefly upon the accuracy with which the various sections can be married up each time the layout is transported. A variety of ingenious methods for joining baseboards has been thought up over the years – the diagram opposite shows the most successful and also one of the most straightforward.

Baseboards are the foundation of a model railway; if portable baseboards are constructed on correct principles then 'portable' need not mean temporary; indeed because of their mobility, portable layouts often have longer lives than many permanent ones.

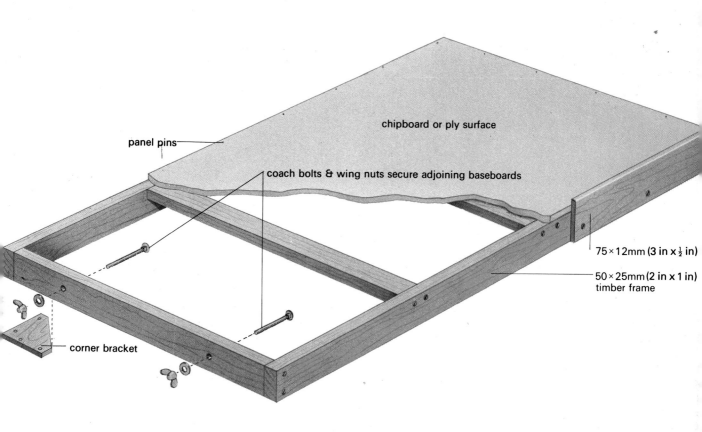

panel pins

chipboard or ply surface

coach bolts & wing nuts secure adjoining baseboards

75×12mm (3 in x ½ in)

50×25mm (2 in x 1 in) timber frame

corner bracket

Above: Simple baseboard construction from 25 × 50mm timber with a chipboard or plywood surface. Coach bolts and wing-nuts make a simple fastening for joining temporary and semi-permanent baseboards.

Right: Two methods of joining temporary baseboards to preserve the alignment of tracks and scenery. On the left, using a modified hinge with removable pin, and right, the baseboards are accurately located by means of headless screws and fastened by metal catches.

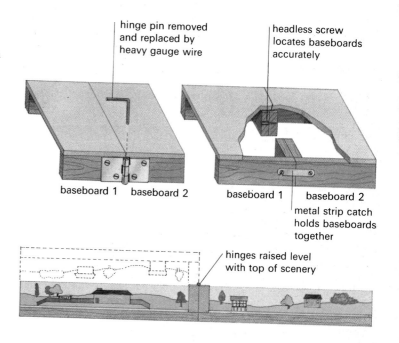

hinge pin removed and replaced by heavy gauge wire

headless screw locates baseboards accurately

baseboard 1   baseboard 2

baseboard 1   baseboard 2

metal strip catch holds baseboards together

hinges raised level with top of scenery

Opposite: An impressive and sturdy layout which has been achieved on a portable trellis-table base by three British modellers. The Wyandotte Transfer layout consists of five easily transportable baseboards.

Above: A hinged baseboard folds to a convenient size for storage. The hinges must be raised above the level of the highest part of the scenery.

Permanent Baseboards

Converting a portable model railway into a permanent layout is a simple matter – simply screw it to battens fixed to the walls and floor. This will give the baseboards increased rigidity while allowing them to be removed later should the need arise. In general the rule applies that the less likely the need to move the railway the larger and more permanent can be the baseboard sections.

In circumstances where the long-term future of the railway is completely secure, sectional construction can be avoided altogether, as for example in the case of many club layouts where the club premises are owned outright. This permanency gives the modeller tremendous scope – he can use the space available in whatever way he likes.

With a permanent baseboard it becomes much simpler to incorporate inclines and have tracks running on different levels. A powered jigsaw is particularly valuable here and can save much laborious work. As long as the top surface of the baseboard is made of flexible material it is a simple matter to cut out a tongue wide enough for a trackbed. Raise it to the required angle with wooden blocks and an incline is formed. The steepest gradient normally used in main line railway construction is 1 in 70 (two per cent). For reasons of space steeper gradients are often resorted to on the model although 1 in 30 (three per cent) is perhaps the maximum advisable.

High-level tracks and stations can be carried on lightweight baseboards. These should ideally be removable if there are tracks running beneath. In OO/HO a clearance of 60mm ($2\frac{1}{2}''$) must be allowed for between levels and so even at the maximum gradient of 1 in 30 (three per cent) a minimum length of 2m (6' 6") is required for one track to rise and pass over another.

Open-topped Construction

With the added complexity of different levels, the use of the flat-topped baseboard begins to impose certain restrictions on layout design. So by limiting the use of flat baseboards to the trackbed itself, and by mounting these on an open-topped framework, it becomes much simpler to design a model railway in three dimensions with hills and valleys, embankments and cuttings, tunnels and viaducts. In real life the countryside that railways run through is by no means always flat. In general, while the railway tries to follow as level a course as possible, the terrain rises or falls.

Many modellers find it difficult to visualize and interpret such a three-dimensional scene in model terms. For those lacking in confidence there are two easy ways out – one is to proceed simply by trial and error, building up the model landscape bit by bit. Such a method has much to recommend it, and many fine layouts have evolved in this way.

Perhaps a more sophisticated method is to build a model of the model, using such materials as card, stripwood and modelling clay. This method also involves trial and error, but has the great advantage that it enables one to visualize the whole railway at once, while naturally being cheaper and easier to alter than the actual layout.

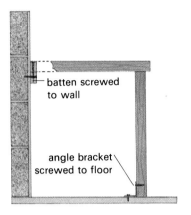

batten screwed to wall

angle bracket screwed to floor

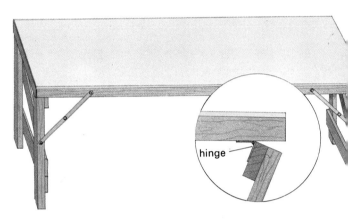

hinge

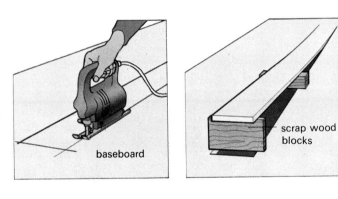

baseboard

scrap wood blocks

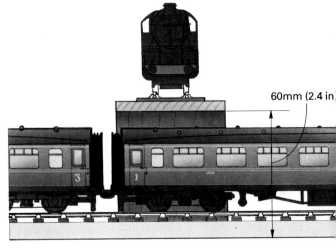

60mm (2.4 in)

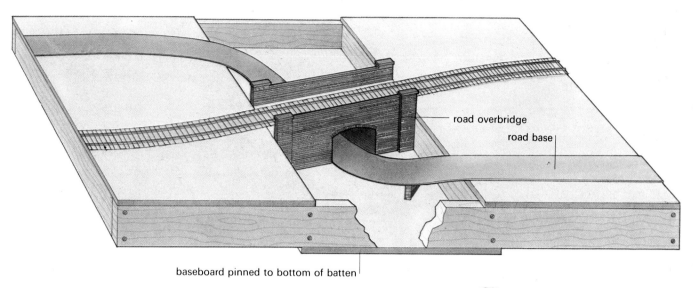

road overbridge

road base

baseboard pinned to bottom of batten

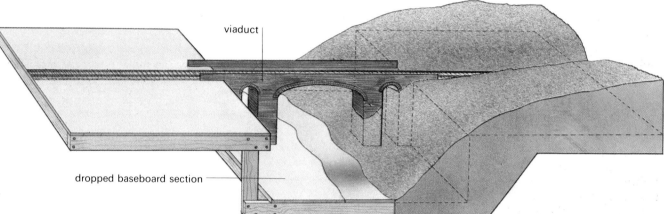

viaduct

dropped baseboard section

Top left: Permanent baseboards can be secured to walls and floors by means of battens and angle brackets.

Upper left: A semi-permanent baseboard can be mounted on hinged trestle-type legs.

Lower left: If the baseboard top surfaces is of plywood or a similar flexible material, a simple method of forming the track-bases for gradients is to cut a tongue in the surface with a keyhole saw or electric jig-saw. Blocks of scrap wood can then be wedged underneath the tongue to adjust gradient.

Bottom left: Where one track crosses another, a minimum clearance of 60mm must be allowed in OO/HO scales between baseboard and the bottom of the track-base.

Top: A shallow underbridge can be modelled by lowering the baseboard surface under the bridge, pinning the baseboard to the underside of the battens.

Above: Deeper scenic features, such as river valleys and ravines can be modelled by 'dropping' the level of the baseboard entirely.

Right: An impressive example of high-level track (right), as a Sante Fe 'Mountain' class 4-8-2 crosses Dry Gulf Trestle on John Porter's North American Lines model.

The L-Girder System

The construction of open-topped baseboards can easily result in a veritable spider's web of timber, with legs, diagonals and supports in profusion. There is however a way to simplify the substructure of permanent baseboards, reducing the amount of timber required, while actually increasing the rigidity of the whole. A further advantage of the 'L-girder' system, as it is known, is that it can use any available sizes of timber, including offcuts.

The L-girder was the brainchild of Linn Westcott, editor *emeritus* of 'Model Railroader'. It is based on a pair of timber girders that look like inverted Ls in cross section. Supported on legs where necessary, these girders run the whole length of the layout. The flat upper edges of the girders provide a firm base on which a light timber superstructure of cross pieces and risers can be built. This in turn supports the plywood or chipboard bases on which the tracks themselves run, as well as providing a lightweight framework upon which the scenery can be constructed.

Methods and Materials

The ideal size of timber to use for the L-girders themselves is 75mm × 25mm (3″ × 1″) for the vertical sections, topped by 50mm × 12mm (2″ × $\frac{1}{2}$″) pieces of equal length. Properly joined and glued the two will form a strong beam. The trackbases are conveniently made from 12mm ($\frac{1}{2}$″) thick material but no other dimension is critical – timber of any convenient size can be incorporated.

Because of the strength of the L-girders, it is possible to build quite a large layout with only two girders and four legs, provided the layout is basically rectangular in shape. However, as the layout design increases in scale and complexity then proportionally more girders and legs will be required.

Each of the various types of baseboard construction described so far has its own particular applications. Flat-topped baseboards are ideal for smaller layouts where the railway itself takes up a large proportion of the space available, and open-topped construction is better if one wishes to show the railway in its setting, but for a fairly large layout where one wishes to show a complete scenic panorama, then L-girder is preferable. The modeller can think in terms of the whole landscape through which the railway runs, while the railway itself can only gain from being seen in context rather than in isolation.

Using the L-girder system by no means necessitates having all the tracks at base level, and it is equally easy to construct a multi-level system. During construction it is a simple matter to adjust the various supports by moving the position of the screws by which they are fixed, until the track bases are either completely level or at the exact gradient required.

Clearly, once it has been constructed an L-girder layout cannot be moved. However, it can easily be dismantled and reduced to a series of re-usable track bases and other lengths of timber. If the overall structure has been sufficiently well conceived, it will be capable of re-erection in a substantially similar form at a new location.

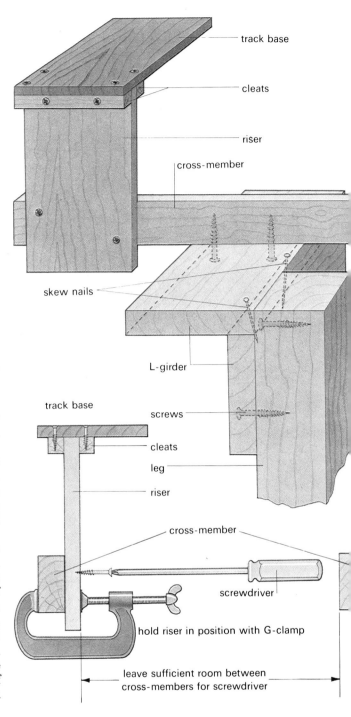

Top: The basic constructional elements of an L-girder baseboard can be made from any rough wood, including second-hand timber. All track bases are supported by risers screwed to the cross-members.

Above: It is important that sufficient room is allowed between the cross-members to allow a screw driver to be used to secure the risers in position. The position of the risers can be adjusted by using G-clamps until the final position is determined.

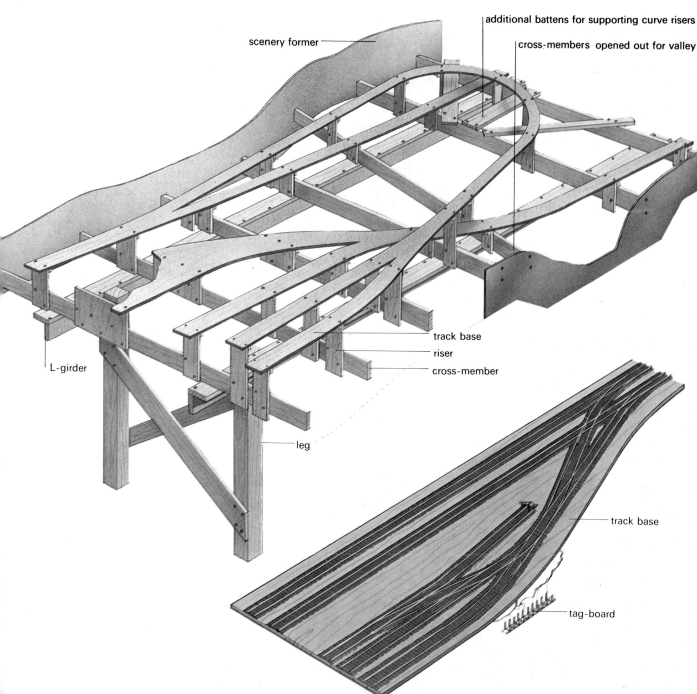

additional battens for supporting curve risers

cross-members opened out for valley

scenery former

track base

riser

cross-member

L-girder

leg

track base

tag-board

Top: A section through an L-girder baseboard, illustrating the total flexibility of this method in allowing for any desired scenic feature. Scenery formers are shown nailed to the ends of the cross-members, the formers for scenery inside the baseboard area are added after the final positions of the track-bases are determined.

Above: Complex track formations are best constructed in modular form, including point-motors and all wiring, before adding to the layout. Wiring can be attached to a tag-board which is then connected to the remainder of the layout wiring.

Right: This detail from the Golden Gate Railroaders layout shows how a combination of wire mesh base and L-girder system can produce an impressive multi-level scenic effect of a very high standard.

Basic Tracklaying

A model railway is only as good as its track. Time and trouble taken with tracklaying will be more than amply repaid by reliable running later on.

Check first that your baseboards or trackbases are level where they should be level, and on a gradient where they should be on a gradient – once the track is down such adjustments will be much more difficult to make. Then before actually fixing the track in place, lay it out to see whether it is likely to fit or not. The use of paper templates, cut to the exact sizes of the various track sections available, will make such planning easier.

Depending upon choice of scale and gauge, three main options are open to the modeller: sectional track, flexible track and hand-built track. Nowadays it is sometimes as expensive to buy component parts as to buy track that is already made up; so unless ready-made track is unavailable in the gauge in which you are working, building your own track will not necessarily save you money.

Section or Flexible?

Many modellers' first introduction to tracklaying is with the sectional track pieces of the traditional train set. Such track has the advantage of being easily taken up and relaid, but its disadvantage is that it is only available in straight or fixed-radius sections. On the real railway, straight track merges gradually into relatively gentle curves, never as sharp and abrupt as those which the trains in model train sets are asked to negotiate.

So while sectional track can have its uses, particularly within the confines of stations, when it comes to laying a stretch of open main line with the sweeping curves of the prototype, then flexible track is best. This is, in any case, often compatible with sectional track, and so the modeller progressing to flexible track need not dispose of the track he already owns.

Because of the difference in radius between inner and outer rails, flexible track laid around a curve will have to be cut to fit. A miniature hacksaw is best used for this and the cutting operation can be made simpler and more accurate if a block is made to hold the end of the track steady. This block can easily be used *in situ*, avoiding the need for elaborate marking out.

In order to make room for the rail-joiners, or fishplates, it may be necessary to cut away part of the sleeper assembly, but so as not to leave an ugly gap, insert a spare sleeper after the track has been laid.

Once the track layout has been made to fit, the track should be pinned down to hold it firmly in place. For each metre or 36″ length use five panel pins, driven home with a flat-ended pin punch. Do not push the pins fully in until you are sure that all the track is correctly aligned.

An alternative method is to stick the track down on a foam or cork underlay. A number of commercial manufacturers supply specially indented foam underlays as accessories for their track.

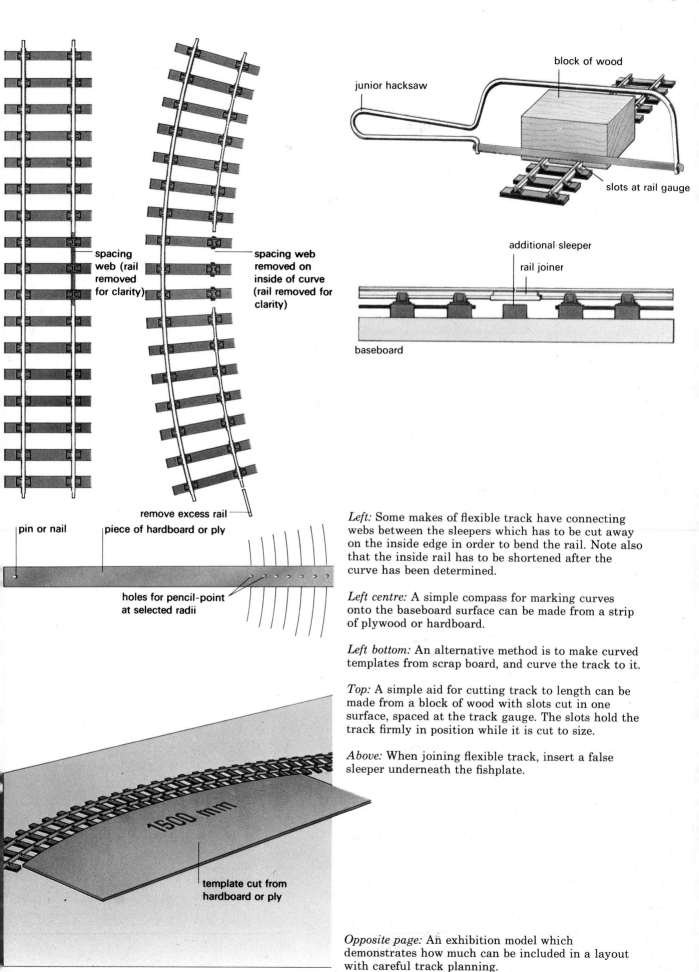

spacing web (rail removed for clarity)

spacing web removed on inside of curve (rail removed for clarity)

block of wood

junior hacksaw

slots at rail gauge

additional sleeper

rail joiner

baseboard

remove excess rail

pin or nail

piece of hardboard or ply

holes for pencil-point at selected radii

1500 mm

template cut from hardboard or ply

Left: Some makes of flexible track have connecting webs between the sleepers which has to be cut away on the inside edge in order to bend the rail. Note also that the inside rail has to be shortened after the curve has been determined.

Left centre: A simple compass for marking curves onto the baseboard surface can be made from a strip of plywood or hardboard.

Left bottom: An alternative method is to make curved templates from scrap board, and curve the track to it.

Top: A simple aid for cutting track to length can be made from a block of wood with slots cut in one surface, spaced at the track gauge. The slots hold the track firmly in position while it is cut to size.

Above: When joining flexible track, insert a false sleeper underneath the fishplate.

Opposite page: An exhibition model which demonstrates how much can be included in a layout with careful track planning.

Turnouts

Having paid large sums of money to obtain your turnouts, treat them with great care. They are extremely delicate, particularly those in the smaller scales. Every reputable track manufacturer provides an instruction sheet, so be sure to read it. While certain liberties can be taken with the laying of plain track, turnouts themselves must be laid with the maximum possible accuracy. Hours spent checking levels and alignments at this stage will save even more time and trouble later on.

It is remarkably easy to bend a turnout in the vertical plane. If the crossing, or frog, is only slightly proud, there is a good chance it will cause a derailment at some time. With a noticeable difference in level, accidents become inevitable.

Start by checking the baseboard with a spirit level and eliminating any unwanted undulations. Then lay your track formation down loosely, using fishplates but not track pins, and then check the alignment. Even when completely satisfied, do not pin the turnouts firmly to the baseboard. Leave the pin heads very slightly above the sleepers to hold the turnout firmly in place while still allowing it to be lifted and relaid without damage, should this be required at a later stage in the construction of the layout.

Turnouts and Trackplans

If you are trying to represent a real railway in model form, then make sure that you use your turnouts in a realistic way. Each railway has its own particular ideas about track formations, but certain overall principles apply, such as the avoidance of facing crossovers on double-track main lines. With the reconstruction and modernization of track layouts there has been a trend towards greater simplicity, with fewer running lines and fewer turnouts. The increased speed of main-line trains in Britain, for example, has led to the virtual elimination of the diamond crossing at junctions and crossovers – a major source of vibration and wear – while the number of facing turnouts has been reduced to a minimum.

Model turnouts are usually made individually, but it is just as common on a full-size railway to see a composite track formation, made up of several turnouts and crossings. Think in terms of crossovers, double junctions and so on, rather than individual turnouts. However wide a range of turnouts is offered by manufacturers, there will always be omissions as in the prototype most turnouts are tailor-made to fit the specific location. This is an area in which the modeller who is able to make his own trackwork will always have the advantage as far as realism is concerned.

On an open-topped baseboard there are also practical advantages in grouping turnouts and crossings in this way. At each end of stations, and at other strategic points around the layout, concentrations of turnouts will occur. If each such assembly is laid out on a single trackbase and treated as a unit, then all the wiring and control gear can also be fixed to this board and can be tested on a workbench before actually being put in place. Later on the layout can be modified or moved without causing damage to these assemblies.

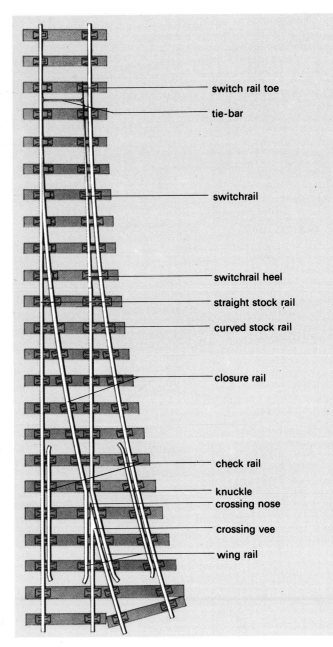

Above: A simple left-hand turnout showing the terminology of the various parts. The section comprising of the closure rails, crossing vee and wing rails is commonly known as the 'frog'.

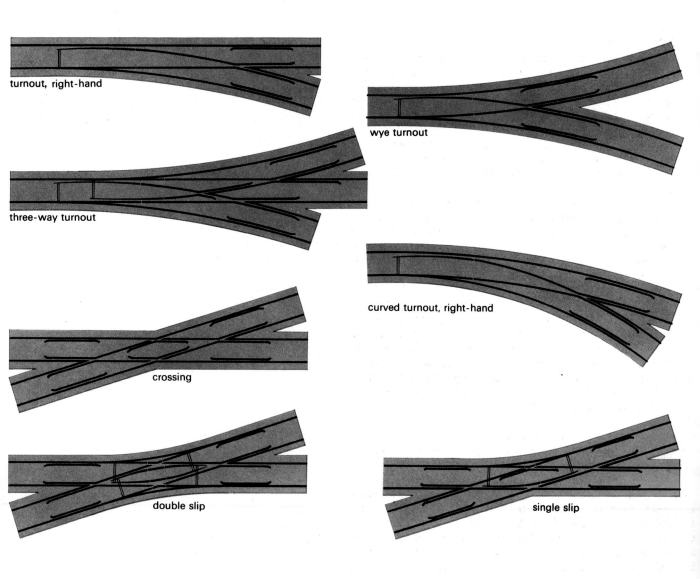

turnout, right-hand

wye turnout

three-way turnout

curved turnout, right-hand

crossing

double slip

single slip

Above: Common forms of turnouts and crossings which are available from proprietary manufacturers.

Below: Note the complexity of turnouts on Rolf Ertmers Altenbeken layout.

Improving the Track

Next time you visit your nearest station, stop for a few minutes and look at the track itself – the 'rail way' upon which the trains run. While rails and sleepers are undoubtedly the most important elements, they must be seen in context. Prototype track is generally laid upon a sub-base and held secure by ballast, while beside the line is the cess or drainage ditch. Other important details are mileposts and gradient posts, lineside fencing and the traditional platelayer's hut. While model track pinned directly onto the baseboard will function perfectly well, it will not resemble a stretch of railway line in miniature unless some of the other ingredients are added.

Beginning first with the sub-base, this will raise the track slightly above the level of the baseboard and so give it the correct cross section. Depending upon the material used, this underlay can provide the added benefits of smoother and quieter running. 3mm ($\frac{1}{8}''$) thick cork is an ideal material for this purpose but tends to be expensive. A more easily available material is linoleum; offcuts can usually be obtained free from furniture shops. Foam rubber is often used as an underlay, and gives a very smooth and quiet ride, but somehow it always tends to look like foam rubber and its springiness makes vertical alignment of the track extremely difficult. Various model railway suppliers have attempted to produce scale ballast, but all have found the cost of screening, packing and transporting to be prohibitive. Grit can easily be screened at home with an old sieve.

Model Ballast

Covering the sub-base and holding the sleepers in position is the ballast. In model form this can be made of cork granules or fine grit. The most realistic material is in this case the real thing, granite chips screened down to scale fineness.

Some modellers mix the ballast with various sticky mixtures and then spend tedious hours coaxing it into place. A much simpler method is to apply the ballast dry, brush it away from the tops of the sleepers, and then, once it is in the right place, apply a solution of 50 per cent PVA white adhesive and 50 per cent water. Add a drop of liquid detergent to reduce the surface tension and allow the solution to soak in thoroughly.

After about an hour the mixture will begin to set, but for best results leave it for a full 24 hours before removing the surplus ballast. This can be done with a vacuum cleaner, but in order not to waste any spare material, cover the nozzle with an old nylon stocking. Car vacuum cleaners are particularly handy as it is possible to collect the spare ballast in the machine itself and empty it out afterwards.

All the ballast needs now to give it the correct appearance is a coat of paint although pre coloured ballast is available but rare. While colour varies from railway to railway, and depends very much on the type of rock or other material used for ballast, the most usual shade is an overall grey. This extends to the sleepers, which although usually modelled as brown, often weather to a dark grey on the prototype. Modern-image modellers, incidentally, should not forget to use concrete sleepered track where appropriate.

A detail of track ballast in preparation by the North London Group for their new layout.

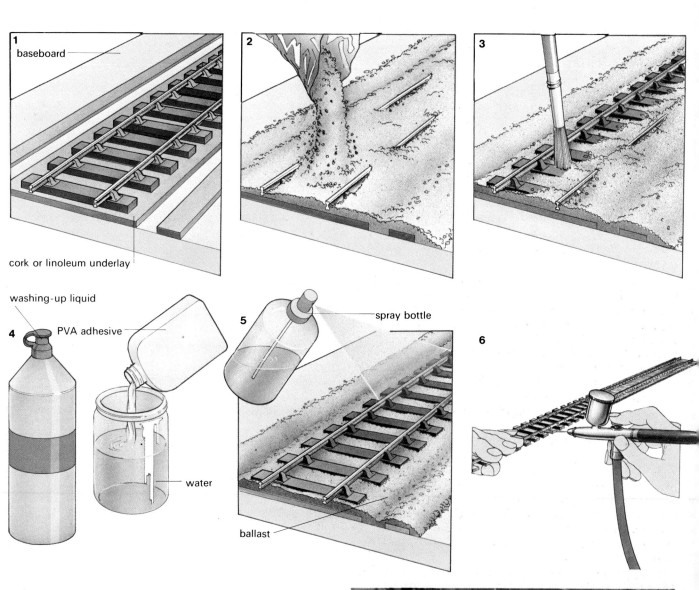

1. Prototype track is arranged with a cess (drain) on either side of the track-bed. To achieve this in a model, strips of cork linoleum underlay are fixed to the baseboard.
2. Scale 'ballast' chippings are poured over the track.
3. Ballast is shaped with a stiff hog's-hair brush and any excess removed.
4. Preparing an adhesive solution with a one-to-one mix of P.V.A. adhesive and water and a few drops of washing-up liquid.
5. Adhesive mixture is sprayed onto the track using a perfume atomiser or garden spray etc.
6. Further realism can be achieved by spraying the sides of the rails a rusty-brown colour with an airbrush before fixing. Any overspray onto the rail surface can be removed with a rail-cleaning block or emery-cloth.

Right: An imaginative use of ballast, as in this detail from the Heckmondwike layout, makes the model extremely realistic.

Simple Landscape

Landscape modelling is a very individualistic art and no two people will recommend the same method. While a certain approach may produce magnificent results for one person, it may be totally useless for another. Modelling a landscape is like painting a picture; each modeller must find the medium that suits him best and develop it in his own way. While innumerable different techniques exist, in broad terms these can be reduced to three main types: the solid, the mat and the shell.

The solid method of landscape modelling came into its own when expanded polystyrene first became available. Here was a lightweight material that could be carved, painted and glued. Another major advantage was its low cost, but polystyrene also had its drawbacks. An extremely disquieting one is that polystyrene is extremely inflammable. Moreover, polystyrene makes a particularly messy material for carving, and can be accidentally melted by certain paint solvents. To keep the mess to a minimum, cut polystyrene with a hot wire. A 300mm (12″) length of resistance wire in an improvized U-shaped holder, connected to the 12 volt transformer, will work as effectively as any commercial tool.

For modelling landscape by the mat method there are various proprietary products available, while surgical lint, dyed an appropriate colour and laid over a foundation of crumpled newspaper, can also be used. One of the most successful techniques has been evolved by the Revd. Peter Denny. First apply hot size, then while it is wet, colour the lint with poster paint. As the lint dries lay it in place, and by the time the lint is completely dry it will have become virtually rigid.

Chicken Wire and Plaster

The third, and most traditional method, is the shell. This requires either a permanent substructure of chicken wire over formers, or simply a sheet of dampened newspaper laid over a crumpled paper foundation. Mix plaster until it has reached a slightly gritty consistency and then dip small pieces of paper towelling in it. Apply successive layers of plaster-coated paper to the foundation until a shell has built up. When it is dry, remove the paper foundation and brush any irregularities over with more plaster.

When covering large areas with the mat or shell method, additional support is needed. Cut series of formers to the approximate profile of the model hillside. As these will remain hidden they can be made of any scrap material such as plywood or card that happens to be available.

Texturing

Scenery made using the mat method will already be textured, and so only needs to be painted to give the appearance of grass. Otherwise it is necessary to cover the surface with a scatter material such as dyed sawdust or flock. Green or brown gloss paint make ideal fixatives but in practice a variety of unholy mixtures tends to be used, the older and stickier the better! Scatter the flock thickly over the fixative, cover it with a sheet of paper and press it firmly down. As with ballast, once the fixative has dried, remove the surplus flock with a vacuum cleaner.

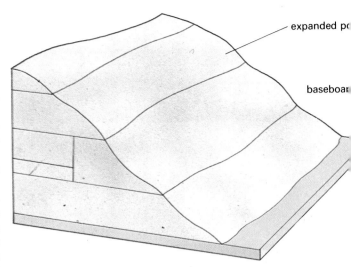

expanded po

baseboar

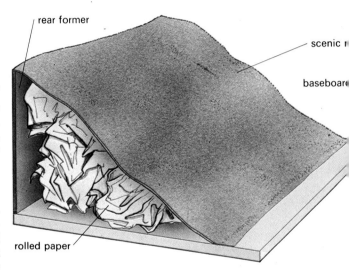

rear former

scenic

baseboar

rolled paper

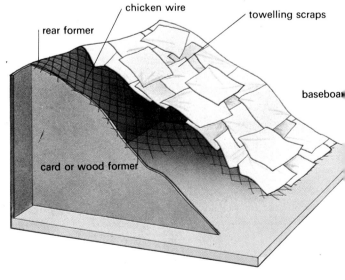

chicken wire

towelling scraps

rear former

baseboa

card or wood former

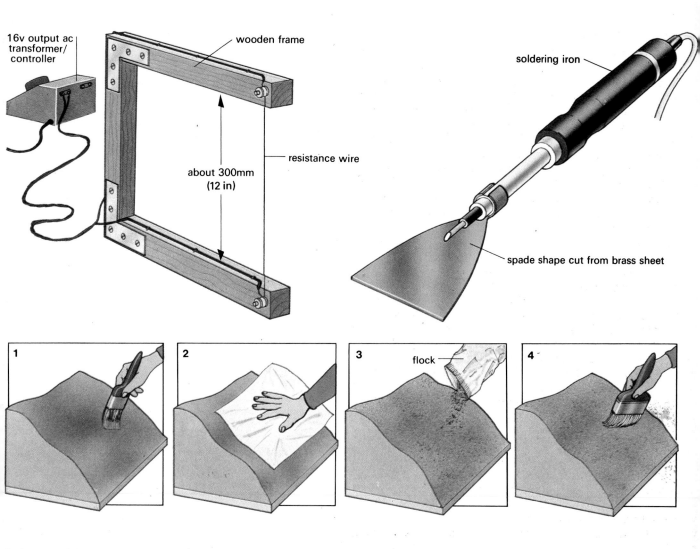

Left: Three of the principal means of scenery construction. At the top is the simplest method using blocks of expanded polystyrene. In the centre is shown the method using a proprietary scenic 'mat' over card or wood formers and screwed or rolled paper. At the bottom is shown the traditional method employing rear and transverse formers with a chicken-wire top surface, moulded to form the scenic features, and overlayed with scraps of towelling or similar material soaked in plaster.

Top: Two simple tools for shaping expanded polystyrene can be simply made. On the left is shown a simple 'hot-wire' cutting frame for shaping large pieces, and on the right is shown a simple modification that can be made to a soldering iron for more delicate shaping of scenic features by adding a brass 'spade' to the bit.

Above: One method of finishing scenery.
1. Paint on a thick layer of old, sticky, green-brown paint.
2. When almost dry, press paper down onto the surface of the paint to roughen the surface.
3. Sprinkle flock powder in appropriate colours onto the tacky paint.
4. When dry, brush off any excess flock powder.

Below: The starkness of a bridge or viaduct can be cleverly transformed by the use of trees and shrubs.

Rocks, Roads and Water

Rocks can be extremely effective in model form. One of the most adaptable methods of modelling them is to build up, and then carve, rock faces from slow-setting plaster. Once the plaster is dry it can be painted appropriately.

The amount of work involved can be much reduced by moulding rocks in quick-drying plaster. A simple mould can be made from crumpled aluminium foil. This is then pressed into the newly mixed plaster and left until the plaster has dried. A little carving may be needed, but in most cases a quick rub with a wire brush is sufficient.

Rocks can also be carved from polystyrene, while with care most effective rock faces can be created from small pieces of slate, set in plaster. The simplest way is to use cork bark, as sold by florists.

Depending upon the medium used, the model rocks will need painting. Use colour photographs and field notes as reference. The more absorbent materials are best painted with a number of thin washes. Water-based paints are best, but be sure to avoid gloss. Streak darker colours in the cracks to simulate shadows, and try to avoid giving an even finish.

Roads

When modelling roads it is important to gauge their visual impact. It is best to avoid modelling main roads, and to reduce the proportions of all roads and lanes by over a quarter. The country lane is an ideal subject for modelling. It is already very narrow, and takes right angled bends where least expected.

As when modelling track, look carefully at the surface of the road, its colour and texture. Traffic signs and road markings have proliferated over the years, so the further back in time the simpler things were in this respect.

Water

There is no single method for modelling water; each of the three methods described here are suitable for different sets of circumstances. Whatever the method used, however, try to avoid the use of strident colours as water usually blends in with its surroundings.

A simple and effective way of modelling calm and level water such as that found in canals is to lay down hardboard, paint it appropriately and then coat it with several layers of varnish. This method is much lighter and more effective than the somewhat unwieldy method of laying ripple glass.

One way of creating a small river or pond is to model the river bed from plaster, adding rocks and weed before painting the whole. Then lay a sheet of thin, transparent plastic sheet across the top. If required, the underside of the plastic should be tinted, while the impression of current can be given by brushing ripples of lacquer over the top.

The most convincing way of modelling water is to use transparent casting resin. This is sold by artists' suppliers for encapsulating small objects. The resin should be tinted and then poured into a prepared river bed; it will flow easily at first, and then set solid. Although expensive, this is undoubtedly the best way of representing water in miniature.

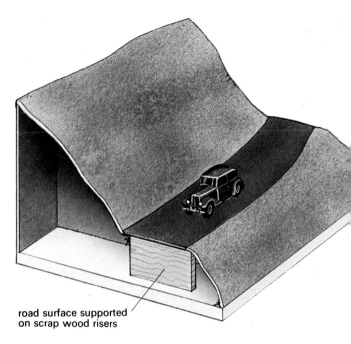

road surface supported
on scrap wood risers

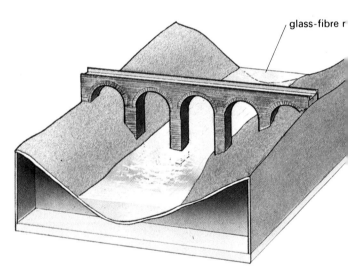

glass-fibre r

Top: Roads can be formed of card or hardboard supported on risers of scrap wood.

Above: Water can be modelled by pouring clear glass-fibre onto a modelled river-bed.

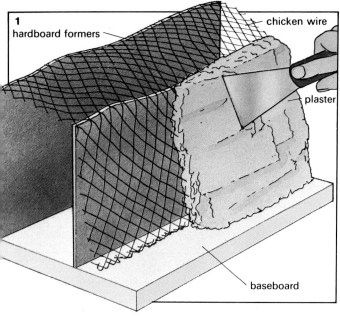

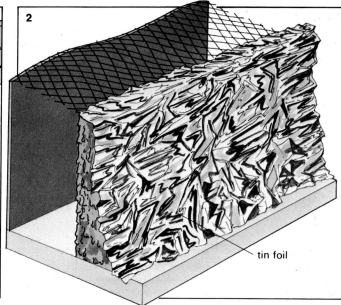

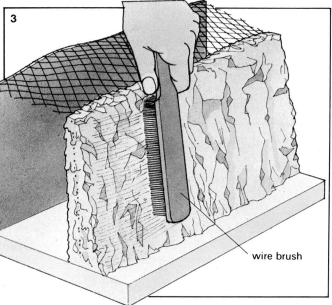

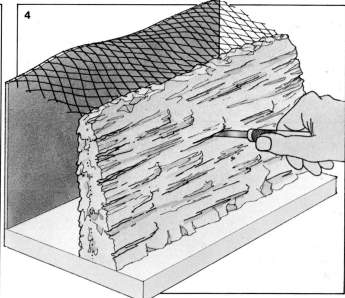

Above: 1. A rock-face is built up with plaster keyed to chicken wire fixed to suitable formers.
2. Press a sheet of crumpled tin-foil onto the plaster before it sets.
3. A wire brush can be used on the dry plaster to add surface texture.
4. a craft knife or sculpting tool is used to finish the rock-face.

Right: Rock faces make an ideal background, providing a pleasing contrast between the precision engineering of the train and the rough texture of the stone.

Trees and Fences

Unless your railway runs through barren countryside, trees will be needed in the model landscape. Trees are not as difficult to model as they might at first appear, and with patience remarkable effects can be achieved. Discover which species are most typical of the area you wish to model, and use relevant illustrations from reference books where possible. Matters can be simplified by treating branches and foliage separately. Indeed, if you wish to model deciduous trees in a winter setting, then omit the foliage altogether.

Carefully selected twigs make useful trees, but they tend to be fragile. A more robust material is wire cable such as that used for car brakes. Unwind the individual strands to make branches and twigs. If necessary, different pieces of wire can be soldered together. Cover the trunk of the tree with bark made from modelling paste.

A bizarre variety of materials has been used to simulate foliage, including dried tea leaves, rubberized horse hair, flock, lichen and wire wool. Techniques vary according to scale and the species of the tree being modelled – experiment to find which suits the purpose best. To apply the material, either stick pieces on individually or first dip the trunk in sticky paint or varnish and then sprinkle on the foliage. To achieve the most realistic results, model trees and shrubs are best painted with an airbrush.

Fences and Hedges

Fences and hedges are used not only to define the boundaries of fields, but often to delimit the edge of the railway itself. There are innumerable varieties of man-made boundaries, many of them specific to a particular locality. Once again observation and a little research will be of use.

For model hedgerows, rubberized horsehair or dried lichen can be used, while foam rubber or plastic are suitable for ornamental hedges in gardens and parks.

Walls can be cut from card and covered in brick or stone paper. 'Dry-stone' walling is best modelled in plaster with individual pebbles for coping stones. Post and rail fencing, typical of lineside fences in Great Britain, is readily built from matches and strip card, glued in place. For a wire fence use metal uprights and sewing thread or filament.

Modelling trees and fences may be somewhat tedious, but it is a means of adding greatly to the character of a model railway. Certain proprietary accessories are available, but they prove expensive if used in quantity. Perhaps a good place to make an exception might be with station fencing, as it is generally conspicuous.

Where a large amount of trees, hedges or fences are required, it is best to set up a form of production line. Almost half the work involved consists of acquiring the right materials and organizing workbench and tools. Once everything is set up, assembly becomes very much simpler and indeed many people find that this type of modelling can be very engrossing.

Apart from adding realism, trees and hedges can be used to hide a number of evils such as baseboard joins. Trees can also be used to soften the transition between model landscape and backscene.

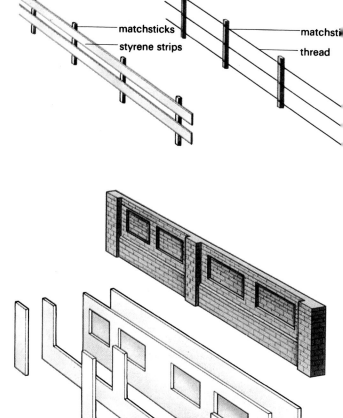

Top: Simple home-made fences can be formed from match-sticks and styrene strip or nylon thread.

Above: Brick walls vary from the plain to the ornate, and all can be easily formed from laminations of wood, card or styrene faced with brick-paper or embossed styrene sheet.

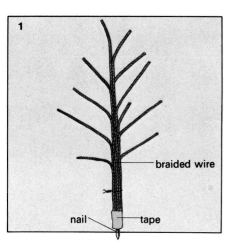

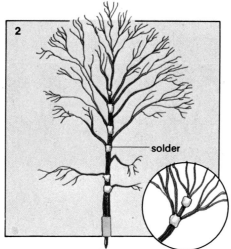

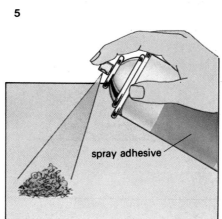

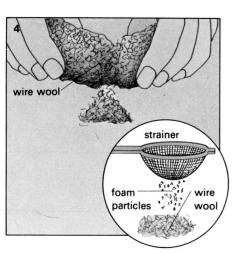

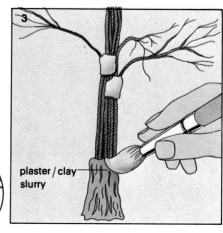

1. Convincing model trees can be formed around an armature made of braided copper wire. The copper wires are wrapped around a nail with tape, the nail serving as a fixing for the finished tree. It is important to refer to photographs of actual trees.

2. The junctions between the branches and trunk are soldered, and the braided wire branches opened out to form further branches and twigs. The principal junctions of these are also soldered.

3. Paint on clay slurry to the wire armature to form the bark, successive layers are built up to achieve depth. Paint the finished bare tree when clay has dried.

4. The foliage is made from a mixture of wire wool and plastic foam particles. Rub two pieces of wire wool together to produce a pile of wire particles. Shred soaked pieces of foam plastic in a domestic liquidiser, dye green, and when dry sieve through a suitable strainer onto the wire wool fibres.

5. Spray a pad of the foam and wire mixture with a setting-type aerosol spray adhesive, carefully lift pad with needles, turn over and spray underside.

6. Lift pad with needles and arrange on branches of model tree. Spray tree with adhesive and dust with flock powder in appropriate colours.

Right: The use of fences in this layout produce a very pleasing composition.

The Urban Landscape

While it is very pleasant to watch trains steaming through the open countryside, the real business of the railway is with urban centres and the movement of goods and people between them. A town gives a reason for a railway's existence and is a main source of traffic.

Obviously there is neither time nor space to model entire towns or cities: the object is simply to suggest the urban character of the railway's surroundings. On a narrow baseboard a useful shorthand is a brick or concrete retaining wall erected behind the tracks, leaving the imagination to fill in the buildings behind. Such retaining walls, so characteristic of urban railway scenes, provide a most effective backdrop and are also very simple to model.

Building Kits

With care and attention to detail it is not too difficult to produce effective model buildings, card being a most adaptable material for this purpose. In the popular scales there are, however, an increasingly varied selection of kits, in card, moulded plastic and wood. It is therefore possible for the modeller to create an urban scene solely by the use of kits, although the result may tend to be somewhat stereotyped unless the kits are modified and adapted.

A disadvantage of card kits is that detail such as lettering and shop window displays is integral and not easily modified. Thus the same high street shops can be seen on hundreds of different layouts.

Plastic kits are more easily altered, because the more prominent features, such as notices and nameboards are not integral parts of the walls, and can be moved, modified or omitted altogether.

Several ranges of kit buildings have a family resemblance, often containing common components and incorporating identical patterns of wall finish. These kits can be combined to form new structures, using plastic sheet to fill in gaps where necessary.

By far the widest range of building kits are of German manufacture. At first sight they appear to portray the national character so well that unmodified they would seem out of place in, say, a British or North American setting; but in some cases, this is no more than a matter of superficial detail. For example, the raised lettering on shop fronts and filling stations can easily be replaced.

Lettering is by far the most noticeable feature of an urban model and immediately sets the character. Crudely made hand painted signs can spoil an otherwise perfect building. There are several sheets of authentic posters and notices on the market, and rub-down lettering can be used with great effect, as can plastic alphabets. An old established way of dressing up buildings is to cut out suitable illustrations and text from advertisements in magazines. The growth of colour advertising makes this idea even more relevant today.

A feature that can add tremendous character to a layout is a canal, preferably at a lock. It brings in another form of transport with possibilities for the trans-shipment of goods, and gives a touch of colour to an industrial scene, since both boats and dock buildings are usually painted in strong colours.

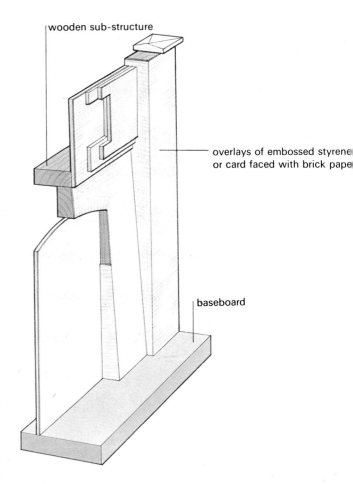

wooden sub-structure

overlays of embossed styrene or card faced with brick paper

baseboard

Retaining walls are evocative of the urban railway landscape and can be easily and convincingly modelled from wood laminated with embossed styrene sheet or printed brick-paper. Note the typical backward slope of the wall and the refuge arches for permanent way staff.

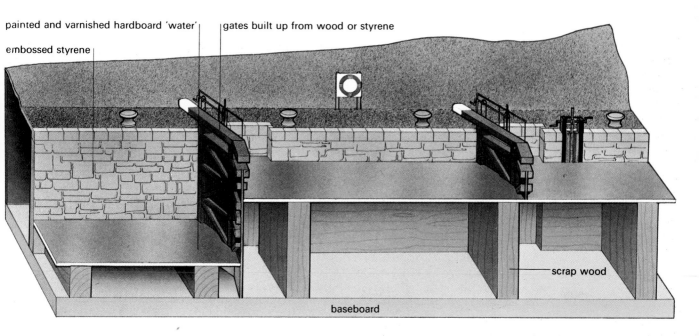

painted and varnished hardboard 'water'

embossed styrene

gates built up from wood or styrene

scrap wood

baseboard

Above: A canal lock makes an interesting model and fits in well in any railway landscape. The still water, characteristic of canals, is modelled in hardboard of card painted in suitable green/blue/brown hues and thickly varnished:— it is important to check that the surface is level. The gates, sluices and other details can be made from strip wood, styrene, card etc. Refer to photographs to ensure authenticity.

The excitement of a railway terminal has been captured by the Sunset Valley Railway with a scene which is bustling with activity on different levels.

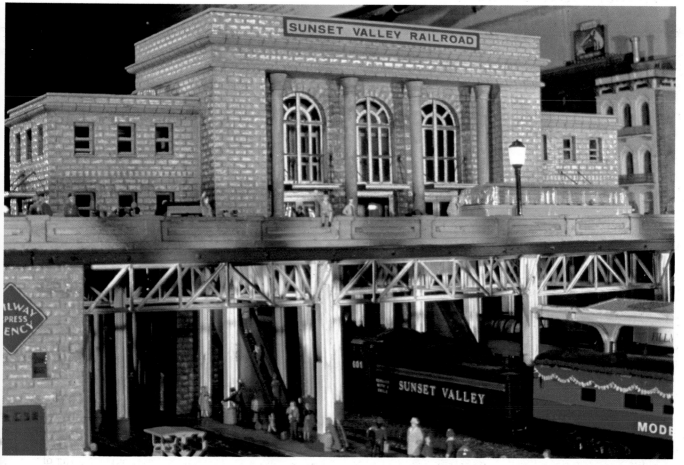

Basic Buildings

Making model buildings is an absorbing and rewarding occupation, and by no means as difficult as it might seem. Even the most complex structures can be sub-divided into manageable sections. Start by building a basic box – say a simple hut with four walls, one window, one door, a roof and a chimney, and from this work up to more elaborate projects.

The three most useful materials are card, wood and styrene sheet, while no more tools are required than a craft knife (with straight and curved blades), a steel rule, a set square and a sharpened pencil. Glues for the materials vary; paper glues are best for card, wood glue or balsa cement for wood and a solvent for styrene.

Obviously a blank sheet of card or styrene cannot represent brick or stone, and therefore a finish of some kind is necessary. Several ranges of commercial brick-papers are available in the various scales. To prevent warping, brickpaper must be applied to the 'box' before assembly, the paper being dried to the surface under pressure. When the glue is dry the paper covering door and window apertures should be cut diagonally and folded back against the inside wall. Try to keep joins in the brickpaper to corners of the building, and disguise the white edge of the paper with matching paint.

Another easy way to produce a brick or stone finish is to use embossed styrene sheet, but as with paper, this does not allow for apertures or ornamentation. Walls must be given additional bracing as the sheets are relatively thin. Great care must be taken with all model buildings to avoid bulges, sags or warps.

Wood-built models can be strengthened at the corners by stripwood, while card and styrene sheet can be laminated for greater rigidity. The number of layers should increase in relation to the size of the wall concerned. A hut would require only two layers, a large loco shed perhaps four.

Painting and finishing

Once the four walls are fitted together, a floor must be fitted to hold the building square. At this stage doors and windows should be modelled. It is worth studying door and window design as these determine the character and authenticity of the building. Model them separately and paint as required, painting the outside walls at the same time. Model enamels are available in a variety of finishes, while poster or emulsion paint give good representation of stucco and plaster.

Once the doors and windows are firmly in place, curtains can be added from tissue paper or painted onto the glazing. Intermediate floors, partition walls and a flat, false roof are added next, while the interior should be painted at this stage if it is going to be visible.

Once the basic shapes have been determined, the roof surface should be modelled. Slate papers or individual scribing can be used, or tiles can be laid on individually. Roof surfaces too should be laminated if strength is needed.

The final work on a model building is to place it firmly on the layout, using plenty of glue to avoid a gap appearing round the edge. Judicious use of flock powders, sand or ash will disguise the join and make the building look part of the scenery.

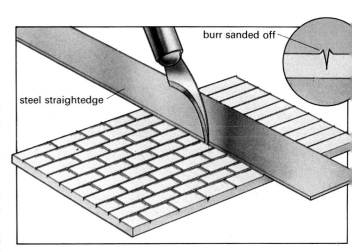

Above: Brickwork is produced by scribing styrene sheet with a curved blade, scribing the horizontal courses first, and then adding the divisions between bricks. The 'burr' produced by the scribing action of the blade is sanded down afterwards. Ready-embossed styrene sheet is preferable for areas of plain brickwork, but this technique is useful for producing arches and so on.

Above right: Windows can be constructed by laminating layers of styrene together, one method of making a simple drop-sash window is illustrated, and this can be elaborated upon or simplified as desired. Similar methods are used to build other types of window.

Above far right: Free-standing chimneys are best anchored to the false roof of the structure, protruding through a hole cut in the roof underlay. The tiles or slates are scribed onto a sheet of styrene of suitable thickness, scribing horizontally and vertically across the sheet to the scale dimensions of the tiles or slates. Horizontal strips are then separated and then overlapped in a staggered pattern onto the roof underlay. Guttering and down-pipes are made from pieces of plastic rod or tube, or from the empty ink-reservoirs of ball-point pens.

Right: An exploded view of a model of a typical British terraced corner shop and cottage, illustrating some of the constructional features to be found in many buildings. Again, reference to photographs and scale drawings, if possible, assists in the detailing of the model.

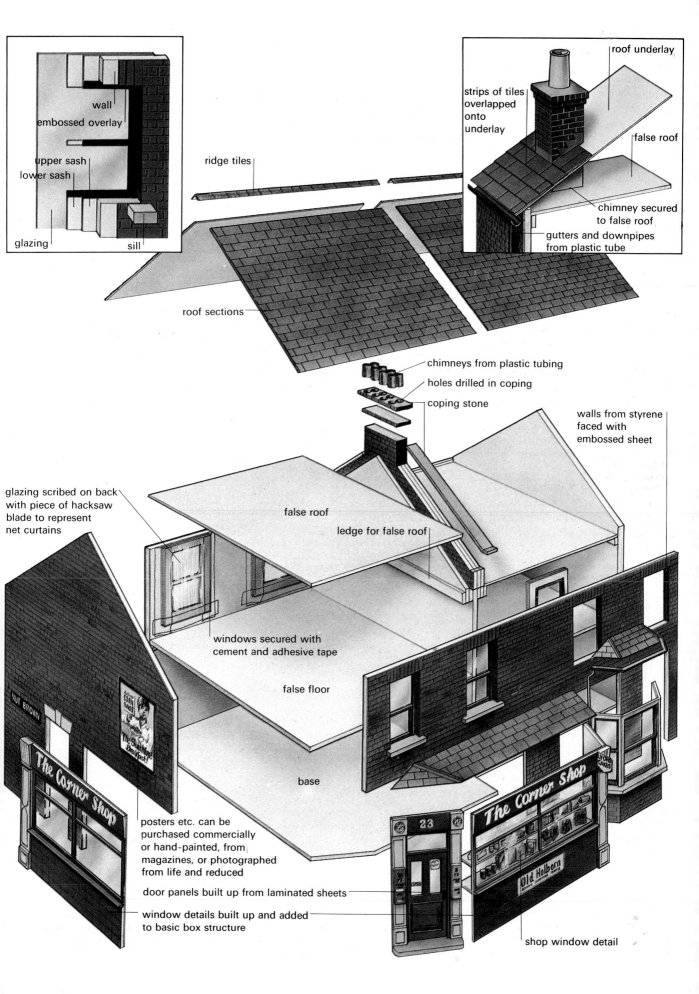

wall

embossed overlay

upper sash
lower sash

glazing

sill

ridge tiles

roof underlay

strips of tiles
overlapped
onto
underlay

false roof

chimney secured
to false roof

gutters and downpipes
from plastic tube

roof sections

chimneys from plastic tubing

holes drilled in coping

coping stone

walls from styrene
faced with
embossed sheet

glazing scribed on back
with piece of hacksaw
blade to represent
net curtains

false roof

ledge for false roof

windows secured with
cement and adhesive tape

false floor

base

posters etc. can be
purchased commercially
or hand-painted, from
magazines, or photographed
from life and reduced

door panels built up from laminated sheets

window details built up and added
to basic box structure

shop window detail

The Corner Shop

The Corner Shop

23

Old Holborn

Railway Buildings

The correct locomotives and rolling stock will only look right in the appropriate setting. The scope and style of railway buildings varied greatly from place to place, and so it is possible to identify the railway company and period by the nature of such structures as station buildings and signal cabins.

While a wide range of kits is available, they may not always fill the precise need, particularly in Britain, where there is still such a profusion of architectural styles. Once again research is necessary here, to determine not only the style of buildings but also their function and size in relation to the importance of the station. Photographs are vital, particularly where drawings cannot be obtained.

Platforms

Perhaps the most obvious place to start is with the platform. On the continent and in North America these are generally just above rail height, with platforms at coach floor height only at metropolitan and suburban stations. At rural outposts it is common for little or no platform accommodation to be provided. In Britain, however, platforms have traditionally been provided at every station, usually 1.07m (3' 6") above rail level.

Platforms can be cut in one piece from solid wood or built up from layered card or styrene sheet framing. Paint the top surface to represent tarmac and overlay a scribed stone edging. The platform face can be covered with brickpaper or embossed styrene sheet. Ramps, a typically British feature, must be carefully cut, either in the platform as a whole, or glued on afterwards.

Station Buildings

For the main station building the techniques described earlier apply, but one or two extra features commonly occur, such as the platform canopy. This is often a lean-to roof, possibly with glazed roof sections, often supported by ornamental brackets or columns. Sections of ballpoint pens make effective plinths and collars for cast iron columns made from cocktail sticks. Valancing, or timber canopy edging, is an extremely important visual element – valancing strips can be bought from commercial suppliers, but otherwise must be individually scribed.

Once the station building is in place, detailing can begin. Posters can be affixed to prepared boards and then to walls, fencing etc. Fencing can be purchased in many varieties, while station nameboards are another vital element, and one which varied greatly in character from railway to railway. To complete the picture there are lamps, platform barrows, seats and figures.

Take a stroll around the rest of the railway property. Goods sheds and loco sheds tend to be solid buildings with few windows. Check height and width of doors where rolling stock is required to enter.

Woodwork should be painted in the correct colour for the period and location, while if possible the building material should be accurate, even down to the shade of brick. Rubbing dirt into the brickwork gives the grimy look often associated with railways – black for the smoke of steam days, brown for the brake dust given off in modern times.

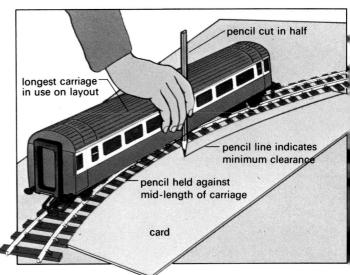

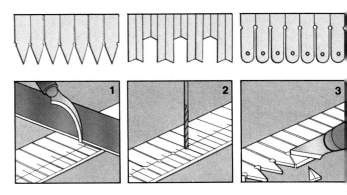

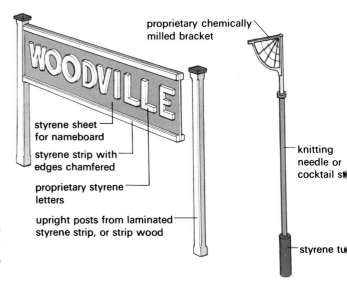

Above: Two examples of railway 'furniture' are shown, illustrating their construction. A simple station nameboard is built from styrene strip in laminations, and proprietary styrene cut-out lettering applied. Simple awning supports can be made from knitting needles, cocktail sticks, pieces of tubing etc. Chemically-milled brackets are available for the more intricate patterns.

Left: The edges of platforms on curved track have to be set back further than on straight track to allow for the overhang of the longer items of rolling-stock. To determine the clearance required for a curved platform, split a pencil lengthwise and hold it against the centre of the longest vehicle in use on the layout for a platform on the inside of the curve, or against one end for a platform on the outside. With a sheet of card butted up to the track or slipped beneath it, run the vehicle around the curve and the pencil will trace the minimum clearance onto the card: allow two or three millimetres more than this for the platform edge.

Left: Ornamental barge-boards and awnings take many forms and three examples are illustrated.
1. To construct a simple 'saw-tooth' pattern awning, mark the dimensions onto a strip of styrene sheet and scribe the planking.
2. Drill the circular cut-outs between each plank.
3. Use a straight-edged blade to 'chop' vee-shaped notches between each plank.

Below Station platforms in the US and elsewhere are simply made from a strip wood base overlayed with a styrene top suitably finished to represent paving, concrete etc., as shown on the left. On the right is shown the raised type of platform as used in Britain and at principal stations elsewhere. The base may be made from wood, or card or styrene, as shown here.

Two examples of scratch built signal boxes by Vivien Thompson, one of which has been 'weathered'.

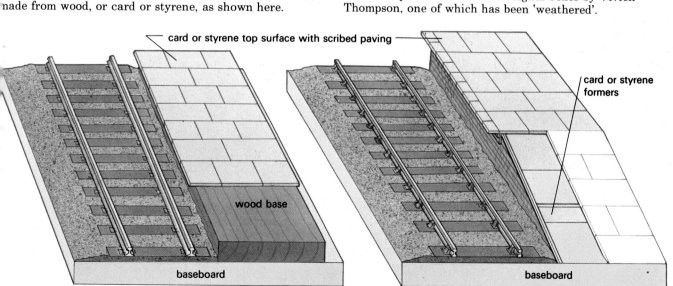

card or styrene top surface with scribed paving

wood base

baseboard

card or styrene formers

baseboard

Back Drops and Low Relief

The object of a backscene is to complete the picture. It functions as a theatrical backdrop, and is intended to create the illusion of distance – of a complete landscape beyond the confines of the model.

While printed backscenes are available, they are repetitive and easily recognizable. An alternative is sky-patterned wallpaper, or a simple wash of light blue or cream emulsion. This goes a long way towards convincing the observer that the railway exists in a wider world, for nothing is more open than the sky itself.

The effect can be improved if a number of fore-shortened, or low-relief, models are placed between the backscene proper and the railway. They offer a lot of scope for originality in very little space, and although only two-dimensional, can be extremely realistic since because of their position they will only be viewed from one side.

In low-relief work the depth of the building can vary considerably, depending upon where the backscene cuts through the building. Roofs are an important factor determining this – with a flat-topped building, for example, it is possible to model a simple facade; but with a gable-roofed building at least one side of the whole roof must be seen. It is however possible to cheat slightly by steepening the pitch of the roof in order to save space – a roof at as steep an angle as 60° will still look correct when seen head on. One important point is to avoid modelling the end rather than the side of a gable-roofed building end-on as the fact that the other half of the building does not exist becomes immediately obvious.

Kitbashing

In most cases, only the side of a building facing the railway need be shown, and so by modifying a kit or two even four buildings can be obtained for the price of one. For example a kit for a small factory or warehouse if opened out in this way might provide a considerable length of backdrop. Low-relief modelling allows many useful short cuts to be taken, the main advantage being that the facade can derive support from the backscene in front of which it stands. Normally a row of houses or shops would take some time to construct, but in low relief it could be quicker to build them than a single free-standing building.

Low-relief modelling is by no means confined to buildings, but allows considerable scope for ingenuity in the portrayal of country settings as well. Once again, the secret is to provide a visual break that suggests to the eye that there is something more beyond. This need be no more than a slight bank, topped with a wall or hedge. A group of trees can be merged into the backscene to give the impression of an entire wood. With relatively high-level baseboards, where the view-point of the observer is sufficiently low down, the horizon can be formed simply by a railway embankment or even a viaduct, with sky behind.

Where applicable it is both simple and effective to suggest distant hills by cutting a long piece of hardboard to a hill-shaped profile, bevelling the top edge and painting it in shades of blue and purple.

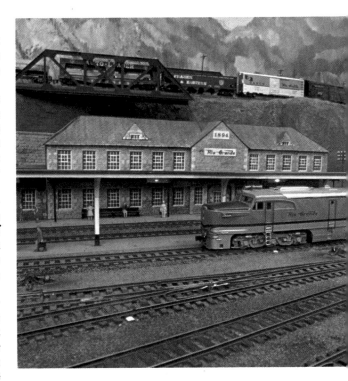

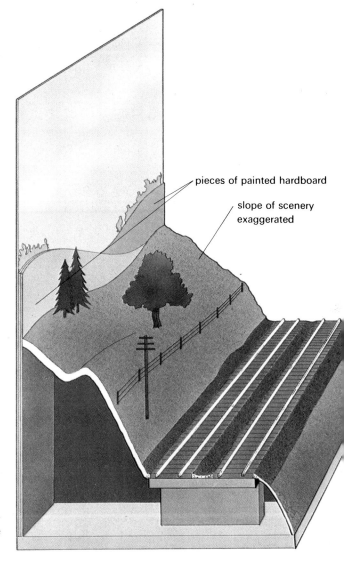

pieces of painted hardboard

slope of scenery exaggerated

Far left: The mountainous backdrop to Cliff Youngs' Denver and Rio grande railway benefits from a high-level track which gives the scene middle-distance depth.

Left: A simple sky background is used here in Frank Roomes' Lutton Branch which does not distract from the activity in the foreground.

Below left: A section through low-relief rural scenery. Note that the horizon is artificially raised and the slope of the landscape exaggerated to create an illusion of depth.

Below: A section through low-relief urban scenery. Again, the slope of the scenery is exaggerated and the depth of buildings, roads, etc. are compressed.

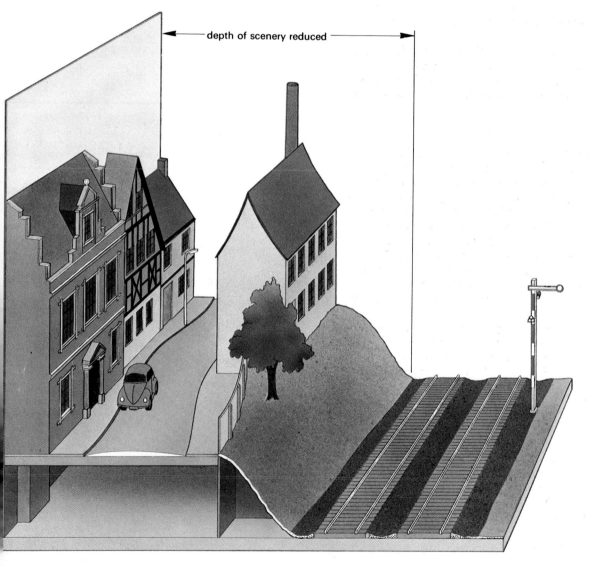

depth of scenery reduced

Bridges

The majority of railway bridges use one of three main types of construction: masonry, concrete or girder; the latter sub-dividing into plate, lattice and cantilever bow-string. Interestingly, suspension bridges are not used to carry railways as they are prone to swing in rhythm with rail-joint beats and break up.

The more elaborate lattice-girder bridges and their derivatives can usually be made from plastic kits, though some expert modelmakers prefer to build them painstakingly from scratch — plastic card being the preferred medium. For the majority of modellers, however, plate girders and masonry bridges are favoured as projects for scratchbuilding.

In most cases the bridge is built around a simple wood and hardboard frame as shown in the sketch. This primitive structure is then covered by the facade of the bridge itself. The most straightforward prototype is a plate girder: this consists of side, top, bottom and end flanges, with a number of strengthening ribs spaced equidistantly along the girder, but usually with the end panels shorter than the rest. Detailing includes rivets and the important flitch plates over the top and bottom flanges, which are not essential but add to the effect if they are correctly carried out. Study of actual plate girders will give a better idea of this.

Since the 1960s the use of pre-stressed concrete girders for railway bridge construction has become widespread. These can be modelled in card or plastic sheet, but the thickness of concrete is more easily reproduced in thin wood. The grain should be filled and the wood sanded smooth before painting.

Masonry Bridges

The most characteristic feature of masonry bridges is the brick or stone arch around which they are built. The facades are particularly conspicuous, with the bricks or stones being arrayed in a curved pattern. In model form the brickwork or stonework is not structural and can be modelled in light materials such as card or embossed plastic sheeting. The interior of the arch can be kept fairly simple as it is not normally seen, but great attention must be paid to modelling the ends of the arch as this is what gives the model its character.

With a stonework bridge, the stones that form the arch are often raised, and this relief effect can be modelled by sticking on individual pieces of card for each stone. A simpler method is to scribe the courses of stonework with a modelling knife.

Brick bridges present similar problems. While the plain brickwork can be modelled with brickpaper or brick embossed plastic sheet and cut to fit, the arch itself is best drawn by hand with a mapping pen on card which has been painted the appropriate colour.

The majority of bridges have abutments, or angled walls, at either side, whose purpose is to hold back the weight of soil in the embankment. Their angle can vary, but is typically between 30° and 45° in relation to the bridge facade. Abutment walls are usually built in either brick or stone and are topped with a capping course.

Above right: A section through a model plate-girder bridge for double track. Wood is used in the basic structure for strength, and overlaid with embossed styrene sheet or brick-paper. The girders are constructed from card or styrene.

Below right: A section through a model brick-built bridge for single track. Again, wood is used for the basic structure overlaid with embossed styrene sheet or brick-paper. Road overbridges of both types are constructed in a similar manner, although lighter materials may be used as the structure need not be as rigid as for rail overbridges.

Left: A layout which demonstrates how bridges can be used in different ways in a landscape.

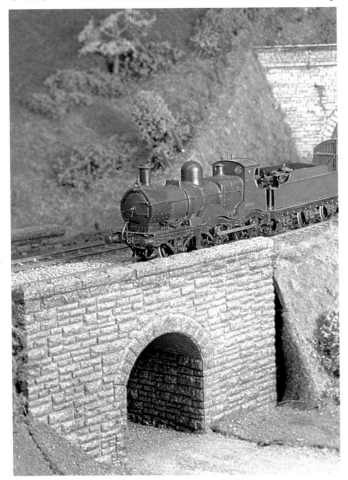

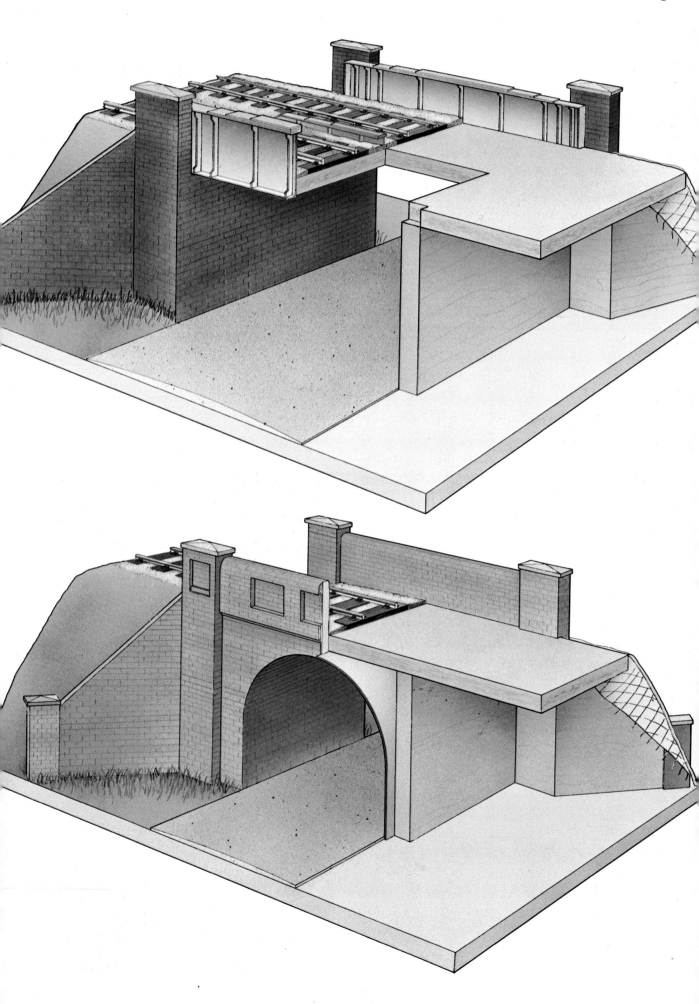

Tunnels

Tunnels tend to appear more frequently on the model than on the prototype, for while in actual railway construction the engineer will try to avoid the difficulty and expense involved, in model terms the tunnel is an extremely useful scenic device.

Imagine for example a model railway line running between two stations. While in real life stations tend to be some distance apart, on the model there may be only the length of two trains between them. If the eye is able to follow a train uninterruptedly on its brief journey, then the distortion will be obvious. The task of the modeller is therefore to create the illusion that the train has travelled a considerably longer distance, by breaking up the continuity of that particular stretch of track. A tunnel is one of the most effective ways of achieving this result.

The tunnel may itself be shorter than it pretends to be, but by providing a scenic break or backscene, halfway between the two portals, it can be suggested that the tunnel mouths are some distance apart.

On and Off Stage

Tunnels are also useful for bringing trains on and off stage – the stage being the fully modelled scene and backstage being the holding sidings or fiddle yard. For example, a model of a through station may have holding sidings at the rear, linked by a continuous circuit. However, so that the observer is aware, neither of the existence of the holding sidings nor of the basically circular nature of the track plan, it is common practice to divide the layout in half with a backscene. Naturally it would be most unrealistic to see trains disappearing through a hole in a piece of hardboard, and so the obvious solution is to disguise the hole with a tunnel mouth.

In a similar way, tunnels are often used on terminus-to-fiddle-yard layouts. A train leaving the terminus station passes through the tunnel en route for the next station and beyond – represented in operating terms by the fiddle yard.

Tunnels are relatively simple to model, since only the portals and the tunnel entrance need be constructed. Within the hillside the train simply passes along a section of concealed track. It is usual to line the tunnel as far inside as can easily be seen. This can be done by simulating brickwork, or by using plain black card.

Tunnel mouths vary from the simple to the ornate, so take care to choose the most appropriate design. On narrow gauge or lightly built lines there may be nothing but bare rock, or at most a few wooden props. At the other extreme are the ornately castellated tunnels built by some Victorian engineers. However, if such a thing can be said to exist, the typical tunnel mouth much resembles the masonry over-bridge and can be modelled in a similar way.

Access to a tunnel is vital, as derailments always occur in awkward places. Often this can be achieved by making the side removable, or by providing some sort of hole in the baseboard. Another approach is to arrange for parts of the scenery to lift out – it is always possible to have a completely removable field with a hedge suitably positioned to conceal the gap.

Above: The Heckmondwyke layout uses a tunnel to great effect on a steeply sloping landscape. *Below:* In contrast, the rugged San Janet range of the Sunset Valley railway makes an impressive backdrop to the brightly painted trains.

Left: Except for 'tube' tunnels as used on the London Underground and elsewhere, railway tunnels are elliptical in cross-section in order to allow room for ventilation and to spread the load on the roof of the tunnel throughout the sides.

Below: A cross-section through a model railway tunnel showing details of construction. Note that the tunnel lining is continued inside the tunnel-mouth for a short distance so as to be visible from the outside. Long tunnels should have some means of access to the interior in case of derailment or other failure. Tunnels along the front of the baseboard can be made accessible through holes in the front of the scenery. Tunnels at the rear of the baseboard can be accessible through holes cut into the bottom of the baseboard, or a removable scenic section can be fitted as shown. The joins in the scenery can be masked by hedges, trees, walls, roads, buildings and so on.

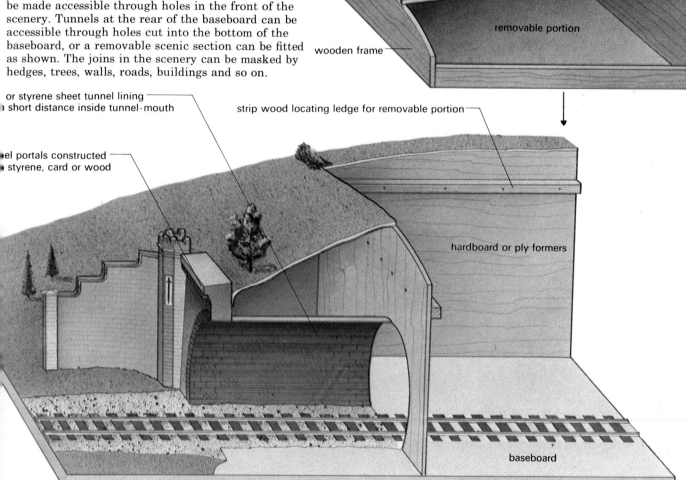

hedges, fences etc. mask joins

removable portion

wooden frame

or styrene sheet tunnel lining
a short distance inside tunnel-mouth

strip wood locating ledge for removable portion

el portals constructed
styrene, card or wood

hardboard or ply formers

baseboard

Turnout and Signal Control

Since electricity is the commonest source of power for model railways, it is hardly surprising that it is also widely used for turnout and signal control. But while it has much to recommend it, electrical control can also be expensive, and the older but well tried methods of mechanical control should not be overlooked. On a large layout a combination of electrical and mechanical control may be advisable, with more distant turnouts being controlled electrically and the trackwork close to the control panel being worked mechanically.

The form of control used with most sectional track systems is a double-solenoid motor, which moves the turnout blades from side to side. A locking mechanism is essential to hold the blades in position, while a pair of push buttons or the electric pencil system can be used to operate the motor.

The latter, home-made system, can save considerable expenditure on switchgear as well as providing a control panel at the same time. A small track-plan is prepared on hardboard, ply or plastic, and two round head screws placed on either side of each turnout. The screws are then wired to the motor, and can be energized by a probe on the end of a flexible wire.

Mechanical Control

Those in search of further economy often think of making their own solenoid motors. It can be done, but there is less work and less cost involved in developing a mechanical system. The most basic of these is a simple push-rod, taken to the edge of the baseboard. A spoke from a bicycle wheel is quite effective, since it is straight, strong and has a handy knob on the end. The spoke slides in holes drilled in the wooden baseboard framing, and at its far end is attached to the tie-bar of the turnout by means of a piece of stiff wire.

The wire-in-tube system of control uses steel piano wire in a small-bore plastic tube. The curves have to be fairly easy and the maximum run appears to be around 2m (6′ 6″). One end of the wire is fixed to the turnout tiebar, the other to a lever frame.

It is also possible to operate turnouts by nylon cord. A return spring is needed at the turnout, and also a number of small pulleys to guide the cord around bends. Nylon fishing line is ideal, being almost indestructible.

Signalling

Mechanical control is particularly suitable for semaphore signals since this is also the method used in the prototype. Although additional pulleys may be required, the principles are the same as for turnouts. The most suitable method of electric control is a single solenoid. The low power needed to work a model signal permits it to be linked to a cheap surplus relay or a home-made solenoid. DC current is essential, since AC produces a loud buzz.

Colour-light signals, obviously, must be electrically controlled. Whilst most commercial types still use miniature lamps, amateur construction today is centred around light emitting diodes. LEDs can be obtained which give red, yellow or green lights, and two, three or four can be cemented together within a suitable housing.

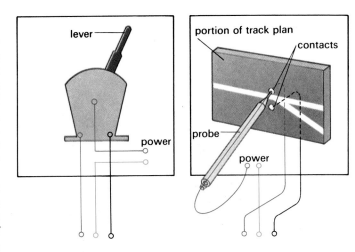

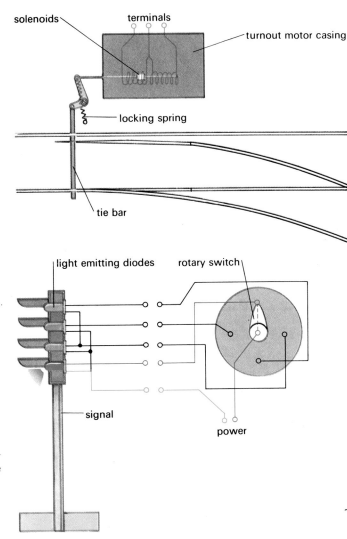

Top: Two methods of electrical control are shown, on the left by means of levers or switches, and on the right by means of an electric probe and contacts on a track diagram. The probe can be simply made by adapting a plastic ballpoint pen case.
Above: A diagram of a typical model turnout motor showing the arrangement of the solenoid, crank and tie-rod.

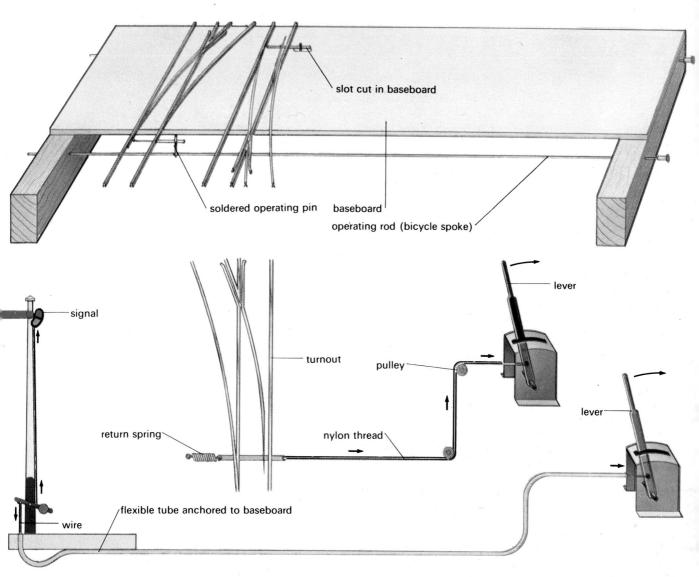

slot cut in baseboard

soldered operating pin   baseboard

operating rod (bicycle spoke)

lever

signal

turnout

pulley

lever

return spring

nylon thread

flexible tube anchored to baseboard

wire

Left: The wiring diagram shown here is for a typical British-prototype 4-aspect colour-light signal capable of showing red, yellow, double-yellow, and green indications operated by a four-pole rotary switch. The circuit is shown for the red aspect.

Top: A simple method of operating points can be arranged using bicycle spokes sliding in holes drilled in the dashboard battens. Upright wire pins, soldered to the spoke are attached to the tie-rods of turnouts through slots cut in the baseboard surface. This method is suitable for small baseboards where the turnouts are grouped together.

Above: Two methods of centralising mechanical control of turnouts and signals are shown in the diagram. Above is shown a method of attaching a lever to a turnout or signal by means of nylon threads and pulleys. A spring must be fitted to tension the thread and return the turnout or signal to its original position. Below, the signal or turnout is connected to the lever by a wire working inside the flexible tube. Bends in the tube must not be too tight, but return springs are not required.

Right: Turnout controls on the Pendon Museum layout, near Oxford.

Wiring

Wiring a layout can be as simple or as complex as the modeller chooses. For those electronic wizards who delight in having banks of switches and coloured lights under their control it holds no fears, but such sophistication is by no means obligatory.

Assuming for the moment that the modeller is working in simple two rail, then one rail takes the current to the locomotive and the other brings it back. If there is more than one locomotive, then isolating sections are needed so that all the locomotives do not move at once when the current is switched on. Electrical isolation can be achieved by cutting a gap in the rails, but even this is not always necessary since the turnouts supplied by most manufacturers are isolating in any case. This means that if a turnout is set for a siding the current will flow that way, but if the turnout is set for the main line, then the siding will be isolated.

One disadvantage of two rail is that owing to problems of polarity, a train cannot be driven right round a reversing loop by one controller. It is essential to reverse polarity in the loop with a separate switch, usually while the train is stationary.

Soldering Techniques

A reliable supply of electric current to every section of track is essential to smooth running, and the best way to achieve this is by soldering every feed wire to the track.

Soldering is not too difficult given a sufficiently powerful soldering iron and cored solder. The secret of success is a clean joint. Freshly stripped wire takes solder readily, but rail can be tarnished, and if necessary should be scraped clean. When soldering always use as much heat as possible.

Allow the iron at least two minutes to warm up first, and then check that it is hot enough to melt solder instantaneously. Simply touch the joint with the hot iron and apply the cored solder, which will flow quickly, resembling mercury. Allow the joint to cool, which it will do in less than 15 seconds, and then tug it gently. A faulty joint will break, so re-solder it.

From the soldered joint, run the wire under the baseboard through small holes in the framework en route to the control panel. Run groups of wires together in wreaths, with a spare piece of wire twisted round to keep them tidy.

A useful wiring technique is to terminate the wires at a tag strip (obtainable from electronic suppliers). This is not only neater, but gives greater flexibility. Provided that the control panel is wired to a similar tag strip, it can be built on a workbench rather than *in situ* so that when it is installed, all that is required from the wiring point of view is to join up the two tag strips.

Wiring Portable Layouts

On portable layouts, wires can be carried from the switch panel to the sections by means of multi-core cable and multi-pin plugs and sockets. Bought new from electrical stores they tend to be expensive, but second-hand sockets can usually be found in electronic surplus stores. For most control purposes, on/off, panel-mounting toggle switches are favoured, and here too, the surplus store can often provide a supply.

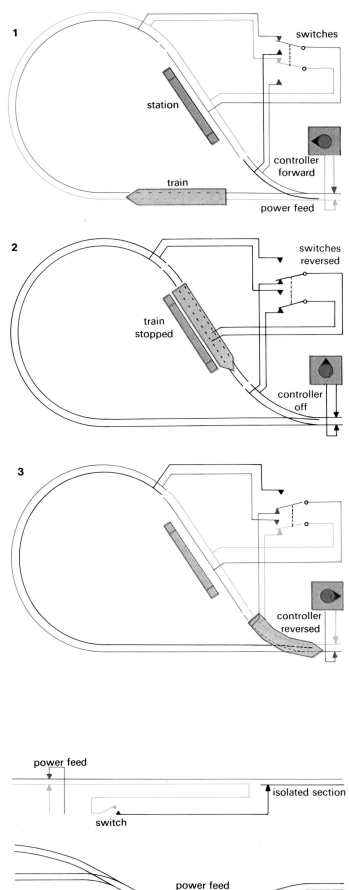

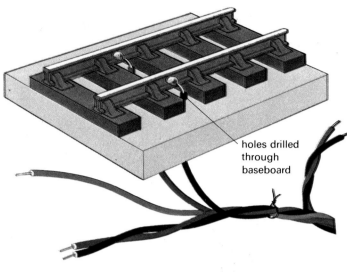

holes drilled
through
baseboard

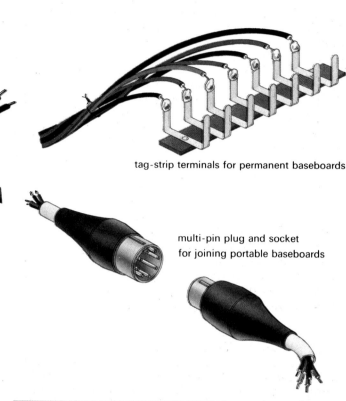

tag-strip terminals for permanent baseboards

multi-pin plug and socket
for joining portable baseboards

Above left: The three diagrams shown illustrate how to wire and operate a return loop by means of section breaks and a double-loop, double-throw switch.
1. The train is run into the loop, and the switch is set to supply power to the station section.
2. The train is stopped at the station and before starting it again the switch is thrown reversing the polarity of the station section with respect to the main line.
3. The controller must be turned in the opposite direction to re-start the train in the original direction of travel.

Below left: Above is shown the wiring for an isolated section which allows a locomotive to stand stationary while another is operated over the same electrical section, as at station terminal roads etc. One running rail has an electrical break in it and the two parts connected together through an on-off switch. Thus the isolated section can be coupled or uncoupled from the power supply as desired. Below, section feeds must be arranged between the toes of the turnouts.

Above: An unobtrusive method of feeding the power supply to the track is to pass the wires through holes drilled in the baseboard, immediately underneath the running rails, and soldering the wires as shown. Wiring beneath the baseboard should be grouped into bundles. Permanent layouts should have the wiring terminated at a tag-board, and the controller connected to this. For temporary layouts multi-pin plugs and sockets can be used to join the wiring between baseboard sections and to the control panel.

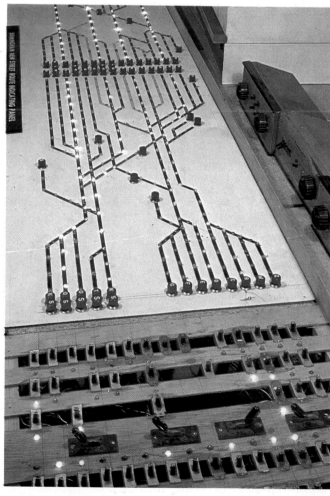

Right: Don Jones' highly sophisticated control panel is a computer-based system with approximately three miles of wire leading to areas of the track. The switches control four main lines. Don has planned for the future by making the end section completely removable so that he can switch to silicon chip technology without altering the panel.

Workshop Techniques

In railway modelling there is a long standing tradition that the best models are produced on the kitchen table, without benefit of elaborate workshop facilities. While it may be true that skill and patience count for more than expensive tools, there is no harm in lesser mortals gathering about them a useful selection of equipment and finding a relatively organized place to work, even if that place is in the end the kitchen table!

The essential tools a modeller requires are few. The following list should cover most eventualities: a good drill with a selection of bits, files (standard and needle), a few different pairs of pliers, tweezers, craft knives, screwdrivers, an engineer's square, a steel rule, a scriber, a centre punch, a light hammer and a soldering iron are all that should be required.

Cutting and Gluing

Most modelmaking consists of cutting out shapes and sticking them together in the right order. Problems usually arise from using cheap materials and blunt tools. A sharp blade goes where it is meant to with ease, whereas so much force is needed with a blunt tool that it is difficult to control.

Modern craft knives have removable blades, which can be sharpened on a fine oilstone slip. Nevertheless it is best to have a selection of blades available so that they can be replaced quickly, and then sharpened in a batch.

Always cut against a metal straightedge – a steel rule or engineer's square is best. Make a couple of light cuts in preference to one very heavy one. Work on a piece of thick card or hardboard which should be thrown away when badly scored lest it pull the knife out of line. Plastic sheet, a very useful modelling material, is best cut by grooving one side and then snapping it. Curves can be scored with a sharp-pointed part of dividers.

Drilling is not as simple as it might appear and requires great care. Before beginning, make a dimple in the exact spot, to guide the drill. A centre punch is needed to indent metal, but wood and plastic can be dimpled with a scriber.

Adhesives

Joining materials is much easier as a very wide range of glues and adhesives is now available. However, old-fashioned acetate cements are still as quick and effective as they were 50 years ago, and indeed for wood and card they are still to be preferred. For polystyrene kits and plastic card, solvents applied with a brush are preferable to plastic cement, which usually strings and takes hours rather than minutes to set completely hard.

Contact cements are excellent if used according to the instructions. For wood joints, the resin glues provide a firm bond. Metal to metal calls for epoxy resins, which tend to expand a little before setting. However, the cyanoacrylate 'wonder glues' need to be used with caution in view of their strength and the speed with which they act. One drop is enough to stick a finger fast to a piece of metal. They should be treated with great respect and avoided as far as possible since it normally is not worth taking the risk.

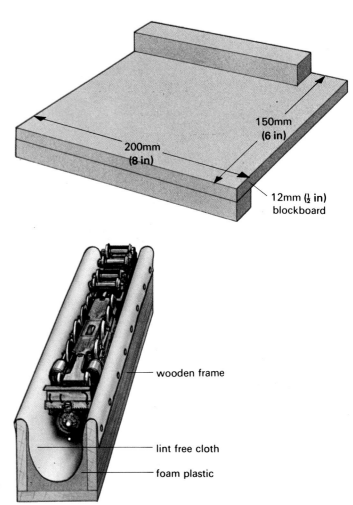

150mm
(6 in)

200mm
(8 in)

12mm (½ in)
blockboard

wooden frame

lint free cloth

foam plastic

Top: A simple bench-hook can be made from scrap wood. When hooked over the front edge of a table or bench, materials can be sawn without damaging the table surface.

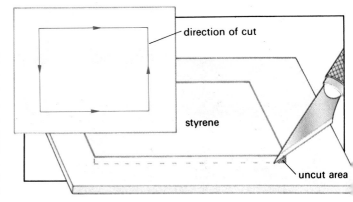

direction of cut

styrene

uncut area

Above: A cradle lined with foam plastic protects the superstructure of locomotives and rolling-stock whilst working on the wheels and running-gear.

When cutting holes in styrene sheet, cut around the edges in the direction shown and then cut again in the opposite direction to remove the uncut areas at the corners.

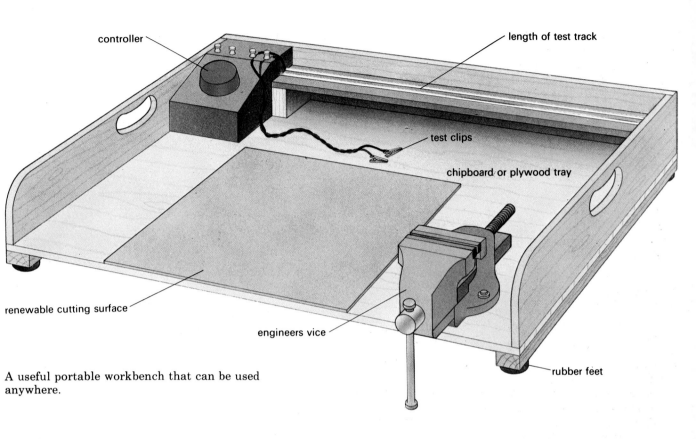

controller

length of test track

test clips

chipboard or plywood tray

renewable cutting surface

engineers vice

rubber feet

A useful portable workbench that can be used anywhere.

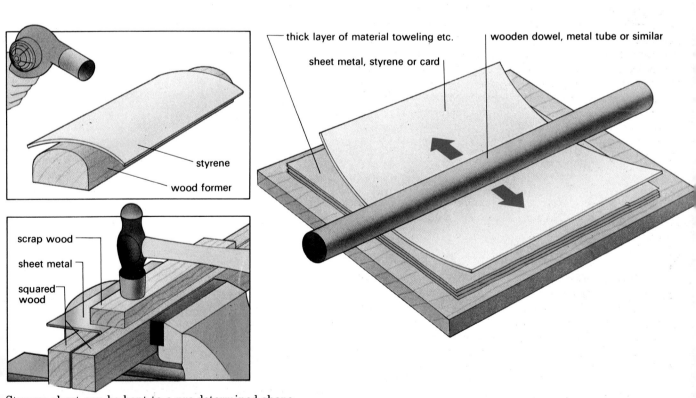

styrene

wood former

scrap wood

sheet metal

squared wood

thick layer of material toweling etc.

sheet metal, styrene or card

wooden dowel, metal tube or similar

Styrene sheet can be bent to a pre-determined shape by heating it with a hair-drier over a wooden former, as shown top left. On the right is shown a method of curving styrene or sheet metal. Left lower shows a method of making right-angle bends in sheet metal. The scrap wood produces a neat fold and avoids marking the metal.

Garden Railways

The ideal answer for the modeller who feels restricted in scope is to branch out into the garden. If he is short of space indoors, he may be able to avoid the usual compromises of shorter trains, tighter curves and so on by building a garden railway.

The modeller will find that he has various new factors to contend with out of doors, but they should be treated as challenges to be overcome. For example, many people worry about the effect of bad weather. The answer to this is to make vulnerable features such as buildings portable, to provide good drainage and to use weatherproof track materials such as stainless steel rail.

There are also the potential hazards represented by animals and even man. The presence of a cat sunning itself on a raised track can perhaps be ignored until trains are run, but rats have been known to take up residence in tunnels and dogs may scratch up lightly laid track. The most serious threat, however, may be vandalism. The best way to avoid this is to build the railway close to the house and to keep the garden well fenced.

Traditionally, garden railways have been built in the larger gauges, such as gauge O and gauge 1. Rolling stock and track has generally been of a robust nature, well able to withstand the rigours of the elements. In some ways, too, the larger the scale of the railway the more it is in keeping with garden vegetation. However,

weatherproof track is now available in OO/HO, and a number of successful small-scale garden railways have been built.

Model railways in the smaller scales tend to use electric propulsion almost exclusively, and this is perfectly feasible outdoors, so long as certain sensible precautions are taken. Mains supplies should be well earthed and transformers insulated, while it is also advisable to supply only low-voltage current to the track and to use portable control panels that can easily be unplugged and taken inside.

Although electricity has much to recommend it, clockwork and live steam traction really come into their own on garden railways. Both are more suitable for larger scales and so can take advantage of the greater space available out of doors.

Many of the earliest garden railways were built on raised wooden trestles. These gave the operator easy access but were unrealistic and sometimes unsightly. Over a period of time, timber sections tend to rot. Nowadays it is common practice to lay the tracks at or near ground level, on a trackbed of concrete, and to try to blend the railway into the real landscape. To avoid the operator having to bend down too much, the line can run along a bank or across a rockery. Alpine rock plants, being miniature in any case, can provide most realistic 'scenery'. Viaducts look most dramatic in a garden setting and can be cast in concrete.

Below: A garden railway arranged along an earth terrace. Wooden stakes pinned to the track hold the track in position. At station areas the level of the ground can be lowered to provide a comfortable operating area, as shown on the right.

Above right: A garden railway arranged on wooden baseboards raised above ground level on concrete blocks.

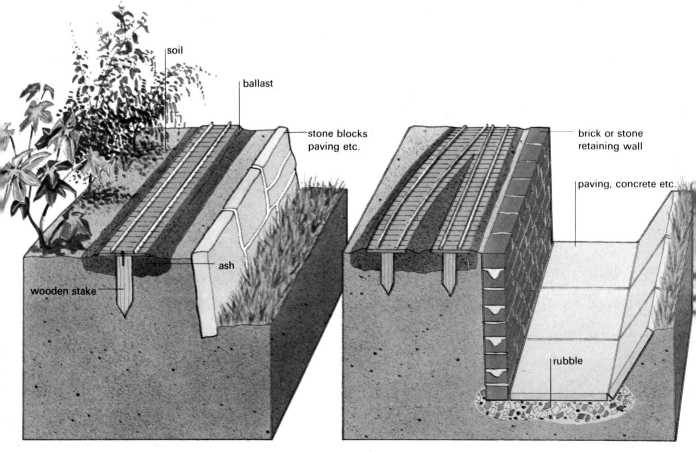

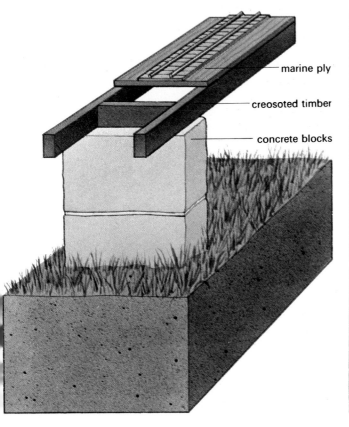

marine ply

creosoted timber

concrete blocks

Above right: A rock garden becomes a natural setting for this King Richard I Great Western 4-6-0.

Below: Heathersfield Light Railway uses handbuilt stock and track.

READY-TO-RUN

While no serious modeller likes being accused of 'playing trains', almost all of us – from the most talented scratchbuilders downwards – will admit, if pressed, to the formative influence of that childhood trainset. We all have to start somewhere, and many of today's leading experts began with a clockwork trainset on the living room floor. It may well be that because of this association with childhood toys, the so-called 'ready-to-run' or 'RTR', model has not always enjoyed the prestige it deserved. However, RTR has now come of age, and the time when the scratchbuilt model was, almost by definition, superior to the manufactured one, has now passed.

In favour of the toy train it can be argued that it reaches a far wider public than more realistic railway models are ever likely to. And it also reaches that public at a formative age. Most boys go through a toy train stage, and whilst most will abandon model railways during their teens, a significant proportion will rediscover their enthusiasm later in life.

Human nature being what it is, many fathers will use their young sons as an excuse to justify the purchase of a trainset that was from the first secretly intended for dad to play with, and in time may become his sole domain. Indeed, many men have been known to dash off to the nearest model shop as soon as their offspring is born. So in this somewhat devious way, the well-being of the model railway hobby can be attributed to the commercial success of the toy train.

Today, such is the quality and the variety of RTR locomotives and rolling stock available in the shops, the purchaser is almost spoiled for choice; and indeed in some cases he may have to choose between two or more models of the same prototype, made to the same scale but produced by different manufacturers. But such competition can only result in higher standards, and the long-term future of ready-to-run models looks most promising.

An early Hornby Meccano train set.

From the point of view of the manufacturer, one of the chief drawbacks of the model railway hobby is its diversity. There is a virtually limitless number of prototypes waiting to be modelled, in at least eight different scales, and so it will be impossible for him to please everyone. Although the number of ready-to-run models is ever increasing, there will always be plenty of scope for kit firms to produce models of the more unusual items that would prove uneconomic for the major manufacturers. Neither is it simply a question of trying to meet every conceivable demand, for among the scratchbuilding fraternity there are many who quite understandably prefer owning models that they have built themselves, regardless of what may be available commercially.

The Model Railway Market
Someone trying to make sense of this somewhat idiosyncratic branch of the hobbies market might well find that three distinct groups of customers emerge.

In the toy train market most of the potential customers (or recipients) are children, and many of these will receive a train set as a Christmas present. Here scale accuracy and detail are none too important, but low cost is essential. Therefore many firms produce a starter range, including simplified models that keep entry into the hobby as cheap as possible. Indeed, super-detailed, and therefore fragile, models are often at a disadvantage as rough handling by children can wreck them within minutes. Scale accuracy is not an important factor in this market as many models are bought by relatives who know little or nothing about model railways.

At the opposite extreme there is the scale modeller who has, traditionally, built all his models himself from basic materials. As the scratchbuilder has always been able to choose his prototype, being only limited by his own skills as to his choice of locos and rolling stock, he has tended to specialize and become something of a purist. If a scale modeller is to use any commercial RTR equipment, accuracy and super detail are essential. Moreover, as his interests tend to be very narrow, he

Below: Kitchen table railway layouts became possible in 1938 with Hornby Dublo's introduction of 'OO' gauge for three-rail operation, 12v DC. Rovex later followed with a two-rail track system.

Opposite: Märklin's gauge 1 Prussian P8 4-6-0.

will only buy an RTR model if it fits his exact needs.

Thirdly, as a halfway stage between the two extremes, we have the proprietary modeller who, whilst taking a serious approach to his modelling, does not wish to, or is unable to, build his own stock. As he is naturally more discerning than the toy purchaser, he is usually prepared to pay a little extra for greater accuracy and detail in his models.

Whilst the proprietary modeller has, historically, had somewhat catholic tastes, given the choice many of them might have preferred to concentrate on modelling one geographical area and one time period. However, until the early seventies the range of RTR models was, with certain exceptions, so small that it was impossible for the proprietary modeller to specialize in the same way that the scale modeller could. Since that time, sufficient models have become available to enable the proprietary modeller in a number of countries to produce a realistic model railway in the sense of being able to purchase correct locos and rolling stock in the appropriate liveries of his country's railway system.

Incompatible

To take the example of Britain, it was almost impossible for the average British modeller of the early 1960s to build a realistic railway from proprietary equipment alone. Of five major OO manufacturers, only Hornby Dublo and Tri-ang offered a complete range and, as their couplings and wheel standards were incompatible, one had to choose one system or the other at the outset. Looking at a Tri-ang catalogue of the period, one discovers that whilst there was a considerable range of locos available, there was no underlying link between them, so that whilst one could not, for example, model a Great Western branch line with the available rolling stock, one could run the latest mainline electric loco alongside Stephenson's 'Rocket'! The proprietary modeller was always at a disadvantage as, in order to obtain enough locos to run his trains, he would have had to recruit a rather motley collection.

But today, in Britain as in many other countries, the proprietary modeller can produce a very realistic model railway with off-the-shelf equipment, without even resorting to the paintbrush. Indeed, with this extra competition, standards have improved so much that commercial manufacturers are in a position to challenge the long-held supremacy of the scratchbuilder.

Commercial models are now readily available for no less than six main scale/gauge combinations – I, O, OO, HO, N and Z – while TT and S are somewhat more limited in distribution and coverage. The largest and the smallest (gauge I and Z gauge) have one thing in common – they are, commercially speaking, the sole preserve of one manufacturer – Märklin of West Germany. Märklin have a long tradition in model railways, dating back to the 1890s. Indeed, they could be said to have produced the first commercially available ready-to-run model railways as long ago as 1892.

Gauge I

Dealing firstly with gauge I, it is slightly ironic that Märklin is returning to this gauge. It is currently the largest in production, but when Märklin introduced gauge I in 1892, it was thought to be the smallest feasible size. Gauge I will always be a minority interest – its sheer size dictates this – but those with sufficient room will find these Märklin models accurate enough for the most exacting scale modeller and yet robust enough to provide hours of fun for the younger enthusiast.

Modellers lucky enough to own a large garden will find gauge I in general, and Märklin's system in particular, well suited to outdoor use. Whilst Märklin's range is not large and all the models are of German prototypes, the quality is excellent. Moreover, by gauge I standards, the prices are ridiculously cheap: a small tank engine in gauge I costs litle more than twice the price of the equivalent Märklin model in HO.

The late 1970s saw a revival in gauge I live steam with small quantities of high quality locomotives being marketed at collector's prices. A fascinating range of live steam models, available in either kit or RTR form, are made in Japan by Aster, and sold in Europe by Fulgurex. Prototypes include a British 'Schools' class 4.4.0. and a US logging railroad Shay.

O Gauge

For a time considered to be an obsolescent gauge, used only by older enthusiasts, O gauge has made a remarkable comeback. The introduction of the Lima range in the early 1970s gave O the boost it needed to re-establish itself. Using the same 12-volt DC two-rail electrification as OO/HO, the Italian-made Lima range includes models of British, French and German prototypes which, in view of their cheap prices, can be considered excellent value for money. Designed mainly as toys, Lima rolling stock can be run on the floor with no ill effects, but it really comes into its own in the garden. Strong enough for young children, Lima products are at the same time sufficiently accurate to satisfy most O gauge enthusiasts, who in general are critical of proprietary offerings.

Two other European O gauge manufacturers are Pola Maxi and Rivarossi, but uncertainties in supply have limited their acceptance.

O gauge in North America is predominantly a builder's preserve, with a large selection of kits and parts available but little mass-produced RTR material. For those able to afford it, however, there are some magnificent hand-built models in brass.

One old stager that refuses to lie down is the famous O-27 system made by Lionel. Basically a toy-train range, it uses three-rail track and 20 volts AC. Flanges and other tolerances are reminiscent of prewar O gauge tinplate on the other side of the Atlantic, but the sheer robustness and massive construction of Lionel trains gives them lasting appeal with North American children.

S Gauge

Of all the scale/gauge combinations, S gauge is undoubtedly the most poorly provided for. Being entirely non-metric, it is unknown in continental Europe and in Britain S gauge is restricted to the scratchbuilder. In North America, however, the gauge has only one main commercial supporter, American Flyer.

HO Gauge in Europe

By far the most popular scale/gauge combination in the world as a whole is HO, or 'half O'. The actual gauge measurement is 16.5mm (0.65″) and scale ratio 87:1 or 3.5mm to the foot. While the dimensions of the track remain relatively constant, there is considerable variation in the precise scale used by the various manufacturers. Indeed the British use of 76:1, or 4mm to the foot, scale is best treated as an entirely separate scale/gauge combination under the heading of OO/HO.

The history of HO in continental Europe once again owes much to Märklin, perhaps one of the longest-running success stories in model railways. But while Märklin has remained loyal to its own three-rail AC system, almost every other manufacturer now uses two-rail.

There are now a significant number of major firms in European HO, each offering a wide selection of locomotives and rolling stock – only N gauge is remotely comparable in available range. Moreover the quality of RTR equipment in HO is so high that only a limited role is left for the scratchbuilder.

To a greater extent than in Britain or North America, the modeller in continental Europe has traditionally been happy to rely exclusively on what was offered by the manufacturers, or often indeed by a single proprietary firm. A modeller using, say, Fleischmann products, would use the Fleischmann catalogue as his bible, and from it would purchase not only locomotives and rolling stock, but every other conceivable item such as track, accessories and so on. The purist might

Collectors' items: This die-cast 'O' scale locomotive from the American Lionel Company has front lights, a whistle in the tender and other realistic features.

argue that this approach was not so much building a model railway as putting together an assemblage of parts, or 'shaking the box'. Certainly, while the excellence of available locos and rolling stock cannot be disputed, their use on sectional track with sharp radii somewhat reminiscent of toy train sets detracts considerably from the realism of the overall effect.

Having said this, there is on the other hand nothing standing in the way of the person wishing to use this superb rolling stock in a more prototypical way. In the case of the Deutches Bundesbahnen (DB), or Federal German Railways, it is possible to buy off-the-shelf examples of virtually every class of locomotive and every type of coach that has run on the system since the Second World War.

Within Europe there are of course considerable variations in coverage – largely in relation to national variations in the popularity of model railways. The example of Western Germany is atypical because as a country it has not only the most manufacturers, but also the most railway modellers.

The commonality of prototypes between East and West German railways places East German modellers in a similarly favoured position, while Austria and Switzerland are also well represented. Italy and France both have independent manufacturers modelling national prototypes, but otherwise coverage of the many remaining countries' railway systems is rather patchy. Modellers are obliged to make do with a large proportion of 'international' rolling stock, fundamentally German in character, and models of perhaps one diesel and one electric class of locomotive specific to their own country.

HO in Europe
The following review of European HO manufacturers betrays the dominance of West Germany, but also shows the growing challenge from Italians, French, Austrian and East German firms.

Ade (made in Germany)
A specialist firm, Ade produces only modern DB coaches, in either RTR or kit form. Whilst fairly expensive, Ade models are of high quality and of fully scale length, but are not widely available.

Below: Kit and ready-built versions of the detailed ADE coaches feature lights, seats and even luggage racks. *Right:* From the Swiss company, Hag, a die-cast BLS class Ae 4/4 electric locomotive.

Electrotren (made in Spain)
The only Spanish manufacturer, Electrotren specializes in colourful goods wagons but the products of this little known firm have only a limited circulation. In order to run broad gauge models on HO track, the axle lengths of Electrotren's RENFE wagons are shorter than scale.

Fleischmann (made in West Germany)
Whilst mainly German, the Fleischmann range includes some models of French, Belgian and Swiss prototypes, and is one of Europe's leading manufacturers. Fleischmann is well known for excellent reliability and after sales service. The Fleischmann DB coaches are considerably shorter than scale, but this is a common European fault echoed by Lima, Märklin and Roco. It is a compromise between very long prototype coaches and the sharp minimum radii of the various sectional track systems.

France Trains (made in France)
France Trains are a small specialist firm producing only French prototype coaches. Whilst somewhat more expensive than some other makes, their range includes many interesting items not offered by the larger firms and is characterized by a fineness of detail not often seen on mass-produced models.

Hag (made in Switzerland)
Hag produces a superbly engineered range of Swiss electric locomotives built in traditional style with diecast metal bodies. The locos run beautifully and are generally regarded as the most powerful proprietary models available; but Hag's Swiss coaches are on the other hand considered outdated in relation to the standards of other manufacturers.

Jouef HO (made in France)
Jouef produces the widest coverage of French prototypes, while their fine range also includes some Swiss
and German models.

Liliput HO (made in Austria)
In addition to their British models, Liliput produces a
magnificent European HO range that includes some of
the finest model locomotives ever offered by any manufacturer at any price. Liliput is also well known for its
excellent range of coaches, which are all scale length
and include full interior detail. Whilst producing
models of prototypes of the usual countries, such as
Germany and Switzerland, Liliput also offers models of
Swedish, Austrian and, unusually, Danish locomotives
and rolling stock.

Lima HO (made in Italy)
Lima makes an enormous range of European models,
but their distribution and availability vary widely from
country to country. However, Lima HO always represents excellent value for money.

Märklin/Hamo (made in West Germany)
Märklin produces a complete model railway system,
using a unique 16-volt AC supply, and stud-contact
track. This has many advantages over the conventional
12-volt DC 2-rail system, including increased reliability,
as the locos are less affected by dirty track and the
wiring is much simpler, especially on larger layouts.
Several of the other European manufacturers, for
example Fleischmann, will also supply their locomotives adapted for the Märklin system. However, to

satisfy the requirements of more conventional
European modellers, some of Märklin's most popular
models are available for 2-rail DC operation under the
Hamo label.

Piko (made in East Germany)
Piko produces a wide selection of models from all over
Europe, including East Germany, Hungary and Poland
and, whilst the quality of their products can vary, their
latest introductions – often based on DB prototypes –
are as good as any manufactured in Western Europe.

Rivarossi (made in Italy)
Specializing in Italian and German prototypes,
Rivarossi has an enviable reputation for quality and
reliability. However, many of their models are made to
the slightly larger scale of 1/82 and this sometimes
spoils their otherwise excellent products.

Roco (made in Austria)
Roco probably represents the finest value in European
HO for, whilst their prices are quite reasonable, Roco's
models are almost impossible to fault at any level. The
locos run smoothly and quietly and their coaches are
magnificent reproductions of useful prototypes. Roco
offers an alternative coupling for all their models which
holds the vehicles so close together that the buffers
almost touch and yet allows the models to negotiate the
tightest curves.

Trix HO (made in West Germany)
Once one of the leaders in HO, Trix now only produces a
small selection of models, including excellent 0-8-0T and
2-6-0 locomotives, based on West German prototypes.

HO gauge Swiss 'Crocodile' freight locomotive class
Be 6/8 of the Schweizerische Bundesbahnen from
Märklin.

HO in North America

Whilst North America is a vast market for HO model railways, American and Canadian modellers, being very kit orientated, have relatively few RTR makes at their disposal in comparison with their European counterparts.

Athearn

The firm of Athearn produces a very wide range of American diesels but, surprisingly, no steam locomotives. Despite their relatively low price, all Athearn models include lights and most have flywheels. In order to keep the price down as far as possible and also to save damage in transit, some details, such as handrails, are left for the modeller to add himself from parts provided. Athearn rolling stock is not strictly ready-to-run, but includes an enormous range of freight stock and passenger cars in the form of simple kits. As these kits come ready painted, it takes, on average, no more than two or three minutes to produce an RTR item in CKD form.

Atlas (made in Austria)

All-wheel drive, cam motors and flywheels help to make Atlas diesels the most powerful and smooth-running available, although for best results they should be run in for over an hour when new. The use of compact motors ensures a correct body-width on hood units. Atlas diesels are particularly noted for their scale accuracy and degree of detail and are the best available. Another bonus is that the range is available in a large variety of road names and liveries.

Bachmann

Well known for an extremely cheap range of diesels, Bachmann have now added several steam locomotives to their range, including a Southern Pacific GS4 4-8-4 in full 'Daylite' livery. Bachmann also produce a relatively cheap range of American freight cars.

Life Like/Model Power (made in Yugoslavia)

There are many low-priced American models made under licence in Yugoslavia, appearing under many different brand names in the US. It is not unusual to see identical models under several different labels. These models, while cheap, represent excellent value for money and are a good introduction to American modelling.

Mantua

Sometimes also known as Tyco, Mantua is a less prominent name, under which is made a range of metal-bodied steam locomotives and some unusual diesels.

Rivarossi/AHM (made in Italy)

Rivarossi produces by far the largest range of RTR steam locomotives. These moulded plastic models are to be found on many HO layouts as they are excellent reproductions and truly capture the gigantic proportions of the originals. No review of the Rivarossi range could be complete without mentioning their famous HO model of the Union Pacific 'Big Boy' 4-8-8-4, the largest steam locomotive ever built.

Left: An Atlas GP-38 'Hi-Nose' Diesel locomotive in Santa Fé colours.

Bottom: Bachmann HO scale South Pacific GS4 4-8-4 in 'Daylite' livery.

Handbuilt Brass

In the history of North American railroads there have been so many different classes of steam locomotive that no single manufacturer could possibly hope to produce a representative range of models. Therefore moulded plastic RTR models tend to be restricted to the most famous types, such as the UP Big Boy and the SP GS4. To fill this enormous gap, a number of small suppliers have introduced a wide variety of models on a strictly limited-run basis. These models are semi-handbuilt in brass by craftsmen in either Japan or Korea, and then distributed in the USA by an importer such as Pacific Fast Mail (PFM). Usually these models are restricted to no more than 1,000 units and sometimes fewer than 50 have been produced. Whilst by mass-produced standards these models are expensive, they include almost every detail and usually feature fully-sprung driving wheels.

The introduction of quality brass models came about in the early 1950s largely through the efforts of an American enthusiast, Max Gray, who commissioned a Japanese watchmaking firm to make him fine detailed models. He eventually imported both HO and O gauge

brass models, for himself and his friends, and by 1954 the demand was so great that he ordered 50 pieces of a Sha in O gauge. Count Giansanti-Coluzzi has done fo European brass models what Max Gray achieved with American outline locomotives.

The reason for the popularity of brass models lies in the excellence of their workmanship: not only in their precision and fine detail but also in the introduction o technical innovations, such as sprung wheels, gea boxes and better motors, which give a vastly improved performance. Their appeal is not solely due to the fac that they fill the gap left by the mass producers who concentrate on popular locomotives, for how do we explain the success of the UPR 'Big Boy' by Tenshodo and similar well-known models?

On the debit side, British outline locomotives are conspicuous by their absence in this field, though a handful of enthusiasts are altering that situation Economic necessity has also forced the Japanese indus try to contract and Korea is now the major producer with the result that originality and advancement have been abandoned to combat over-production, and stan dards have dropped.

Below: One of the first companies to produce hand-built brass models was Japanese manufacturer Tetsudo Makei Sha, whose JNR Class C 62 4-6-4 is shown here.

Above: A highly detailed GWR 'Castle' Class 4-6-0 brass model made by Fulgerex in 1974. Only 200 were produced and numbered for Peco.

Below: An early brass model, circa 1958, of a Wabash 2-6-0 by AHM (Associated Hobby Manufacturers). Though lacking in detail it was good for its time.

OO/HO in Britain

There was a tremendous increase in interest in model railways in the early seventies which encouraged many new firms to enter the British OO/HO market. There are now ten manufacturers actively involved. Of these, Hornby, Graham Farish, Liliput (formerly Trix) and Wrenn are well-established OO makes. Jouef, Fleischmann, Lima and Rivarossi have long been producing European HO but are new to the British scene, whilst Airfix and Palitoy Mainline are well-known British toy companies not previously associated with model railways.

The position has always been complicated by the British use of OO (4mm to the foot) when the rest of the world uses HO (3.5mm to the foot), and consequently these new manufacturers were faced with the choice of either adopting the worldwide HO standard, and therefore having to re-educate the British public, or accepting the status quo and continuing with the traditional British OO standards.

Three of the newcomers tried to introduce British HO – Lima, Fleischmann and Rivarossi. Lima produced an extensive range of very cheap HO models, using the standard European coupling, but could not entice British modellers away from OO. In a short space of time, the HO range was soon replaced by a new Lima system in OO, using the British tension-lock coupler. Fleischmann introduced one excellent diesel loco and matching coaches in HO but, by the time these reached the shops, the cause of British HO was already lost. Rivarossi's venture into British HO, was an unrebuilt LMS Royal Scot.

The other new makes, Airfix, Mainline and Jouef, all successfully launched their models in OO, using a coupling similar to the established tension lock pattern. With this massive new reinforcement, any chance that Britain would surrender to the rest of the world and adopt HO gauge was lost forever. As a result the range of British RTR models in OO has increased to the point where the proprietary modeller can buy his entire stock off the peg. At the same time, due to this increased competition, standards have improved to such an extent that many scale modellers are now turning to RTR equipment in preference to scratchbuilding or kits.

Left: Wren OO gauge 4-6-0 'Castle' class locomotive in BR experimental blue livery.

Below: OO gauge LMS Fowler Class 2P locomotive from Hornby.

Right: Oldtime American 4-4-0 locomotive of the Union Pacific, from Airfix.

Right below: An Airfix tank locomotive of British Rail.

Airfix

Although Airfix is one of the newest entrants in the field of model railways, their models stand comparison with the very best from any manufacturer in the world. Indeed, if one were to award a prize for the best RTR model of a British prototype, it would surely go to Airfix's Great Western 0-4-2T which, with its companion autocoach, makes up a complete branch-line train. Airfix's LMS carriages are not merely BR coaches repainted in pre-nationalization livery, but scale models of particular prototypes using correct bogies and underframes. Airfix was the first British firm to produce coaches with flush fitting windows, a feature

that improves their appearance dramatically. On the layout, Airfix locomotives perform as well as they look; indeed, in a well-publicized test, one of their diesels hauled 105 coaches, setting a world record.

Graham Farish

Graham Farish is a small manufacturer who, whilst not offering a complete range, produces a variety of carriages and wagons. Unfortunately some of the private owner liveries, especially on the box vans, are fictitious, and therefore of little use to the serious modeller. Although representing good value, the coaches are basically all the same pattern, merely re-painted into the various liveries.

Hornby Railways

The trade name 'Hornby' is so well known to the general public that it is not surprising that Hornby is the undoubted market leader. Unfortunately, Hornby have slightly raised the buffer height of all their models in order to allow their somewhat large tension-lock coupling to work efficiently. Whilst this does not greatly affect the look of a locomotive or coach, it does give a short four-wheeled wagon a rather upright look. Moreover the somewhat plastic-seeming finish on Hornby wagons appears toylike when compared with the excellent matt surface achieved by, say, Airfix and Mainline.

However, Hornby's coaches are more convincing and, despite using a standard BR-style bogie they can, in

Below: British Rail class 25 Bo-Bo multi-purpose diesel-electric locomotive from Hornby.

Bottom: An Airfix GWR Class '61xx' 2-6-2 'Prairie' tank locomotive in British Railways livery.

Below right: A fine scale LMS 3rd Brake Coach by Mainline/Palitoy.

general, be recommended. The LNER teak coaches are especially good and a great boon to all East Coast modellers as teak is a very difficult finish to simulate. Hornby has made many real improvements in the locomotive range over the past few years and these models now include many features until recently found only on continental products.

Jouef (made in France)
Unfortunately Jouef's OO range has to date been restricted to a class 40 Diesel and matching Mark III coaches, which is a pity as their products so far are in all respects superb. The coaches are full scale length, with a good paint finish, spoilt only by the grossly overscale flanges used on all Jouef models.

Liliput OO (made in Austria)
Liliput have greatly condensed the old Trix range and now concentrate on their excellent LNER steam locomotives. These fine models were the first to feature scale-size wire handrails, and as they perform as well as the better European makes, they deserve their excellent reputation.

Lima OO (made in Italy)
Once thought of merely as toy manufacturers, Lima have produced some very fine models in recent years, and while some of their models are still toylike – for example, their four-wheeled wagons – others, such as their Deltic diesel locomotive, are by any standards excellent and, at the prices charged, extremely good value. Lima's coaches are all based on British Rail Mark I types and therefore the pre-nationalization liveries are incorrect, but for the BR modeller they are a good buy. In 1978, Lima up-rated all their steam locomotives and their latest GWR 2-6-2T is a worthy addition to the Great Western scene. Lima produces a fine range of models and they are ideal for a youngster's first introduction to model railways.

Mainline/Palitoy (made in Hong Kong)
Mainline's LNER J72 0-6-0T was the first of the new generation of models to arrive in British model shops and it set the standard for others to follow. Their BR Mark I coaches are excellent, spoilt only by the non-flush fitting windows which show up the thick coach side, but despite this they have proved very popular with BR modellers. However, Mainline's LMS corridor coaches are as near perfect as one could imagine, and even a fine-scale modeller would be hard pressed to find fault with them. One of the best features of the Mainline range is the excellent coupling, which, while compatible with all other makes, is less obtrusive and holds the vehicles at scale distance apart.

Wrenn
Wrenn inherited the old Hornby Dublo range which, until original withdrawal in the early 1960s, had been the most scale-orientated proprietary system. Certain improvements have been made, such as metal bogie wheels on the locos and pin-point bearings in the wagons, but many features, such as flangeless centre drivers for six-coupled locomotives, remain; and although they were acceptable when the models first came out in the 1950s, they are anachronisms today. Furthermore, except for some livery changes, no really new models have been introduced to the range since it came under the Wrenn label. Many of these new liveries are purely fictitious, and while they may appeal to the toy market, they are of little use to the scale enthusiast.

TT Gauge

Once hailed as the gauge of the future, TT failed partly because the emergence of N scale took place before it had had time to develop fully. TT gauge was seen as having neither the detail of OO/HO nor the space-saving advantages of N. However, in Eastern European countries, TT is more popular and some of the East German Berliner Bahnen models are fairly widely available. TT is also represented in the United States, but has only a minority following.

N Gauge in Europe

When N gauge was first introduced by the German firm of Arnold Rapido in the early 1960s, it was assured of a very bright future. The space-saving advantages of this miniature size were obvious, and Arnold's engineering standards were very advanced for their day. N gauge was taken up with enthusiasm by a number of other European manufacturers and a very full range of models is now available to modellers of continental European railways. Part of the appeal of N gauge is the almost complete interchangeability of products with, for example, the original type of automatic coupling being universally adopted. N gauge is now second only to HO in Europe, but owing to its tiny size is less popular in the toy train market.

Arnold Rapido (made in West Germany)
Pioneers in the field, Arnold are still market leaders thanks to a policy of constant development. The range of models offered is very wide indeed and includes much North American material. Many working accessories are available, as well as automatic block control and smoke-producing locomotives – a feature normally found only in OO/HO.

Fleischmann (made in West Germany)
Fleischmann produces an excellent range of German models, including steam, diesel and electric prototypes, with representatives of other countries such as Sweden being added. They were the first to introduce scale-length coaches in N and have constantly set new standards of detail and authenticity.

Minitrix (made in West Germany)
Minitrix produces a very large European series of mainly DB prototypes which, unlike their British range, is constantly being expanded.

Roco (made in Austria)
Roco is the newest of the European manufacturers in N gauge and has started by offering scaled down versions of the superb HO range – with little apparent loss of detail, despite the smaller size.

Rivarossi (made in Italy)
Rivarossi make a small European range of German and French prototypes that has not been expanded in recent years. North American models are also produced and the firm seems to have been concentrating on this series lately.

Top: A Roco Multi-purpose electric locomotive class 144 of the Deutsches Bundesbahn.

Centre: A Freight locomotive class 151 of the Deutsches Bundesbahn by Minitrix.

Bottom: Fleischman Class 94 0-10-0 tank locomotive of the Deutsche Bundesbahn.

N Gauge in North America

American and Canadian layouts, or 'pikes', have traditionally been on a more lavish scale than their counterparts across the Atlantic. This is in keeping with the prototype, where mile-long freight trains are a common feature of operation. HO has long been established as the leading scale/gauge combination in North America, but the introduction of N gauge was met with much enthusiasm. It allowed the man with very little space at his command to build a respectable layout, and it also made it possible for some vastly impressive model railroad empires to be dreamed up, with even greater track mileage than had been possible with HO. The European lead in N gauge has meant that a number of continental firms produce North American models for sale on both sides of the Atlantic.

Arnold (made in West Germany)

The European success of Arnold has been duplicated in the North American market where the Arnold range is of an equally high standard.

Bachmann

This leading American HO manufacturer also produces a large range of both steam and diesel locomotives in N gauge with a complementary range of freight cars and passenger coaches to match. The prices are extremely reasonable and represent excellent value for money, although not all the items are available in Europe.

Con-Cor

Con-Cor sell a fine range of locomotives, passenger cars and freight cars, all of which are available from specialist model shops. Their locomotives are particularly well engineered and their passenger cars deserve special mention as they are available in a large selection of road names unobtainable from any other manufacturer.

Kadee

In addition to the magnetic couplings for which they are well known, Kadee also produce a superb range of N gauge freight cars, available fitted with either their own or the Arnold Rapido type of coupling. It is unfortunate that Kadee do not produce any locomotives as the standard of their freight cars is truly remarkable, exceeding that of most equivalent HO models.

Life Like (made in Yugoslavia)

Life Like offers a very wide selection of well-modelled diesel locomotives – the N gauge equivalent of the popular HO range.

Atlas (made in Austria)

Not to be confused with the old Atlas range now retitled under the Rivarossi label, these new Atlas models are made in Austria by Roco, and are accordingly of typically high quality. They set a new standard for N gauge: for example, the FA1 diesel is one of the first to feature flywheel drive.

F7 of B & O by Arnold. First to produce N-gauge commercially.

Bachman EMD F9 Diesel. Santa Fe.

Kadee 40ft Box Car with single door.

Atlas FA1 Diesel Locomotive, Wabash.

N Gauge in Britain

N gauge first arrived in Britain as a continental import, and at first only models of continental outline were available. For a while Minitrix was the only manufacturer to make models of British prototypes. In time, however, a pair of British N gauge firms emerged, and Minitrix dropped into the background.

The tiny size of N gauge models has deterred all but the most determined scratchbuilders, and for those dependent in any case on the RTR market, the choice of British prototypes available is still somewhat limited. Despite the introduction of white-metal body kits for RTR chassis, N gauge in Britain has nothing like the scope of OO/HO, and so many British N gauge enthusiasts base their layouts on European or North American practice.

Graham Farish

Graham Farish produces the largest range of British N gauge steam locomotives, and all their models are based on pre-nationalization prototypes. Special note must be made of their Pullman coaches, which are the best ready-to-run coaches available to the British modeller.

Lima (made in Italy)

Lima have produced a comprehensive range of models, featuring both steam and diesel prototypes, and by keeping the prices very competitive have done much to bring newcomers to this section of the hobby.

Minitrix (made in West Germany)

The German firm of Minitrix was one of the first manufacturers to produce British outline models on existing European chassis. Regrettably, however, few new models have been produced in recent years.

Lima LMS Fowler class 4F 0-6-0 steam locomotive.

Lima British Rail Mk I Corridor Composite carriage.

Z Gauge

Until Märklin pioneered Z gauge in the early 1970s, N had been considered the smallest gauge suitable for commercial development. The technical problems involved with N gauge were considered difficult enough, so when Märklin announced Z both the model trade and the hobby at large were astounded. However, unlike N, which has attracted many manufacturers throughout the world, Z gauge is virtually confined to the German outline models made by Märklin. Despite their diminutive size, Z gauge models are very authentic, and indeed, if anything, they seem more accurate than their larger N equivalents.

As Z gauge has been developed by a single manufacturer, there is no possibility of the conflicting standards and problems of coupling compatibility that have so beset most other scales. Since Märklin continues to develop the range – now including most of the features available in HO – Z gauge appears to have an assured future. Whilst not really aimed at the toy market, as many children would have difficulty with such a small size, Z is ideal for the adult enthusiast looking for something a little different.

Above: Märklin Mini Club Class 41 2-8-2 of the Deutsche Bundesbahn.

Below: The Märklin Z gauge Mini Club set was first introduced without a transformer, because it was 9 volt DC, giving USA and British enthusiasts the opportunity to adapt it to their own supplies.

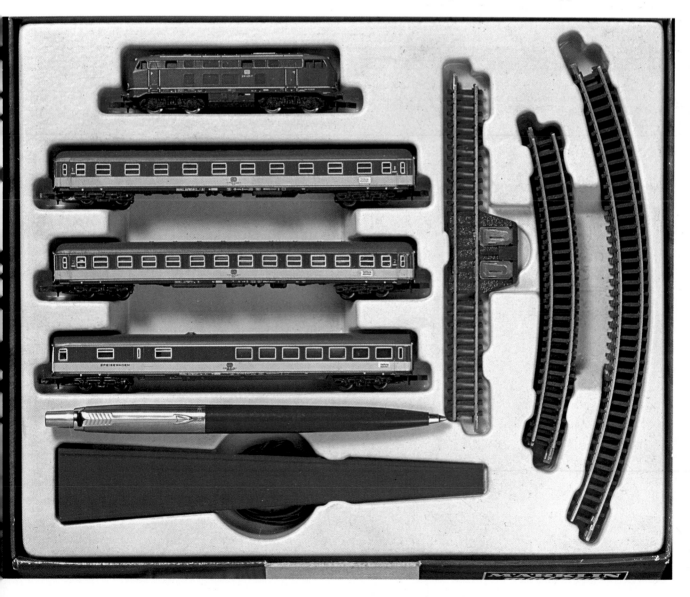

KIT BUILDING

After a period of using ready-to-run equipment, many modellers want to broaden their horizons and start to think in terms of building their own locomotives and rolling stock. The choice available ranges from assembling very straightforward CKD (completely-knocked-down) kits to building a model entirely from home-made components – a labour of love that may take months or even years. In broad terms, however, the field may be divided between kitbuilding and 'scratchbuilding' – literally, making things from scratch.

Kitbuilding and scratchbuilding have always been significant in Britain as in the past the standard of RTR equipment was not always as high as it is today. On the continent of Europe, however, the opposite has in general been true, and RTR locomotives and rolling stock predominate. In North America, the immense variety of steam prototypes that once existed, and the kaleidoscope of railroad liveries that still exists, leaves tremendous scope for model building as commercial manufacturers can never hope to cover everything. On the other hand, CKD kits have very wide currency, particularly as they are a convenient way of despatching virtually finished products by mail, leaving final assembly to the customer.

Building kits is a most useful way for the modeller to gain experience. As he builds more of them, he widens his knowledge of construction techniques and identifies those that work best for him. In addition, viewing each vehicle as an assembly of components gives the modeller insight into the way model locomotives and carriages can be built – a great asset to the man who may eventually want to tackle scratchbuilding.

It is difficult to draw the line between kitbuilding and scratchbuilding, particularly as some kits leave much construction work for the modeller to do himself. However, most modellers would accept that a model may properly be called scratchbuilt if the bulk of its main components have been fabricated from basic raw materials, even if some use may have been made of prefabricated parts.

All that a modeller requires to make a HO passenger car, from American kit manufacturers Wm K. Walthers Inc.

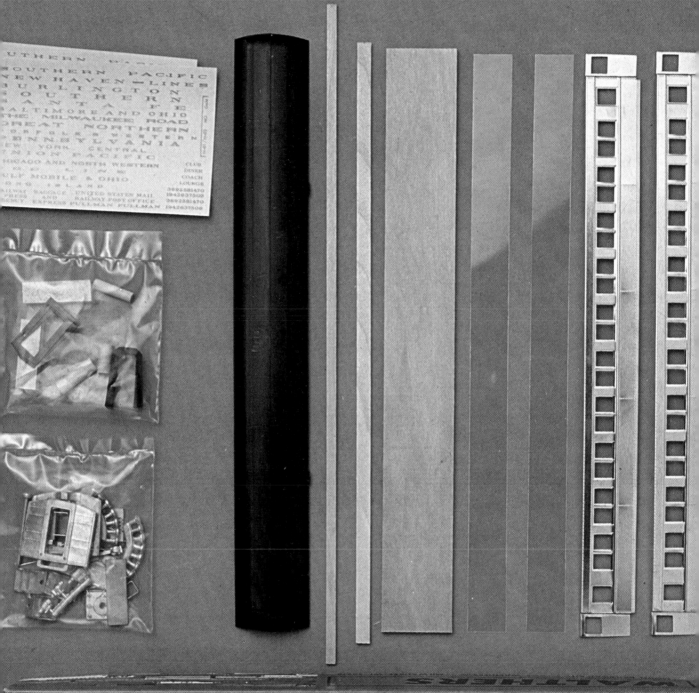

Materials

The materials available to the kit manufacturer – and for that matter the scratchbuilder – include card, wood, moulded plastic and sheet plastic, as well as cast, punched and etched metal. Kits are usually engineered to make the maximum use of a single material, turning to others only for complex components such as wheels, although there are a few multi-material kits on the market.

Card

The use of card as a material for kits dates back to the early days of the hobby when few alternatives were available. Proper use entailed several layers of card – preferably coated with shellac to stiffen it, make it cut cleanly and protect it from damp and warping. Card was once used for entire bodies, but there are few such survivals on the market today.

However, card continues in use as an overlay for other materials – occasionally in coach kits, but more especially in freight vehicle construction. For example, the British firm of Peco specializes in four-wheeled open wagons which come with blank metal sides. The intricate and often colourful private-owner livery is printed on thin card embossed to represent planking, strapping and rivet details. This technique is quite effective, though the embossed detail is not as crisp as that achieved with moulding.

When cutting the overlays, the effect can be greatly enhanced if the glaring white edges of the card are touched up with a suitable paint. Once the sides are glued in place, an overspray of matt varnish will help to seal the surface and protect the card from damage and wear.

Wood

Wood is another traditional material for kit construction. In Great Britain, the use of wood has declined considerably. Only one very limited range continues to employ it for bodysides, although wood is still used for floors, roofs, or to give hidden strengthening. In the larger scales, it can be used most effectively to model wood-planked carriages and wagons. It can also be made weather-proof and this, in combination with its strength, makes wood particularly suitable for vehicles running on outdoor layouts.

North American kit manufacturers have not been in such haste to abandon wood, and they still commonly use it for HO and O gauge boxcars. The wood is usually milled pine or basswood, and needs a sanding sealer and a rub down with fine steel wool to achieve a smooth finish. This is of course especially true where a wooden model is based on a metal-bodied prototype – in such a case the grain effect would undermine the appearance of the vehicle rather than enhance it.

If a wooden roof is supplied with a kit, to avoid the grain showing through it is easy to cover it with thin card, taking care to disguise the join where the roof meets the sides and ends. Incidentally, the texture of roof canvas can be simulated with a layer of tissue paper glued over the structural roof.

For wood-to-wood joints, white PVA adhesive is probably the best, while general purpose glues or cements should deal satisfactorily with wood-to-metal joints and so forth. Where the manufacturer lists a preferred adhesive, check whether it offers any real advantages over similar types which you may have in stock. But don't take risks – it's heartbreaking to watch a well-assembled model fall apart when incorrectly used adhesive starts attacking the components.

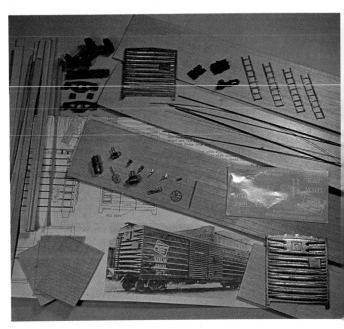

Parts of an American 50ft automobile box car belonging to the Milwaukee Road, produced in O gauge by Ambroid. It is mainly of wood, despite the prototype's metal construction, and detail parts are stripwood, wire or cast metal.

Moulded Plastic

While moulded plastic is reviled by some and revered by others, there is little doubt that its introduction boosted the overall standard of railway modelling considerably. Scratchbuilding was no longer necessary in order to achieve models of high quality, and finely detailed, accurate models came within everyone's grasp.

Plastic itself may be cheap, but the cost of moulds can run into four or five figures. Consequently manufacturers try to get as much use out of them as possible – sometimes more than perhaps they should. A mould is usually comprised of two or more pieces of metal clamped together, but as wear develops, the pieces may begin to clamp up slightly out of register. This produces two effects: flash (surplus plastic squeezed out round the edge of mouldings), and offset halves with an obvious mating line. The manufacturer also has the problem that unless either the mould or the plastic is very flexible, he must avoid the use of 'undercuts' that will lock the finished item in the mould. This is why handrails, for example, are often only modelled in low-relief rather than being shown as free-standing.

Some of the simplest kits are CKD – completely knocked down – being capable of assembly within half n hour with only a screwdriver. However, most kits are supplied on a network of sprues and the final appearance of the model depends very much on the way individual components are removed from these sprues. Avoid the temptation to twist them off! Parts are best cut away with a piercing or jewellers saw, any remaining

stub being removed with a Swiss needle file. The flash mentioned earlier can be trimmed with a sharp craft knife – or, if it proves stubborn, with a needle file. Imperfect matches are more difficult to remedy, especially if they appear across convex surfaces such as brake cylinders or buffer heads. Such flaws can be

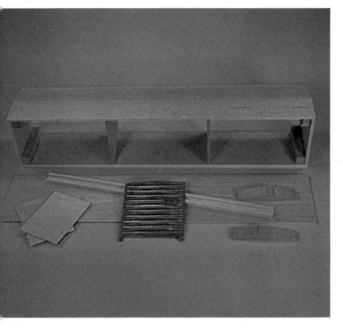

Construction begins with the main box which holds everything else together. It must be firm and square before the next stage is commenced.

Truck bearers and the chassis spine are supplied to shape; the ribs are cut from stripwood (a tight fit increases strength).

The underframe cylinders and pipework are formed from metal castings and wire of several thicknesses. When this is complete the remaining body details can be attached. Some details, such as the roof walk, are best painted before fitting.

Brush painting is quite practicable but many modellers prefer an airbrush. Spraying gives rapid colour build-up, quick drying and allows several coats in one evening. Waterslide lettering, from the kit, needs to be protected with varnish.

dressed with a file, but replacement may sometimes be the only answer. Paying attention to detail in this way takes little time overall, but impatient modellers are tempted to overlook it – thus setting at risk the appearance of the finished vehicle.

Plastic 'glues' are in fact usually solvents, melting and welding the various parts together. This makes it particularly easy to ruin a kit by letting the solvent stray. At some time or another, most people have left an unintentional but almost indelible fingerprint in the side of one of their plastic models. If this occurs in the middle of a highly detailed area, it probably cannot be made good. In plainer areas, allow the damage to harden for over 24 hours, fill depressions with body filler, and when this in turn has dried, smooth the surface down with emery.

Liquid solvents are preferable to tube cements because they are more easily controlled – especially if you reduce the number of bristles on the brush which is usually supplied with the solvent. However, cements are normally stronger, and will bind some plastics that liquid solvents fail to hold. Do not press parts hard together when bonding them, or molten plastic may weep out along the joint. If this happens, leave it to harden before trimming or your knife could damage the softened area nearby.

Plastic models are very light, so when assembling them, look for places where you can hide a little ballast. Light vehicles trapped between heavy vehicles in a train are prone to derailment, especially when propelled round curves or across turnouts. Keeping similar vehicles to as near a standard weight as possible makes running more reliable. A rule of thumb for OO/HO is one ounce per axle.

Sheet Plastic

The term 'plastic' is taken to include a wide variety of materials such as PVC, polypropylene, acetate, polystyrene, nylon compounds and so forth. These are usually supplied in sheet form and they tend to be used in combination with other materials, their main uses being for vehicle shells, sides, or simpler underframe components.

One form of kit provides the modeller with a preformed shell of clear PVC, to which he glues screenprinted PVC sides carrying the livery of the prototype. This method can be simple and effective, although the coach sides may lack rigidity, and there is a risk of waves or depressions appearing along the body. However, it allows the manufacturer to produce several types in the same coach family simply by substituting different sets of screen-printed sides.

Because the materials tend to be somewhat slippery, surfaces should be roughened before gluing so as to give the adhesive a key. Glues can be a problem – some hardly affect sheet plastics at all, others attack them too vigorously, so follow the recommendations of both kit and glue manufacturer carefully.

If possible, avoid using the acetate sometimes provided for glazing. It is very unstable, and can expand and pull away from its intended location, even if well glued. Clear polystyrene, though rather easily scratched, is far less troublesome.

Cast Metal

While one or two North American firms produce die cast locomotive kits in hard zinc alloy from metal moulds, a very large variety of kits are made from soft lead-based white metal. The moulds for these are simply two rubber discs clamped together. Molten white metal is poured down a hole in the centre while the discs are spun, and centrifugal force thrusts the metal through the paths in the mould.

The process – but not the metal – is extremely cheap and according to price and demand may cover its cost over as few as 300 copies. However, the moulds wear fairly rapidly and need replacing. Registration of the moulds is sometimes imperfect, and cylindrical shapes are liable to distort.

White metal is widely used for detail castings and for larger items such as coach ends, while in Great Britain particularly it is also used for wagon and locomotive kits. One drawback is that for a variety of reasons quality can be variable. Problems include indifferent masters, low-grade metal (leading to blow-holes, etc.)

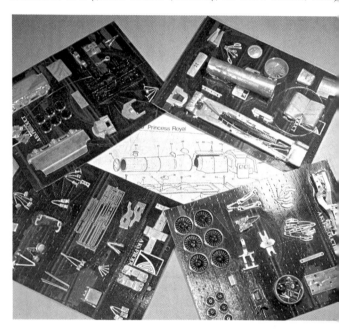

N. & K.C. Keyser's OO white metal kit for a London, Midland & Scottish Railway *Princess Royal*. The castings are sealed to their cards with clear film to prevent losses.

contraction, poor finishing and flash – plus the problems of degradation, imperfect matching and distortion already mentioned. White metal contracts by about two per cent on cooling, which occasionally leads to parts refusing to fit together. A file may cure this, but if the mis-match is serious, return both parts to the manufacturer. Blow-holes in flat areas can be cured with filler, but ragged t-strap flanges, for example, may not be worth rectifying. The most troublesome kits are generally well known, so if in doubt check with your dealer for advice.

Preparation of white-metal kits requires a knife, needle files, and a fibreglass brush. Most parts will have casting marks that need to be cleaned off, while the smaller components such as whistles and safety valves may still be attached to a 'tree' and are best left there until needed. The fibreglass brush is pen-like in appearance, and used carefully on dull castings will bring them up like pewter. Over-used, it will erode detail, round off corners that should be sharp, and so on. While in use the brush produces a fine dust of glass fibres which can cause considerable skin irritation, so it is best to work over a large sheet of newspaper and tidy up

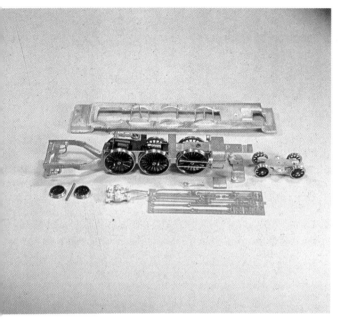

The driving wheels are fitted temporarily to identify rough spots and obstructions. The footplate is cleaned and tried in place. Low footplates help to hide motors but cause electrical short circuits if the wheels touch them.

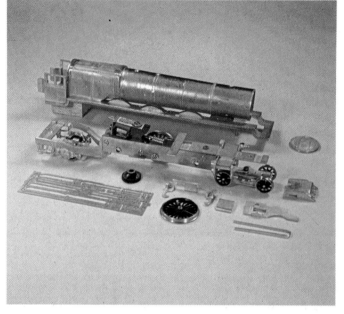

The wheels are removed to allow the chassis to be painted. Careful filing and adjustment cured an imperfect fit of the boiler and firebox. The model greatly benefits from such attention to detail, even though it is time consuming.

With the wheels replaced and the cylinders completed, the Walschaert's valve gear can be built up from the etched fret provided. Ensure that the driving wheels rotate readily with the coupling rods on and that the crosshead has sufficient free travel.

The entire superstructure is sprayed red, masked as required, and sprayed black. The lining is guided by adhesive tape, but some brushwork may be necessary. Nameplates are provided with this kit but for sentimental reasons a different name was obtained from the King's Cross range.

thoroughly. Be sure to rinse your hands carefully in water – but without rubbing them – before proceeding with construction.

There are various means of fixing suitable for use with white metal: adhesive filler, epoxy resins, or instant glues. The ease of using some of the glues is offset by their life expectancy. Glues eventually break down, although it may be ten years before this happens. One guide is that the faster a glue dries, the shorter is its effective life. Throughout its career, a model will be subject to frequent vibrations and occasional knocks, which will speed up any decay in the adhesive.

If properly made in the first instance, a soldered joint will be permanent, but normal solder has a melting point higher than that of the castings, with obvious risks. However, a low-melt solder, used with a cooler soldering iron (wired through a dimmer switch or in series with a mains lightbulb) is a much safer proposition provided all surplus flux is removed from time to time during construction.

For major sections, or where strength is vital, use solder. Car body filler is ideal for the remainder. Filler will also join metal to plastic, although it is advisable to roughen the plastic on the bonding surfaces. Bonding with filler can be messy, and the joint will be fragile during the drying period. About 15 minutes after the joint has been made, excess filler can be carefully peeled away with the point of a sharp knife, allowing detail smudged with filler to be reclaimed. The joint is still delicate when this is being done, and should not be stressed at all. Nevertheless, with this method it is possible to hide joints completely – as filler does in fact fill, and without contracting as it hardens. When dry, it can be filed smooth.

Sooner or later, a hot soldering iron is going to sli and damage a casting. Such damage – on simple components at least – can be repaired either by blobbin fresh solder onto the area or by building up with fille In either case, when the medium is hard it can b trimmed and filed, and eventually burnished with th fibreglass brush until the damage is indetectable to an but the closest scrutiny.

Punched Metal

Punched metal is a medium particularly suitable fo coach kits. Other metals such as brass have bee employed, but the metal normally used is aluminium Being soft it forms readily, although modellers shoul be warned that it scars or deforms just as easily whe scratched or bent in any way. Coach bodies can eithe be pressed complete (except for the floor and ends), o with sides and roof separately stamped and formed. Th first method can lead to problems in forming th cantrail correctly at either edge of the roof, while common flaw with separate sides and roof has been tendency for the windows to be punched too low although the inaccuracy is not great. Punched metal i only suitable for relatively two-dimensional parts, an so it is common to find it used in conjunction with othe materials such as wood, white metal or plastic.

It should be realized that aluminium is a very slipper metal – like stainless steel, it has its own chemica shield which swiftly re-establishes itself after an abrasion. With the correct flux and sufficient hea aluminium can be soldered to aluminium or othe metals, but the surface of the joint must be adequatel cleaned immediately beforehand. Similarly aluminiur can be glued, but unless the same careful preparation i

Ex-GNR Class C12 4-4-2 Tank locomotive in LNER condition, circa 1930, from Craftsman Models in 4mm scale kit.

Tyco's General steam locomotive and tender kit 4-4-0 for advanced modellers contains 82 precision parts.

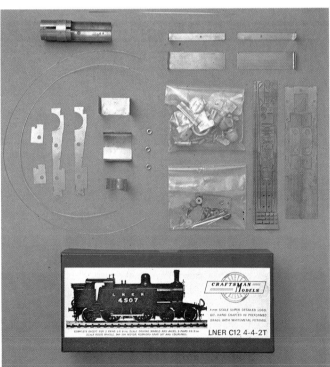

made, even joints made in strong epoxy glue will shear under stress.

The metal will drill quite readily, but swarf tends to twist up the drill flutes. If this is allowed to continue unhindered, the drill will seize fast in the hole. However, a drop of liquid detergent will prevent all this as it lubricates the cutting edges and keeps the swarf from bonding.

Aluminium takes paint beautifully if degreased and wiped clean of all fingerprints, but the finish will be more permanent if a self-etching primer is used. This virtually digs its teeth into the metal, making the finish far more resistant to chipping and stripping. Etching primer is also recommended for painting other metals.

Etched Metal

Process-engraving is a traditional block-making technique used in the printing industry. It involves printing a negative on to sensitized zinc, and acid-etching the result. The method has been adopted by kit makers, but only to a limited extent. Its main disadvantage is that only one surface of the metal is etched, which means that if any surface detail, such as panel beading, is to be reproduced, the windows cannot be etched away and must be punched or laboriously sawn and filed out.

At the beginning of the 1970s, brass kits began to appear on the market which had the metal etched from both sides. It became apparent that although the new process was sophisticated, it was now possible for intelligent amateurs to produce kits from their own artwork and negatives with a relatively small investment. In consequence, a tremendous range of etched kits has evolved, particularly in the United Kingdom. The strengths and weaknesses of etching – including its high cost – led initially to a concentration on those exotic vehicles which responded well to etching but were difficult to produce by other means – mainly panelled coaches and bogie freight stock. But the scope has since broadened to include four-wheeled wagons and locomotive kits.

Separating components from the etched fret can be accomplished with tinsnips, a piercing saw, or a small chisel and mallet. In all cases, the remaining stub should be filed away or it may undermine structural strength by preventing parts fitting snugly. As with white-metal castings, components should only be detached as necessary as they have a well-developed faculty for escaping! Some modellers find it beneficial to have a large sheet of polythene under the workbench and chair to catch most of the items without having to indulge in a search of the entire floor area.

Assembly is best done with solder – the rudiments of this 'black art' can be learned in five minutes, and skill rapidly builds up with practice.

For the finer details, it is best to forsake solder for glues, such as epoxy or cyano-acrylate. Five-minute epoxy is excellent where only one or two items are being glued, but where a lot of small details are being fitted, the original 24-hour-setting epoxies are better – only one mixing may be necessary for the whole job, and there is no urgency to fix delicate items in place. Simply load a pin with glue, spot it where required, and manoeuvre the detail into place with tweezers.

The sophistication of etching has made it possible to combine strength with elegance. Some manufacturers are already producing vehicle kits with wheel compensation – though not true springing – to ride over rough areas of trackwork. And modellers can now have something approaching the thinness of prototype parts after years of being forced to accept greater thicknesses due to the limitations of plastic moulding – deeply recessed coach windows being one example, thick smoke deflectors another.

On the other hand, etched metal cannot reflect three-dimensional bulk. It cannot, for example, represent deep outside framing on box vans, unless it is elaborately and expensively built up in layers. Another problem is that all detailing must be on one of two levels rather than on several. The metal is attacked from both sides by the etching acid. If there is 'resist' on both sides, the metal will retain its full thickness. If the resist is partly missing from one side, the metal will be etched from that side to produce panels, plank-grooves, etc. If there is no resist at all, the metal will be etched from both sides, and no metal will remain. This limitation is important, but a Scandinavian firm has been working on three-level etching with some success, and multiple level etching may become normal as chemical milling techniques are developed.

Whatever its drawbacks, etched metal is ushering in the next generation of kits, introducing a quality that is almost indistinguishable from expert scratchbuilding.

An American 40ft composite reefer by the All Nation Line. This kit is an O gauge made up of metal and wood.

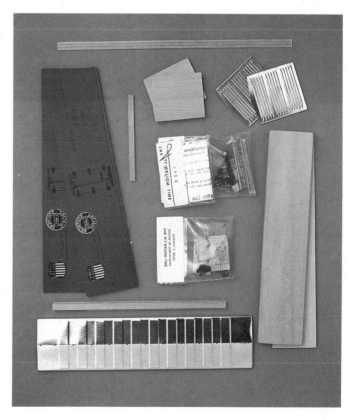

Improving Kits

Many beginners make the reasonable assumption that the parts in the box will produce a complete model, but this is by no means always so. Often the complexity and also the cost of the kit can be reduced by leaving out such finished parts as wheels, couplings and motors. This has the added advantage of allowing for the varying range of standards in the hobby. The first improvement is therefore self-evident – to complete the kit!

A modeller prepared to build his own chassis to go under a locomotive body kit should first obtain a reliable drawing of his prototype (and photographs if possible), and compare the kit parts with it. First, are they the same length? The kit design may have been compromised to fit a commercial chassis. Second, if the wheel-spacing is incorrect, can it be rectified without serious difficulty? Third, are the overall proportions right? A firebox marginally too high or too wide might alter the character of the locomotive considerably.

Further detailing might include sand-pipes and brake-rigging for the driving wheels; new chimneys and domes; substituting wire for moulded pipework; fine turned fittings instead of split pins for handrail knobs, etc. US firms such as Cal-Scale and Kemtron provide a wide range of cast parts for detailing North American prototypes, but European modellers are less fortunate. British steam prototypes require few, since their lines are probably the cleanest in the world, with most ancillary items out of sight. This makes it all the more important to model what should be there.

Many steam locomotives were substantially rebuilt during their lives, with different boilers, fireboxes, smokeboxes, cabs, cylinders, and sometimes even wheel arrangements. All these alterations lie within the scope of the ambitious kit-basher prepared to buy a model in one state and modify it to another; indeed, many modellers prefer drastic kit-surgery to the alternative of scratchbuilding. Requirements include the drawing and photographs already mentioned, a clear plan of action, tools, the victim, and some courage to make the first saw cuts!

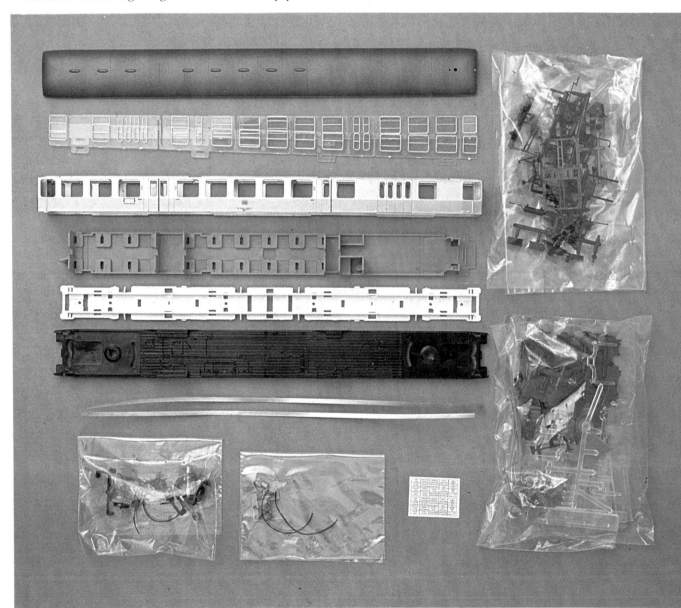

Reducing lengths is a fairly simple operation, but increasing them demands internal supports and an appropriate filler. When altering the length of a model steam locomotive, do not cut the boiler into several pieces just to retain the boiler bands – the fewer cuts the better. New bands can be made from thin paper, Scotch tape, or metal, and other parts may be scratchbuilt or purchased as required.

Rolling stock can also be improved and modified – by finishing off incomplete underframes and substituting metal where plastic might be insufficiently robust; by improving crude brake gear, replacing wrong bogies or axleboxes, and adding wire handrails; by fitting metal handwheels in place of moulded ones, refitting glazing to avoid deep recesses and so on.

When modifying plastic kits, try to locate cuts where they can easily be disguised, and rub the seams down till they blend with the surrounding material. Joints can be backed with polystyrene sheet, if necessary, while welding solvents make them quite strong if allowed to dry properly. If you have gaps between two parts being mated, dissolve scrap plastic in a little solvent. The resultant thick 'goo' can be applied like a body filler (but carefully) and rubbed down when hard.

Getting your models on the road

Showcase models need not run, but working models will benefit from tuning. First check freedom of movement, especially in couplings, axlebearings and bogie pivots. Eradicate stiffness wherever you find it – preferably by lubrication – although it may take a knife or file to remove some roughness or stray paint. If your locomotive binds, though the linkage seems free, check the quartering of the driving wheels. Inducing extra slop in a coupling rod bearing is something of a coward's way out in engineering terms, but it may solve the problem.

The root of the trouble may lie deeper, of course, so check the operation of the motor. Usually a motor will go slightly faster in one direction than the other, but the difference should not be pronounced. If it is, then run the motor for a few hours in each direction to see if it cures itself. If this fails, then get a new motor. Where the gear train is indirect, check for free movement down the line, and ensure that the meshes are neither loose enough to slip nor tight enough to jam.

Sometimes a chassis works well on its own, but misbehaves when a metal body is fitted. The cause is likely to be a short, so try lining the inside of the shell with tape to insulate it. Watch also for a short transmitted through metal couplings between stock, or between engine and tender. Other possibilities are that the motor brushes are fouling the interior and the brush pressure on the commutator is being increased or reduced; or that the weight of the body alters the balance of the chassis, perhaps forcing it down far enough to be struck intermittently by the pony wheels. Finally, if the model has a sprung or compensated chassis, make sure the springs are of the correct tension.

Having now looked in some detail at the practical problems facing the modeller who wishes to assemble kits, it is time to consider the position of those enthusiasts who prefer the satisfaction and challenge of building their own locomotives and rolling stock from scratch.

Left: An ADE kit, before assembly, showing the large number of parts which go into making these fine models.

Below: The kit fully constructed.

SCRATCHBUILDING

It is difficult to draw the line between kitbuilding and scratchbuilding, particularly as some kits leave much construction work for the modeller to do himself. However, most modellers would accept that a model may properly be called scratchbuilt if the bulk of its main components have been fabricated from basic raw materials, even if some use may have been made of prefabricated parts.

What are the reasons for the existence of this absorbing branch of the hobby? The most fundamental motive of the scratchbuilder is to create something with his own hands. Building a model steam locomotive, for example, can be a lengthy business, but if carried to a successful conclusion can be tremendously satisfying. But there is much more to it than that. Creativity can also be expressed in a great many other aspects of railway modelling, and it is undeniably true that there are many creative modellers who have no experience of scratchbuilding whatsoever.

The special attraction of scratchbuilding – as opposed to kitbuilding – is that it enables the modeller to possess something which is totally unique: a creation which fulfils his desire to own a particular model coupled with the satisfaction of developing and using hand crafts to produce it.

To succeed as a scratchbuilder requires a host of skills, from detailed initial research in libraries or archives to handling a wide variety of models. When these combine at their best the results are outstanding, and the world's finest models are invariably scratchbuilt.

LNER V2 Class 'Green Arrow' 2-6-2 mixed traffic
locomotive circa 1936. This 4mm scale model is soon
to be produced in brass by Mega Models, London.

Perhaps the most powerful reason for building from scratch is that the modeller achieves something totally unique and individual. It is of course perfectly possible to build a convincing model railway – certainly in the more popular scales – utilizing nothing but commercial products, be they ready-to-run or in kit form; but having achieved this, there is always the knowledge that even if a kit or RTR model of that prototype exists, his scratchbuilt example is unique – and for some, this is sufficient reason for making it themselves.

However, for many people, scratchbuilding truly comes into its own when the modeller, for whatever reason, desires to own a particular model for which the trade does not cater. Only then, in his view, can he really stamp some personality onto his efforts. This, one suspects, is the main reason why many scratchbuilders practise their art today. The models they build are not only unique, but are also uniquely different, and therein lies their attraction.

A third reason for scratchbuilding which is less valid now than formerly is the feeling on the part of the modeller that he can produce a better product than the trade. In prewar days this was undoubtedly possible to achieve without any great exercise of individual skill, but such is the quality of many modern kits and RTR offerings that there are probably few modellers nowadays who can honestly claim to be able to produce better results than those of the best commercial products. Thus, scratchbuilding, proportional to the hobby as a whole, accounts for a smaller fraction of finished models than was once the case.

A further justification for scratchbuilding can be summed up in the word 'pride'. We are all human, and the chance of being able to say proudly 'this is all my own work' can provide a powerful stimulus – even if the end product is well below perfection, or even below the standard of the commercial equivalent. Many modellers feel slightly guilty at assembling their systems wholly from commercial parts, and who is to say they are wrong?

Finally of course, there is the cost factor. In most cases the finished cost of a scratchbuilt model is much lower than that of a commercial offering of comparable quality, since raw material is cheaper than finished components. For this reason, many modellers often resort to scratchbuilding as an economic necessity. Time, however, is not without its own value. The modeller gives his time for nothing – at least as far as his own models are concerned – but many people would perhaps be amazed at the true cost of scratchbuilt models if it were to be calculated in relation to the amount of time spent.

Be that as it may, high-quality scratchbuilding is, even to those who do not practise it, generally regarded as the pinnacle of the model railway hobby. There can be no real doubt that the majority of the finest models to be seen around the world are those which, for the most part, have been individually hand-crafted.

The Requirements of the Scratchbuilder

It is one thing to want to create; it is quite another to know what to create or how to go about it. Essentially, however, good scratchbuilding is pre-eminently a combination of knowledge and skill.

The first issue is one which cannot be circumvented by the would-be scratchbuilder – knowledge of the prototype. This does not mean that he should have been perfectly familiar previously with the object he wishes to model, but merely that he must be well-provided with relevant information. To be certain of this, it is of course necessary to undertake research.

Research can become quite a time-consuming business in itself, involving the need to hunt through libraries, archives, drawing collections and the like. If the relevant locomotive, carriage or wagon still exists, physical inspection may be possible which, in turn, will prompt the need for notes, measurements, drawings or photographs. Even after having obtained such data, the modeller may still feel that he cannot yet make a start. In what livery should the model be painted? Did the prototype look the same in, say, 1960 as it does now? These, and others like them, may be crucial questions to which the modeller can find no satisfactory answer; and, as with so many other facets of this hobby, he alone will decide whether or not to proceed.

Regardless of how much individual research the modeller is willing to undertake, two types of information are virtually indispensable during the actual construction of a model. One is a good drawing, and the other is an ample supply of adequate illustrations. It is almost impossible to make a good model without a good drawing, and it is very difficult to proceed far without accurate pictures (usually photographs) which will indicate whether there are any significant departures on the real prototype from the details shown on the drawing. The more attention given at this stage, the better the chances of success, and it is no coincidence that some of the most knowledgeable railway historians

are to be found among the ranks of the fine model makers. The quality of observation and attendance to detail displayed by the good model maker is also the hallmark of a good railway historian.

Having discovered, researched and assimilated the requisite amount of information, the modeller then has to ask himself some fundamental questions relating to his own ability to turn wish into reality. In other words, 'Have I the skill to make a satisfactory model?'

Skill in model making is quite impossible to define, although we can all recognize it when we see it. Some may regard it as an in-bred quality, others as something which can be learned. It is probably a combination of the two, but with a heavy leavening of hard work, willingness to learn from others, and experience – something which can only be gained with time. Were one to ask the vast majority of skilled modellers to describe their first efforts, they would either blush or come out with some quite unprintable comment. This can only be reassuring for the novice, and nobody should fight shy of scratchbuilding simply because they have never tackled it before.

Almost by definition, scratchbuilding is a diverse occupation, covering every possible scale, gauge and prototype, including some impossibly obscure ones. The materials available to the scratchbuilder are equally varied: they include all those outlined earlier with reference to kitbuilding, as well as many more – in fact, anything on which the model maker can lay his hands.

Because of this diversity it is difficult to lay down practical guidelines. The best advice to any would-be scratchbuilder might be to progress gradually from simple to more elaborate kits, thereby obtaining experience of a wide variety of materials and techniques, before embarking upon his chosen field. To cover the subject of scratchbuilding thoroughly would take another book; but for those interested to learn something about the practical techniques involved, two typical examples are illustrated.

Ex-LSWR luggage van scratch-built by Vivien Thompson.

Detail of rail car from Robert Hegge's scratch-built Crooked Mountain Lines.

Great Eastern Railway 2-4-0

This example is of a scratchbuilding project covers the production of a 4mm scale (OO gauge) model of a Great Eastern Railway Class T26 mixed traffic 2-4-0 tender locomotive designed by James Holden.

Of 100 locomotives built from 1891–1902, the LNER in 1923 took over the whole class redesignating them Class E4. Throughout their lives the engines, affectionately known as the 'Intermediates' were employed on all types of traffic on branch lines and cross country routes in East Anglia. In the mid-1930s, six engines were transferred to the old North Eastern area of the LNER to work the Darlington–Penrith line and as a result had side window cabs fitted. Gradual withdrawal commenced in 1926 but ceased during the Second World War and 18 engines remained to be passed into British Railways ownership on nationalization in 1948. They were the last 2-4-0 tender engines working in Britain, and No. 490, the sole survivor of the class was preserved and restored to its original condition when withdrawn in 1959.

This basic piece of prototype research was followed by an in depth survey of the class, to pin down the individual locomotive to be modelled, how it varied from its sisters and in which period it was to be shown. For this exercise, as many photographs as possible were studied and notes made on variations from the working drawings obtained. All engines are different, even if of the same class, and often the works general arrangement drawings can only be relied upon to give basic facts and dimensions.

The next stage was to plan the construction – scanning numerous trade catalogues to find that the boiler fittings, tender axle boxes, buffers and smokebox door were available commercially. It also became apparent that with a tiny boiler and an open cab, a tender drive mechanism would be preferable, possibly with the electrical pick-up being made through one set of wheels on the locomotive.

For a first attempt, the superstructure could have been built from styrene sheet, but the material chosen was in fact sheet brass .025mm (0.010″) and .037mm (0.15″) thick. The frame material was 125mm × 16mm ($\frac{1}{2}″ \times \frac{1}{16}″$) strip brass, using square section bar for spacers. In addition to the earlier shopping list of specific commercial items the following had to be purchased – wheels, driving and pony axles, axle bushes, sheet and bar section brass, handrail wire, split pins, nuts, bolts and the tender-drive unit complete with wheels.

The critical part of any scratchbuilt locomotive is its chassis, and the critical part of the chassis construction is the acuracy with which the frames are cut and drilled. The accuracy of the driving axles in turn depends on the coupling rods since they must be used as a drilling jig for the axles. In this case the coupling rods were commercially available; if this had not been the case, two pieces of bullhead rail could have been sweated together, filed to shape and drilled. There are however, a number of photo-etched coupling rods now on the market and these save much time and trouble.

Two identical pieces of frame brass were sweated together along the top edge with a very hot soldering iron. With a sharp scribe the outline of the frames and the centres of all holes were then marked. Using the coupling rods as a guide a pilot hole was now drilled through the frame for each driving axle, this hole then being enlarged to accept the frame bush. It is essential

Below: A typical selection of reference material necessary to building an accurate model.

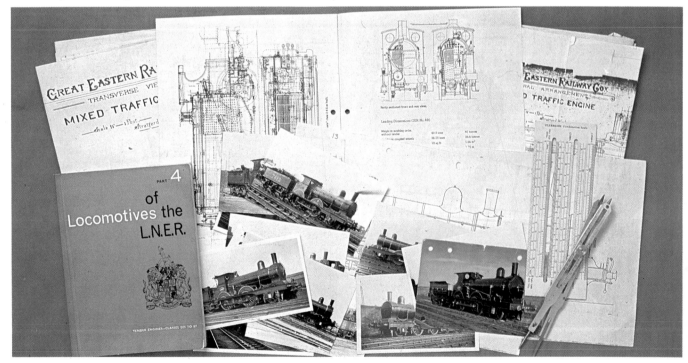

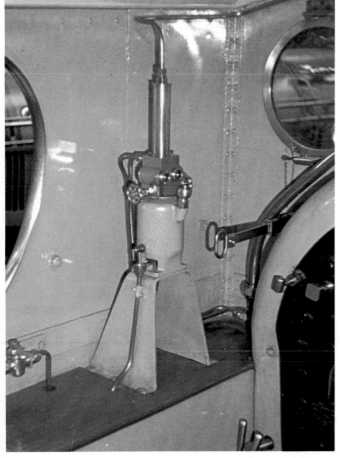

These detailed photographs are particularly useful when constructing an accurate model.

Above left: A safety valve and whistle on Great Eastern 2-4-0.

Below left: Sight-feed lubricator in cab.

Top right: Coupling rod pin and bush.

Centre right: Top of Westinghouse pump.

Bottom right: Detail of tender axle box and springs.

that all these holes are drilled at right angles. The remainder of the frame was then shaped and drilled – the outer face of the frame spacer screw holes being countersunk so that the screws (8 BA) lie flush with the chassis side. The chassis frames were then split under heat and cleaned with emery paper. Next the frame spacers were fashioned from square brass, drilled and tapped to accept the frame screws and body mounting screws. Remember that providing all holes are drilled square, the frames should assemble square.

Preparing the Wheels

Crank pins can be fitted in a number of ways, but in this case shouldered screws were used to fit into 10 BA tapped holes. One set of wheels was mounted onto two axles and checked for true running, fitted through the frame bushes and the other wheel fixed with its axle nut. The chassis was checked on the same track at this stage to ensure squareness and free running, without which it would be pointless to continue. The coupling rods were added and again the chassis was checked for free running. If the wheels bind with the rods fitted it is normally because there is a minor discrepancy between the crank pin centres and the axles. The remedy is to case each crank pin hole and try again until free running is obtained.

The remainder of the chassis was now completed and the pony truck built up as shown in the drawing. The electric pick-up is shown comprising spring handrail wire soldered to the heads of screws which are, in turn, mounted in an insulated block. The wire bears onto the backs of two driving wheels with rim insulation – the return part of this circuit being through the chassis, through the drawbar and to the tender drive unit. At this stage, with the tender unit connected, a trial run was made to ensure free running and the efficiency of the pick-up system. Note that the tension of the wire pick-ups can be critical and some experiment may be called for.

Above: Tender buffer beam, draw-gear and couplings of the Great Eastern Railway 2-4-0.

Right: A typical scale drawing prepared specifically for the railway modeller and published in the model press or historical railway society journals, while others are available commercially. The drawing shows the Great Eastern Railway 'T26' class 2-4-0 mixed-traffic tender engine as originally built, and incorporates scrap views which enable the modeller to produce a model of a locomotive of this class at any period in time. Copies of the original makers' general arrangement drawings are available from some sources, or can be found in railway engineering journals contemporary with the building of the particular prototype. Apart from requiring a more detailed knowledge of reading engineering drawings, they naturally do not show the later modifications made to the design.

Drawing reproduced courtesy Lyn D. Brooks, Great Eastern Railway Society.

Below: Key to the drawing opposite.

Key to fittings		
A	Roscoe displacement lubricator	(see B)
B	Furness lubricator	(later replaced A on 417-446)
C	Continuous handrails	(later fitted to 417-446)
D	Later blower valve	(see E)
E	Final blower valve	(later fitted to 417-496)
F	Flanged smokebox	(later fitted to 417-446)
G	Macallan variable blastpipe	(later fitted to 417-436, removed from 1926 onwards)
H	Later smokebox door	(fitted from c.1915)
J	Frame patches	(fitted from c.1900, some locomotives only)
K	Later alternative buffers	
L	Pop safety valves and altered whistle	(from c.1930)
M	Later chimney	(fitted from c.1930)
N	Brass beading removed	(from 1929)
P	Side window cab	(Nos 408/11/6/63/78/96, 1935)
Q	Raised cab roof	(fitted from 1933)
R	Rivetted smokebox	(from c.1935)
S	Steam heating equipment	(fitted from 1910)
T	Washout plugs	(fitted from c.1935)
V	Vacuum brakes	(No 474 in 1901, others from 1928)
Note: * Right-hand side only † Left-hand side only		

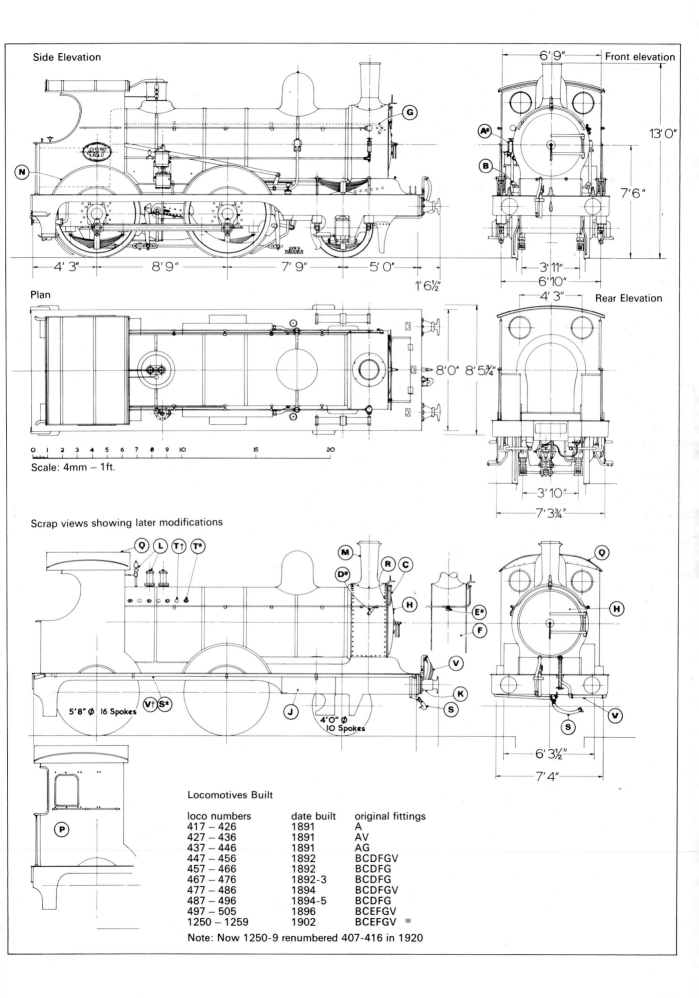

Side Elevation

Front elevation

6'9"

13'0"

7'6"

4'3"   8'9"   7'9"   5'0"

1'6½"

3'11"

6'10"

Plan

Rear Elevation

4'3"

8'0" 8'5¾"

0 1 2 3 4 5 6 7 8 9 10   15   20

Scale: 4mm – 1ft.

3'10"

7'3¾"

Scrap views showing later modifications

5'8" Ø 16 Spokes

4'0" Ø
10 Spokes

6'3½"

7'4"

Locomotives Built

loco numbers	date built	original fittings
417 – 426	1891	A
427 – 436	1891	AV
437 – 446	1891	AG
447 – 456	1892	BCDFGV
457 – 466	1892	BCDFG
467 – 476	1892-3	BCDFG
477 – 486	1894	BCDFGV
487 – 496	1894-5	BCDFG
497 – 505	1896	BCEFGV
1250 – 1259	1902	BCEFGV

Note: Now 1250-9 renumbered 407-416 in 1920

Scratchbuilding

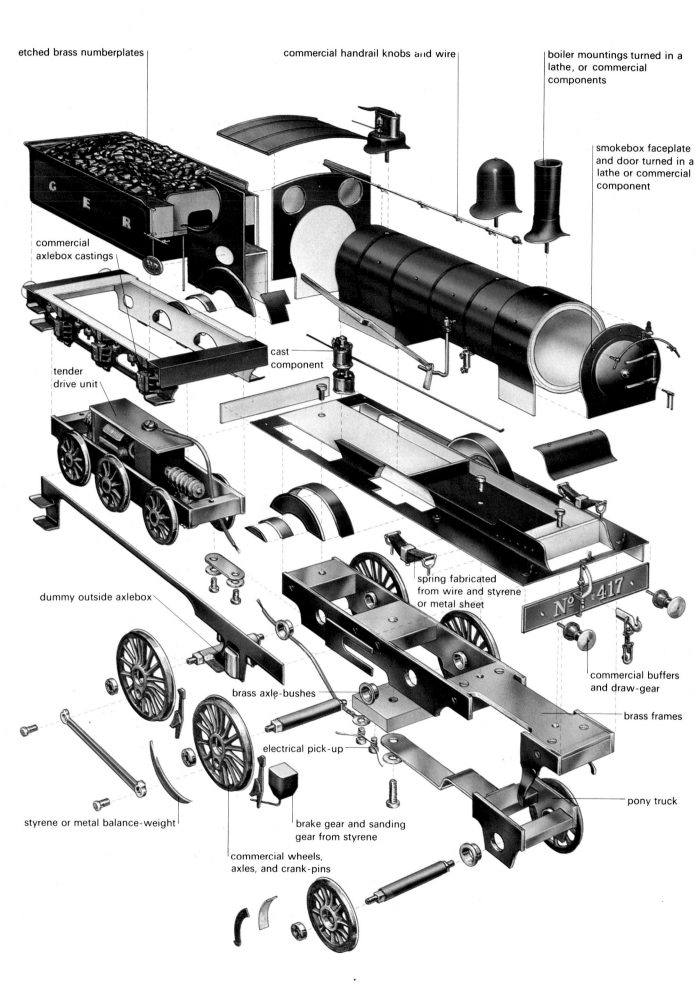

etched brass numberplates

commercial handrail knobs and wire

boiler mountings turned in a lathe, or commercial components

smokebox faceplate and door turned in a lathe or commercial component

commercial axlebox castings

tender drive unit

cast component

dummy outside axlebox

spring fabricated from wire and styrene or metal sheet

brass axle-bushes

electrical pick-up

commercial buffers and draw-gear

brass frames

pony truck

styrene or metal balance-weight

brake gear and sanding gear from styrene

commercial wheels, axles, and crank-pins

The next item to be tackled was the main footplate. This was cut with a piercing saw from 0.37mm (0.015") brass sheet together with the valances, smokebox saddle, buffer beams and draw beam. Wherever two identical parts were required, like the valances, two pieces of brass were sweated together and both cut at the same time. This ensured that they were identical, and made cutting easier.

Each part was carefully cleaned, using emery paper followed by a glass fibre brush. With a very hot iron, soldering commenced, wherever possible from the inside, until a basic box structure was completed. The other footplate fittings were added, checking at each stage that the body did not foul the free running of the chassis. The most difficult fabrications on this model were the driving splashers. These were formed as a full circular dish and when complete, quadrants were cut off with a piercing saw to fit the footplate.

Having built a strong square footplate, the boiler was now prepared from a piece of 18mm (0.71") diameter brass tube. The centre line for the boiler fittings were marked and holes drilled, and the same for the handrail supports. A smokebox wrapper was made from 0.37mm (0.015") brass sheet and the firebox cut and folded out to fit between the frame extensions on the footplate. Boiler bands were not fitted at this stage since they were to be applied ready painted and lines on the finished model. The smokebox front was left off until the handrails and boiler fittings were complete so the soldering iron could still be used.

The next section to be tackled with the boiler in place was the cab. Spectacle plate, cab sides and roof, together with interior splashers and finally the cab roof, ensuring that this sat square and did not dip towards the tender. The beading round the cab cut-out was fashioned from flattened split pins soldered to the edge of the sheet. Providing all ran well, the remaining detail fittings could now be added. The handrails were mounted using split pins crimped to the size of the handrail rather than model handrail knobs which tend to be overscale.

The axle boxes, and any other castings, can either be glued or soldered using a cool iron and special low melting point solder. A hot iron must not be used.

The main part of the tender body was made in one long piece, carefully folded to shape. The flare on the top edge is difficult for form; the method used in this case was a preshaped wooden former over which the top edge of the tender side was shaped by tapping with a wooden block and a pin hammer. The resultant sides and end were soldered into position and the coal plate and other detail added.

Before the model was finally prepared for painting, every available space inside was packed with weight, either lead or plasticine; this improved the riding, adhesion and electrical contact.

Left: An exploded view of the principal parts of a scratch-built model of the Great Eastern Railway T26 class 2-4-0. The main body structure can be made of a variety of materials, and some of the smaller fittings may be available commercially. A tender drive unit is shown, although the model may alternatively have the motor mounted in the locomotive itself, and driving on one of the driving wheel axles. The frames are made of brass, and the wheels and axles are of a type commonly available. The wheels on one side have insulated centres of two-rail electrification, as the opposite wheels, axles and frames are electrically live. The electrical pick-up is from the tyres of the insulated wheels, the pick-up itself being mounted on an insulated block attached to the frames. Return is through the frames and un-insulated wheels. The leading carrying axles of the prototype had a small amount of side-play in the axleboxes for traversing curves, but due to the sharper curves generally employed on model railways, a 'pony truck' is fitted to the model.

A 4mm-scale model of the GER T26 Class 2-4-0 from the collection of Major H.R. King. This particular model, although slightly inaccurate, nevertheless shows a high standard of scratchbuilding.

Southern Railway Driving Coach

The construction of model coaches is basically the same in all scales, the thickness of materials being the main difference. Illustrated opposite is the driving coach (code MBSO) of a Southern Railway '4COR' electric unit which exemplifies most of the techniques used in building modern metal panelled stock.

Starting halfway up the coach, the first part to be cut out is the floor. This is laminated from two layers of 1mm (40 thou.) styrene sheet, both the same width i.e. taking the wider top dimension, and when set chamfering the floor to the narrowest width at the base of the sides; this gives the tumblehome at floor level. Most British corridor stock of this period (LMS excepted) had bow ends, therefore the floor must be cut at each end to take this, allowing for the thickness of the vertical end pieces. It is also as well to mark both centrelines, first to locate the bogie bolts and then for underframe detail later. Drill out the bolt holes. In modelling the MBSO, one coach floor must be cut out to take the motor bogie, allowing enough room for the bogie to swing freely.

The sides are drawn out on 0.5mm (20 thou.) styrene sheet; if several coaches of the same type are required, mark all out at the same time as this eases the drudgery. It is best to mark out the MBSO sides top to top as they are mirror images. The inset driver's door must be marked on a separate piece to permit overlap behind each side of the door for strength. The window apertures are cut with a new blade, each cut to within two or three millimeters (0.1″) of the corner, then cutting across on the diagonal and removing the blanks. A needle file will give the required radius in each corner. On the MBSO the top corners are right angles.

As with most Maunsell stock, windowframes are needed; an overlay of 0.25mm (10 thou.) styrene sheet is used for each window and blanks are cut to the right size, being glued over each aperture. When dry the blanks are cut through from the rear and cleaned up. The MBSO has sliding frames at the top and these are also cut from 0.25mm (10 thou.) and glued in position. The tumblehome is formed on a wooden ruler by rubbing the craftknife handle along.

A template is formed from 1mm (40 thou.) to the shape of the ends, and scribed rough on 1mm (40 thou.) sheet; the resultant scoremark filled in with pencil and cut out with an old pair of scissors, cleaning up with a file as necessary. The centre portion is removed and glued in place to the floor, followed by the two flanking pieces. The MBSO needs more detailed treatment at the driving end: this end is cut from two layers of 0.5mm (20 thou.), the driver's window removed and corners filed.

Bulkheads are made from 1mm (40 thou.) in rectangles, carefully stacked together and secured with adhesive tape. The end template is offered to the top one, and scribed round on one side for the shape of the tumblehome. The block of bulkheads is then clamped in the vice and filed down to the scoremark, taking care that this is done accurately – it should ensure that all bulkheads are equal! these are then separated and glued in place, putting the metal rule along them from end to end and adjusting any discrepancy. Toilet partitions can be cut from 1mm (40 thou.) and secured to the bulkheads.

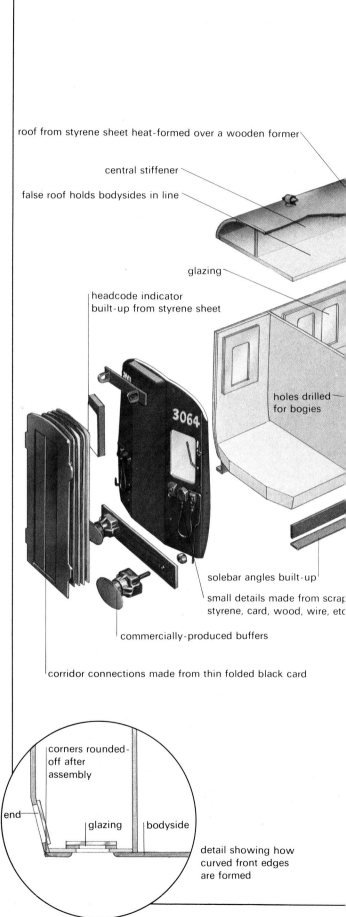

roof from styrene sheet heat-formed over a wooden former

central stiffener

false roof holds bodysides in line

glazing

headcode indicator built-up from styrene sheet

holes drilled for bogies

solebar angles built-up

small details made from scrap styrene, card, wood, wire, etc

commercially-produced buffers

corridor connections made from thin folded black card

corners rounded-off after assembly

end

glazing

bodyside

detail showing how curved front edges are formed

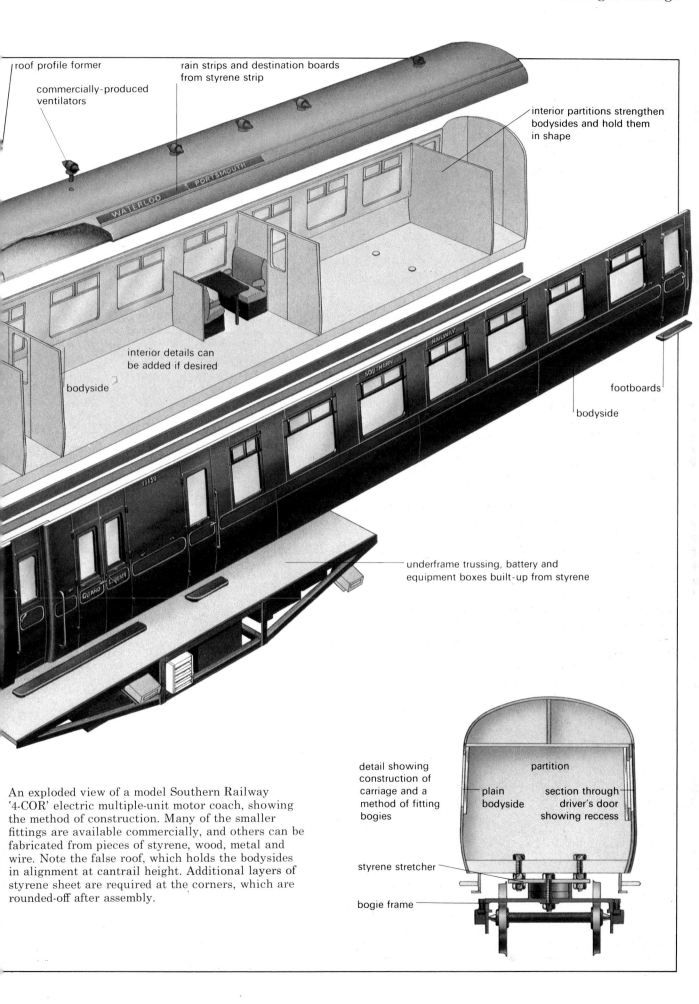

roof profile former

commercially-produced ventilators

rain strips and destination boards from styrene strip

interior partitions strengthen bodysides and hold them in shape

interior details can be added if desired

bodyside

footboards

bodyside

underframe trussing, battery and equipment boxes built-up from styrene

An exploded view of a model Southern Railway '4-COR' electric multiple-unit motor coach, showing the method of construction. Many of the smaller fittings are available commercially, and others can be fabricated from pieces of styrene, wood, metal and wire. Note the false roof, which holds the bodysides in alignment at cantrail height. Additional layers of styrene sheet are required at the corners, which are rounded-off after assembly.

detail showing construction of carriage and a method of fitting bogies

partition

plain bodyside

section through driver's door showing reccess

styrene stretcher

bogie frame

The corridor partition is cut from 0.5mm (20 thou.) and marked out to the same dimensions as the compartment side windows, allowing for the thickness of the floor 2mm (80 thou.) and measuring 1mm (40 thou.) below the height of the sides. (All corners are right angles in the windows.) This partition is glued to floor and bulkheads.

Scribe door openings on the sides, not too deep but enough to prevent clogging with brush painting. With a corridor coach, it is best to leave off the corridor side until the interior has been painted, so secure the compartment side to floor and bulkheads first, paint as required inside and complete with other side. 0.25mm (10 thou.) droplights can now be glued in position, some in the open position.

Below the Footplate

Attention is now turned to the part of the driving coach below floor level. The headstocks are shaped from 1mm (40 thou.) sheet, with the same thickness but narrower and shorter for backing to take the solebars. Drill out for buffers. Secure headstocks and backing to floor. Bogie bolsters are two layers of 1mm (40 thou.) sheet, 28mm × 12mm (1.10″ × 0.47″) drilled out to take bolts. Solebars are cut from 1mm (40 thou.) and glued to headstocks and bogie bolsters. The bogie bolts can now be pushed through the floor and bolsters, using plenty of glue to anchor top in place and tightening nut beneath bolster.

Interiors can be detailed to taste, but if possible add seats – suitably upholstered in the correct colours. First class compartment seats are made from three pieces of 1mm (40 thou.), thirds (seconds) from two while saloon seats require more pieces. When ready these are glued in place, taking care not to use too much solvent. Paint the compartment or saloon floors and ends of seats when in position.

The sides are now painted. Brushes can be used, but of course these days many modellers employ an airbrush, masking the sides as necessary, and this often gives a much better effect. Usually two thin coats will suffice, making sure windowframes are well covered. With the MBSO the driver's side end is painted now also.

Glazing is next. When droplights are fitted in compartment stock, three pieces are required: one for the door, two for the quarterlights. Even on the corridor side it is better to use short pieces to ensure that each is thoroughly glued and not likely to sheer off when the roof is in place. Be more careful with solvent in this operation than any other – it is so easy to ruin glazing with careless brushwork. When this is dry, drill out all holes for commode and door handles, then should the glazing be loose, it is simple to re-glue.

A flat false roof is fitted of 0.75mm (30 thou.) styrene, shaped to fit the ends. This will make sure that the sides are straight and the end well supported. This is left to dry for at least 24 hours. With the MBSO the motor bogie is either secured through a hole cut in the false roof or left to rotate in the hole; I prefer the latter for ease of maintenance. To prevent sag in the centre of the roof, two strips of 1mm (40 thou.) the height of the ends, are laminated together; then they are glued to the false roof and ends.

Far right, above: A method of cutting window apertures with radiused corners by leaving a fillet in each corner, finishing off with a round, rat-tail swiss file.

Far right, below: Simple carriage door handles can be made from filed down blackened-brass track-pins or from bent and filed brass wire.

Below: Two methods of fitting motor-bogies to model multiple-unit stock or diesel and electric outline locomotives are shown. The method shown above is for bogies having a centre-bearing. The bogie can be secured to the body by adding a nut to the bearing pivot before fitting the roof, but it cannot then be removed for maintenance. Below a different form of motor bogie is shown, having lugs which fit over radiused edges in the floor and support the vehicle.

Below near right: Three methods of laminating carriage bodysides: from top to bottom; old-style pannelled stock; LNER Gresley-pattern pannelled and beaded stock; modern flush, curved sided stock.

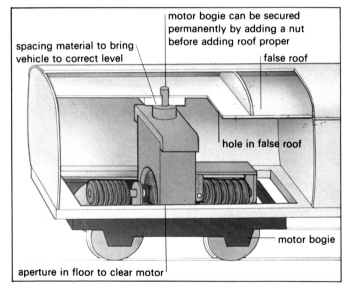

spacing material to bring vehicle to correct level

motor bogie can be secured permanently by adding a nut before adding roof proper

false roof

hole in false roof

motor bogie

aperture in floor to clear motor

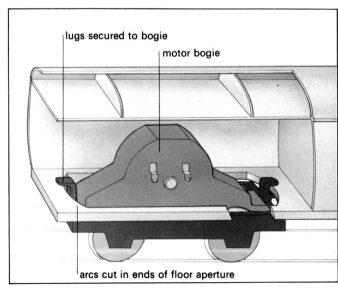

lugs secured to bogie

motor bogie

arcs cut in ends of floor aperture

The actual roof is made from 0.5mm (20 thou.). This is bound to a wooden former with string and then immersed in boiling water and left to cool. Other modellers achieve the correct shape by cooking over a former in an electric oven. The resultant roof is glued to the sides and ends. The cantrail strip is 0.25mm (10 thou.) and welded to side and roof to hide join. Rainstrips are formed from similar material and carefully shaped and glued in place. Holes are drilled to take torpedo vents, most modern types are available commercially. A force fit is required, but not too tight or the roof will tear. An electric coach needs more detailing than normal: use cotton for cable runs, with scraps of plastic rodding; periscopes can be shaped from styrene.

Underframe details differ from coach to coach, but most coaches of this period had trussing and this is built up from strips of 1mm (40 thou.). Non-electric stock require battery boxes, dynamo, v-hangers, brake cylinders – all available commercially. Wire completes brake rigging. In older coaches gas cylinders replace the electric equipment, and these coaches need gaslamp tops on the roof. Electric driving coaches are the most arduous to model: arc shutes, resistance frames, fuses, compressors, are just some of the equipment required, and are built from styrene.

Ends must be detailed, too. Most ordinary coaches need little more than lamp brackets and jumper cables, but electric coaches have far more bits and pieces, including a destination box (with opposite route number) and these again come from various gauges of wire and scraps of styrene. Corridor connections can be built entirely from styrene, though it is very effective to make the bellows from black photograph album paper. Footboards of 0.5mm (20 thou.) are glued to 1mm (40 thou.) square blocks and complete the actual coach construction.

When the final painting has been done and the coach embellished with all transfers, it may be mounted on its bogies. A wide variety is available commercially, but some types either have to be built up from styrene or adapted from those available. Wheels are left to choice as are couplings.

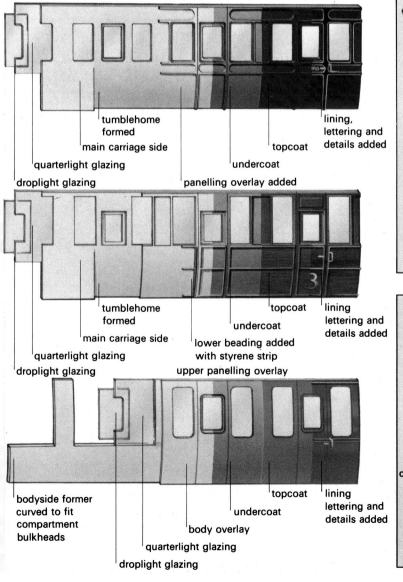

tumblehome formed
main carriage side
quarterlight glazing
droplight glazing
panelling overlay added
undercoat
topcoat
lining, lettering and details added

tumblehome formed
main carriage side
quarterlight glazing
droplight glazing
lower beading added with styrene strip
upper panelling overlay
undercoat
topcoat
lining lettering and details added

bodyside former curved to fit compartment bulkheads
droplight glazing
quarterlight glazing
body overlay
undercoat
topcoat
lining lettering and details added

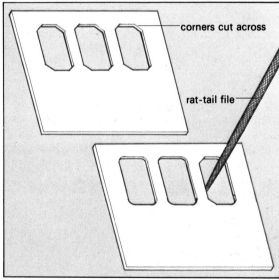

corners cut across
rat-tail file

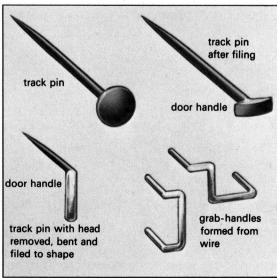

track pin
track pin after filing
door handle
door handle
track pin with head removed, bent and filed to shape
grab-handles formed from wire

Painting and Weathering

Painting, if carried out carefully, can put a proprietary model into the exhibition class, but equally, if carried out without thought and preparation, can spoil an otherwise perfect scratchbuilt model. Individual preferences play a large part in the finish which is to be achieved, and some discussion on this point is worthwhile before exploring materials and techniques. Historically, most models have been finished in an exhibition condition, i.e. looking as they would when first built or refurbished. Unless the model is for exhibition only, this is a little unrealistic, and in recent years there has been an increase in the trend for modellers to make locomotives and rolling stock look as though they have seen some service. To get the right effect, it is important to look carefully at the prototype and notice the way in which rust, soot, oil, diesel exhaust, graffiti or even indiscriminate cleaning have an effect on appearance.

Similarly, the right use of colour has a dramatic effect. There have been so many examples of the frailty of human memory when it comes to colour, that unless you are an expert on particular liveries, it is as well to stick to colours which have been carefully matched by the manufacturer. In matching these colours, scale is often taken into account. To illustrate this point; if the Great Eastern locomotive described earlier were to be painted in the original GE dark blue as used on the prototype, it would appear almost black, because the colour is not in scale with the area covered on the model. The paint used therefore, has to be several shades lighter. The converse applies to light colours, and white, in particular, should never be used in a pure tone; a pale grey being the best substitute. The final finish must also be in scale and a full high gloss varnish would reflect too much light. Depending on the cleanliness to be depicted, the varnish finish should be satin through to completely flat.

Equipment

Quality is of paramount importance and brushes should be of the best quality kolinsky or sable. The range of brushes should be from size '0' for detail through to size '4' for larger areas. Do not purchase brushes smaller than size '0', they hold far less paint, and have just as fine a point. The most important thing to look for when selecting brushes is the point, and a good artists' supplier should not be surprised if you ask to check this aspect by damping and pointing the brush in a glass of water. Having purchased some really good brushes, it is now equally important to look after them properly. They should be stored flat or stood point upright, possibly with a polythene tube for protection. They should never be left standing on the point, nor should they ever be put into paint so that the ferrule is covered, since this causes paint to get into the base of the hairs from whence it cannot be removed. They should be thoroughly cleaned after each use, firstly in the relevant thinners, then with water and detergent worked into a lather and finally in clean running water, repointed and stored. Brushes treated with this care should last a very long time.

Brush painting has its drawbacks, and many model-

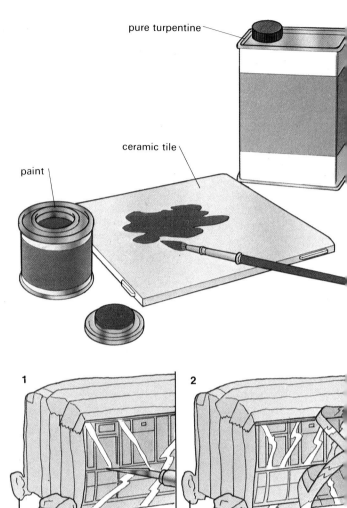

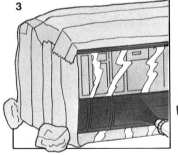
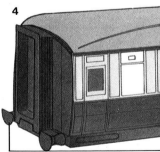

Top: Paint should be thinned down and applied in several coats for best results.

Above:
1. When spray-painting a model, cover the part to be worked on in clear tape or masking film in order to be able to see to cut away the mask for the area to be sprayed. Use masking tape on all surrounding areas.
2. Masking film is pulled carefully away.
3. Spray the area in light even strokes, taking care to avoid runs in the paint.
4. When dry, carefully remove masking.

Above right: A simple spray booth prevents overspray onto surrounding area.

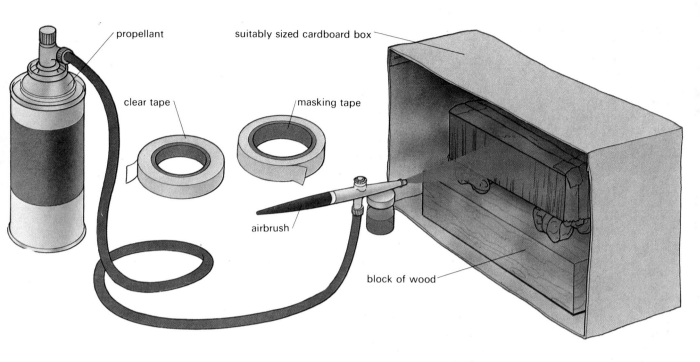

propellant

suitably sized cardboard box

clear tape

masking tape

airbrush

block of wood

A ready-to-run model of DB class 41 2-8-2 freight locomotive modified and realistically weathered by Jerry Veit.

lers in all spheres of the modelling hobby now use airbrushes. For the uninitiated, an airbrush is a miniature paint spray with a capacity for fine adjustment and short paint runs. They can be costly but are well worth the expense. To power the airbrush, cans of compressed air may be used, but a small custom-built compressor, while expensive in the first instance, is a considerable economy in the long run. As with brushes, thorough and regular cleaning is most important. An airbrush is a precision instrument and without blowing through with clean thinners after each use, it will soon clog and become useless. One word of warning, whenever using an airbrush, with any paint or thinners, it is essential to use a face mask.

For lining, where transfers are not available, a designer's bowspring ruling pen is hard to equal, but it must be a good one, preferably with jaws that open to 90° for cleaning.

Materials

Most countries have their own particular brand of specialist model paint, and depending on the basis of the paint, different methods should be adopted. In the United Kingdom, Humbrol and Precision have ranges which are oil-based and can be brushed or sprayed without problems. They have been carefully matched to British prototype colours and use finely ground pigments compatible with model work. They dry within 24 hours. In North America—and to some extent elsewhere—Floquil is similarly available, but this paint has a xylene base which, especially when sprayed, is highly toxic. Since xylene attacks plastics, this paint requires a barrier coat for work with non-metal models. It is however, very fast drying and dense, covering in one coat. Unfortunately, cellulose paint is not generally available to the modeller in matched colours but it dries with a very hard and even finish. However, commercially available primers may be used on metal models and where a plain black finish is required semi-mat automotive finishes are suitable. Cellulose must be sprayed, taking the necessary precautions, but never over enamel or oil based paint, on which it acts as a stripper.

Finally, a selection of varnishes will be required, to protect each item painted so that handling and minor knocks do not affect the paintwork, transfers etc. Both oil based and polyurethane based varnishes are available, and described as gloss, semi-gloss, satin or mat. Oil-based varnish drys slowly but gives the work more depth and the colours more warmth. Polyurethane varnishes dry quickly with a hard surface, but lack warmth and tend to be ultra glossy.

Painting

Taking a scratchbuilt or kitbuilt model in metal, the first consideration is complete cleanliness. The model should be stripped to its main components and the motor removed. If necesaary, the previous paint finish should be removed with a water soluble paint stripper. The next step is to give each component a good scrub with a toothbrush and a foaming type household abrasive detergent in hot water. This will remove all traces of oil, flux, glue resin, finger grease and leave a surface, when dry, which is ready to take paint. Now a good quality primer should be painted or sprayed, especially on brass or nickel silver, since paint, on an unprimed surface has a tendency to flake off in use. In some areas a self etching primer is available, which has a slight acid effect and in this way keys into the metal surface. Since this substance also keys inside the airbrush, it should not be sprayed!

If the model is being built and painted by the same person, it is useful to bear in mind that some areas are less accessible once construction is complete, and for this reason it is best to paint the chassis before fitting wheels, and the wheels before mounting on axles. Where the wheels are to be lined, each wheel should be mounted on a false axle with a central dimple, into which one leg of a bowspring compass can be mounted. The wheel can thus be painted and lined before it is attached to the chassis.

Below: An early LMS 50ft parcel van, circa 1925.

Right: A superbly weathered and 'kit-bashed' Fleischmann heavy tank locomotive by Jerry Veit.

No mention has yet been made about the working environment. Ideally this would be in a warm, light and well aired studio with a dust free atmosphere. The average modeller however, can rarely achieve this, and so therefore every effort must be made to minimise dust and dampness in particular, and to have a convenient drying container, into which items can be placed, undisturbed to dry.

Returning to the task in hand, a further coat of grey primer should be applied, remembering that two or more fine coats are better than one heavy one which runs and leaves blemishes. Grey is an ideal colour for the next stage, which is to check that the surfaces are all flat and without lumps. Rectify any such blemishes with a scraper or fine wet and dry paper, and then the model is ready for the main body colour. Do not waste time at this stage by masking except where a bright metal part is concerned; it is easier to mask after the main coat has been applied, and then only for areas that have straight edges. Areas of colour other than the main body colour—smokebox, buffer-beams, cab roof etc.—may now be filled in, usually with a brush.

When dry the model should now be ready for lettering and lining. If proprietary transfers are being used, the manufacturers instructions should be followed, taking your time, and checking first from photographs the exact locations of each character or design. If available, use proprietary lining, but if not, use the bowspring ruling pen loaded with paint or designers colour mixed to the consistency of milk. Regrettably there is no hard and fast formula, and each modeller will have to try several consistencies on a scrap board before achieving passable results. Lastly apply a coat of the desired varnish, and here it helps considerably if the varnish is thoroughly warmed before use, since the heat thins the liquid and thus helps to achieve an even, thin coat.

Firstly to achieve the right effect a spray or airbrush must be used. Secondly, because the paint must dry quickly and to resemble dirt must be mat, xylene based colours are the most effective. The paint should be very thin – the consistency of water – and the spray as fine as possible. Start by spraying the wheels and chassis, using a rusty mixture, and spray one fine coat from each angle. Change to a dirty purple black for steam locomotives or a jet black for diesel locomotives and spray the roof to give the impression of soot or exhaust. The exact density of weathering must be a question of personal preference, and fortunately this is one area where layers of paint or rather, 'dirt', can be built up until the desired effect is achieved.

Weathering

Other tricks which can be employed are to partially clean away the sprayed dirt over numbers, names and handrails using thinners and a rag, to apply dribbles of yellowish white round safety valves, glands, and whistles on steam locomotives, and to paint very thin gloss black round hornblocks, springs, locomotive valvegears, and diesel underframes to denote where fresh oil has been used during maintenance.

OPERATING

The essential difference between a model railway and a trainset is the way in which they are operated. It is possible to put together an elaborate layout and then just sit back and watch the trains chase their tails, but much more satisfaction can be derived from operating according to full-size railway practice.

In order to make the transition from prototype to model possible, however, it is necessary to simplify and adapt. This must be so, for to follow prototype practice exactly one would need a room full of drivers and firemen, signalmen and guards, inspectors and shedmasters and so on. It is up to the individual to decide for himself which aspects of railway working interest him most. Of the three examples that follow, one layout features block signalling methods on a single-track branch, the second focuses mainly on freight operation and the third is a complete railway system in miniature, running to a realistic timetable.

Each of these layouts is worked to an established pattern which has taken many years to evolve. The fact that some of the methods employed may seem complex need not deter anyone from simplifying or adapting them as required. There is, for example, no reason why Cliff Young's system could not be applied to freight working on any layout, while block signalling, or its equivalent, can always add interest. Similarly, although the Sherwood Section uses clockwork power, many of its concepts are equally valid for electrically controlled layouts, large or small.

In operation there is perhaps only one hard and fast rule: to ensure that over a period of time the movement of trains is balanced. At Lutton and Sherwood this means that every item of rolling stock is back in its original position at the completion of the full 24-hour timetable, while with Cliff Young's waybill system, the freight cars will always be evenly distributed. But should all your rolling stock finish up at one end of your layout, then it is time to look for a new system.

'Tilbury Tank' No. 79 class 4-4-2 T on shed at Lutton.

The Lutton Branch

The scene is a country station, deep in the Bedfordshire countryside, in the early years of this century. Even in this apparently bucolic branch line terminus, however, a surprisingly large amount of train movements can occur, and indeed the signalman appears to have a slight problem at this moment.

A goods brake van and two coal wagons sit impassively on the main line outside the signalbox as the shunting of a freight train slowly proceeds. At the same time a passenger train is due, and the block instrument bell rings once to call the signalman's attention. Can the signal clear the station approach in time for the arrival of the Bedford train, or will it be held at the home signal by the tunnel, whistling impatiently?

In a sense this scene exists only in the imagination, but for the visitor to Frank Roomes' fine-scale O gauge layout it is very real indeed. For that same visitor is asked to put on a signalman's cap and try to cope with the many and various trains that are scheduled to arrive and depart from the Lutton terminus in the course of a day – but actually condensed into a two-hour operating session. The visitor therefore has a very real problem, and if he delays the Bedford train he will hear funny (electronic) whistles from the tunnel and later probably hear all about it from the driver, perhaps a fellow visitor too, but certainly someone with an easier job.

But all is not as chaotic as it sounds and, indeed, the novice signalman is in capable hands. For the Lutton branch follows the rulebook of British block signalling – an almost totally foolproof method of achieving safe control of railway working; while its master of ceremonies, Frank Roomes, is among other things a professional signalling instructor.

A while before the train from Bedford is due to arrive, the signalman at Lutton will be contacted by his colleague at Winwick, the next station down the line (or in actual fact by Frank Roomes, who will be operating the fiddle yard). The method of communication is a system of telegraph bell codes based on Midland Railway practice.

Block Signalling

In effect the Winwick signalman is sending Lutton a series of messages, which Lutton acknowledges by repeating the relevant bell code. So after the single beat 'call attention' has been acknowledged, Winwick offers Lutton a passenger train, by ringing: three, pause, one. Lutton is not being asked whether the road is clear right up to the buffer stops, but merely whether the main line, or 'block section', between Winwick and Lutton is clear as far as that home signal.

So although shunting may still be in progress in the station, the Lutton signalman is able to accept the train turning the pointer on the block instrument in front of him from the normal 'line blocked' position to 'line clear'. This indication is automatically shown on the instrument at Winwick. Shortly after, as the train leaves Winwick for Lutton, the Winwick signalman again calls the attention of Lutton and then sends the two-ring code for 'train entering section'. Once the train is on the block section and no further train can depart from either Winwick or Lutton until the line is clear.

In single-line working on a full-scale railway, the driver of the train would carry a token, giving him the authority to traverse the block section. It would be passed to him by Winwick box, and he would have to give it to the Lutton signalman on arrival. In model terms such a manoeuvre would be impractical, but this is one of the very few concessions made as far as the authenticity of signal operation is concerned.

Assuming that the shunting is now over and the freight engine is waiting in the headshunt prior to going on shed, the Lutton signalman can pull off the outer home signal and watch the Bedford train trundle into the station. Having in theory relieved the driver of the token as he passed the box, our signalman can now call up Winwick and tap out: two, pause, one – 'train out of section'. When that is acknowledged he can return the pointer on the block instrument to 'line blocked'.

Frank Roomes insists that reliability of motive power and stock is a must, and by using O gauge with stud contact, automatic coupling and uncoupling, obeying signals and shunting at the correct speed, a 'day's' operations can pass without derailment or the need to prod a locomotive into activity.

Once the Bedford train has arrived, the next departure may well be a connecting train for Kenbrennan Castle, and this too will have to be protected in a similar way. To make matters even more complicated, the overworked signalman also has to cope with the trains on a small industrial tramway, which have a habit of creeping up to the main line when least expected. However, the rules of railway operation can be relaxed slightly for a tramway, which in this case is worked on the 'one engine in steam' principle, only one engine being allowed down the tramway at any one time.

Top left: The lever frame at Lutton Signal Box.

Left: These instruments were collected over some years by Frank Roomes and now adorn the Lutton Signal Box.

The sequence-timetable for the Lutton Branch

	LUTTON TIMETABLE			
No.	Train		Platform	Remarks
1	To	Kenbrennan C.	Pass. 4	
2	From	Bedford	Pcls. 2	Shunt to 3, move 8
3	From	Kenbrennan C.	Pass. 1	
4	To	Bedford	Pass. 1	
5	From	Tramway	Pass. 2	RQ
6	From	Kenbrennan C.	Pass. 1	RR, shunt to 4
7	To	Tramway	P/F 2	RQ
8	To	Kenbrennan C.	Pcls. 1	
9	From	Bedford	Pass. 2	
10	To	Kenbrennan C.	Pass. 4	
11	To	Bedford	Pass. 2	
12	From	Tramway	P/F 2	RQ
13	From	Kenbrennan C.	Pass. 1	RR, shunt to 4
14	From	Bedford, London	Pass. 1	Shunt to CS after move 17
15	To	Tramway	P/F 2	RQ
16	To	Kenbrennan C.	Pass. 4	
17	To	Bedford	ECS CS	
18	From	Kenbrennan C.	Frt. 1	Shunt for move 21
19	From	Bedford	Frt. 3	Shunt for move 26
20	From	Bedford	Pass. 2	
21	To	Kenbrennan C.	Frt. 1	
22	From	Tramway	P/F 1	RQ
23	To	Bedford	Pass. 2	
24	To	Tramway	Pass. 1	RQ
25	From	Bedford	Pass. 2	
26	To	Bedford	Frt. 3	
27	From	Kenbrennan C.	Pass. 1	RR, shunt to 4
28	From	Bedford	Pass. 1	
29	To	Bedford	Pass. 2	
30	From	Bedford	Frt. 3	
31	To	Kenbrennan C.	Pass. 4	
32	From	Tramway	Frt. 2	RQ
33	To	Bedford	Pass. 1	
34	From	Bedford, London	Pass. 1	Shunt to CS after move 37
35	To	Tramway	Frt. 2	RQ
36	To	Bedford	Frt. 3	
37	To	Bedford	ECS CS	
38	From	Bedford	Pass. 1	Shunt to 4, move 41
39	From	Kenbrennan C.	Pcls. 1	Shunt to 3, move 42
40	From	Kenbrennan C.	Pass. 1	Shunt to 4 after move 42
41	To	Bedford	Pcls. 3	
42	To	Kenbrennan C.	Pass. 4	

Pass.	Passenger train	RR	Run round train
Pcls.	Parcels train	RQ	Runs if required
Frt.	Freight train	CS	Carriage siding
ECS	Empty Carriages	P/F	Pass./Freight

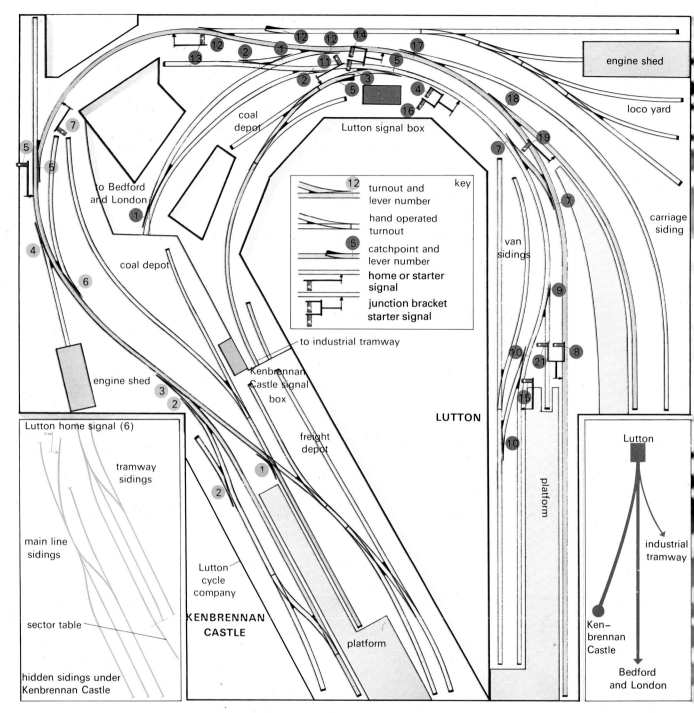

The diagram includes the following labels:

engine shed

loco yard

carriage siding

to Bedford and London

coal depot

Lutton signal box

key

	turnout and lever number
	hand operated turnout
	catchpoint and lever number
	home or starter signal
	junction bracket starter signal

van sidings

coal depot

to industrial tramway

Kenbrennan Castle signal box

engine shed

freight depot

LUTTON

platform

Lutton cycle company

KENBRENNAN CASTLE

platform

Lutton home signal (6)

tramway sidings

main line sidings

sector table

hidden sidings under Kenbrennan Castle

Lutton

industrial tramway

Ken-brennan Castle

Bedford and London

Above: Track diagram for the Lutton Branch showing the lever numbers for the signals and turnouts controlled by Lutton and Kenbrennan Castle. The small diagram on the left shows the layout of the 'hidden sidings' beneath Kenbrennan Castle, and the diagram on the right shows the geographic location of the imaginary line.

Opposite top: This diagram shows the operation of the block system as employed on the Lutton Branch, and shows a section of single-line railway between two signal boxes 'B' and 'C'. For clarity, signals are only shown for the 'down' direction of running, and the

passing loops at the signal boxes have been omitted. The section of line between each signal box's home and starter signals is termed 'Station', or 'Section Limits'. The section between the starter signal and the next signal box's home signal is the 'Block Section'. Whilst more than one train can stand within 'Station Limits', depending on the track layout and signalling provided, only one train is permitted to travel through the 'Block Section' at a time. Also shown are the 'staffs' or 'tokens' for single line working: train drivers must be in possession of the relevant 'staff' for the section of line that they are travelling over, and as there is effectively only one

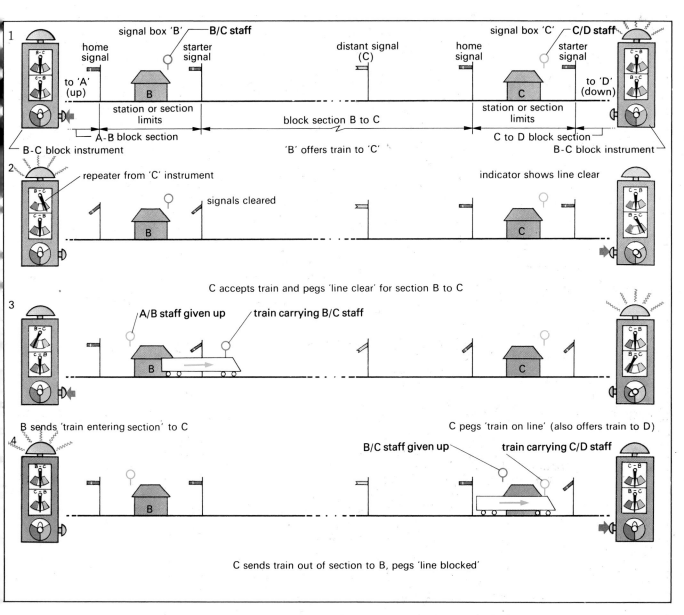

staff for each section, two trains cannot be travelling in opposite directions on a single-line section.

1. Signalman 'B' wishes to send a train to 'C' and 'offers' it to him by means of a system of bell-codes between the signal boxes.

2. Signalman 'C' 'accepts' the train by repeating the signal back to 'B', and sets his block instrument for the B/C section (down trains) to 'Line Clear'.

3. When the train arrives at 'B', the staff for the previous A/B section is exchanged for that for the B/C section. The train passes into the B/C section and 'B' sends the signal 'Train entering section' to 'C'. who 'pegs' his block instrument to 'Train on line'. These indications are repeated on 'B's' instrument. 'B' replaces his signals to 'on', or 'danger' after passage of the train.

4. When the train arrives at 'C', the staffs are again exchanged, and 'C' sends the signal 'Train out of section' to 'B' and sets his block instrument to 'Line Blocked'. 'B' repeats the signal back to 'C' to acknowledge that his repeater has operated correctly.

Bottom right: The B/C section block instrument from signal box 'B' in the diagram above.

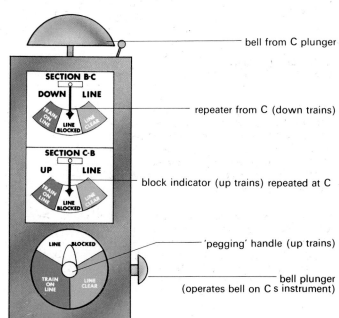

O Gauge in Four Metres Square

This complex railway network is modelled in gauge O, but incredible as it may seem, Frank Roomes has managed to fit it into a spare bedroom measuring less than four metres square (12′ × 12′). Apart from Lutton itself, only Kenbrennan Castle station is actually modelled, the tramway and the main line to Bedford disappearing into tunnels.

During an operating session, Frank Roomes generally presides over all three destinations, assuming alternately the characters of the tramway driver, Winwick signalman and Kenbrennan Castle signalman. All this is more than enough to make beads of perspiration break out on the brow of our novice signalman, and indeed the confidence of some visitors, who thought they knew all there was to know about railway operation, has been shattered by the machinations of their host behind the scenes.

However, Mr. Roomes is not totally without mercy, for at least the operating sequence does not have to be carried out against the clock. Time at Lutton is completely flexible, and so if the beleaguered signalman needs to stop for a well-earned cup of tea then he will probably be allowed to do so.

The signalman's control position at Lutton resembles an actual signal box as closely as possible. Mounted on the wall are two authentic block instruments, one connected to Winwick and the other to Kenbrennan Castle. Down by the track is the lever frame with which the signals and turnouts are controlled; the row of 24 numbered levers makes an impressive sight. Although obviously much smaller than a prototype lever frame, it works in a similar way, and even has the same type of interlocking. This is a simple safety mechanism, which prevents the relevant signals being 'pulled off' – and thus a train movement taking place – until the road for that train has been set.

Having looked in some detail at the life of the signalman on the Lutton Branch, let us now examine the work of his colleague, the Midland Railway driver.

The Lutton Branch Driver

Waiting quietly in Platform One with a passenger train for Bedford (first stop Winwick), is locomotive No. 2123, an ex London Tilbury and Southend Railway tank engine. Movement of No. 7 crossover gives the first indication to the driver that the road is being set, then up by the signalbox, No. 4 starter signal drops, followed immediately by No. 21, the starter signal for Platform One.

The (imaginary) guard gives the right away, and as the driver opens the regulator gently, No. 2123 draws the train slowly out of the platform, snaking over the crossover onto the main line. With flanges squealing in protest, No. 2123 curves away past the signalbox, where the driver collects the staff, before accelerating the train away into the tunnel en route for Winwick.

The work of the driver, while not as onerous as that of the signalman, is equally rewarding as he has responsibility for a delightful fleet of some dozen pre-grouping locomotives, all of them hand built. To add variety to this basically Midland Railway stud there are locomotives from some of the Midland's subsidiary and joint companies: for example a royal blue 4-4-0 from the Somerset and Dorset joint, and a distinguished looking 4-4-0T in the mustard livery of the Midland and Great Northern. One or two 'foreigners' in Great Western green have been known to put in an appearance, but the atmosphere is still predominantly Midland.

Power is supplied by the stud-contact system. This provides a somewhat unexpected bonus in that the intermittent noise of the skates as they pass over the studs between the rails, very closely resembles the squealing of flanges so characteristic of full-size steam locomotives traversing curves or turnouts at low speed. Despite the use of fine-scale track with sharp curves and a 1 in 30 (three per cent) gradient, the running of the trains is totally reliable – as it needs to be if the concentration of the operators is not to be interrupted.

A 24-hour timetable exists for both passenger and freight trains on the Lutton Branch, but since there is no clock by which to run the trains, operation is carried out according to a simple sequence table. This lists in order of occurrence the 44 arrivals and departures at Lutton during the course of each theoretical day. At the end of the sequence all locomotives and rolling stock will end up in their original positions, ready for the following day's trains.

A two-hour operating session is the norm, and in this time an experienced pair of operators might well be able to run a full day's trains, while beginners might only manage 12 movements. Locomotives and rolling stock are left where they are at the end of the evening, but they do not have to wait long for service to be resumed as the Lutton Branch is worked very intensively.

Among the visitors to Lutton are many railwaymen, while even officers of the Royal Corps of Transport may be seen at work there occasionally. Now that the training school and military railway at Longmoor have been abandoned, army personnel are sometimes sent to Lutton for a spell of signalling practice. What better endorsement of the authenticity of Lutton's operating methods could there possibly be?

trailing junction shown at the top with the lever numbers for the turnout and signals. The levers in the signal box are connected to locking bars which have an arrangement of notches cut in them into which fit the tappets connecting the locking bars together. At the bottom of the diagram, the locking bars are shown as set for a train proceeding from A to B. The turnout lever no. 5 is normally set for the straight route and thus is not moved. Levers 1, 2, and 3 control the distant, home and starting signals respectively and when pulled 'off', or 'reversed' the locking bars move downwards as shown. The notch in bar 2 pushes tappet 'y' to the right and into the notch in bar 5, and thus the turnout cannot be moved once the signal is cleared. Bar 1 is for the distant signal, which cannot be moved until the home and distant signals are cleared and tappet 'x' can slide to the right into the notches in bars 1 and 2. Bar 4, for the junction home signal, cannot be moved as tappet 'z' is prevented from moving to the left by bar 5. Thus the signalman cannot send a train from C into the path of the train from A to B. Similarly, when the road is set up for a train from C to B, layers 3, 4, and 5 are reversed. Movement of lever 5 for the turnout moves Bar 5 downward forcing tappet 'y' to the left, locking bar 2 and preventing it from being moved. Bar 4 is now free as the lower notch in bar 5 is opposite tappet 'z', and movement of 4 moves the tappet 'z' to the left, locking 5 in position. The distant signal, 1, is locked as although the notch in bar 3 is opposite tappet 'x', the tappet is prevented from sliding to the right by bar 2. Thus again, the signalman cannot clear a train movement across the path of the train from C to B.

Left: The 'Tilbury' Tank No. 1 Class 4-4-2 standing at Lutton Station.

Above: Prototype signals and turnouts are interlocked in order that conflicting train movements can not be made. A simple 'interlocking' is shown here for a

The Denver and Rio Grande Western

The railroads of North America are noted for their emphasis on the movement of freight traffic over long distances. Passenger traffic, on the other hand, is by no means so intensive as it is in Europe and so the operation of a passenger service can be seen as providing a little light relief amid the general pattern of freight operation.

Translated into model terms, freight working can provide tremendous operational interest. In time-tabled passenger operations the unit is the passenger train and its movements are entirely predictable. But with freight, the units can be as small as individual car loads and the timing of their movements unpredictable. The adoption of a system of freight operation can greatly increase the variety of possible train timings and train formations on a given layout. Freight and passenger operation are by no means mutually exclusive, and it is up to the individual to decide upon the most suitable balance for his own purposes.

North American modellers have developed a variety of methods to operate freight-based systems. Some people prefer switch lists – printed forms on which the destinations of the cars are written in by the 'boss' of the railroad. Others drill holes in their cars and insert lettered drawing pins of various colours which when decoded show where each car is to be delivered. But the

Top: Route diagram of the Denver and Rio Grande Western System showing the stations and principal industries.

method which has gained steadily in popularity since it was described by Doug Smith in the Model Railroader (December 1961) is a card and waybill system which Cliff Young modified for use on his own layouts.

After a year of planning, the layout in Cliff Young's present home was started in October 1969 and the first full operating session took place on January 1st 1971. The railway room is 2.5m (8' 6") wide and 6.3m (21') long; but over 150m (500') of HO gauge track – including a main line 60m (200') long – were packed in, while still leaving room for four operators to work comfortably.

Westwards from Denver

The railroad which provided the inspiration for Cliff Young's layout is the Denver and Rio Grande Western; and in particular its main line from Denver to the west which climbs 1,200m (4,000') to the Moffat Tunnel at a height of 2,750m (9,200') above sea level in a distance of only 80km (50 miles). The ruling grade is two per cent (1 in 50). After piercing the Rockies through the Moffat Tunnel, which is over nine kilometres (six miles) long, the main line continues to Salt Lake City and Ogden, where connections are made with the Western Pacific and Southern Pacific Railroads respectively. These few details are necessary to understand the traffic flow, which is incorporated in the operation of the layout.

Bottom: Diagram showing how the layout is fitted into the available space.

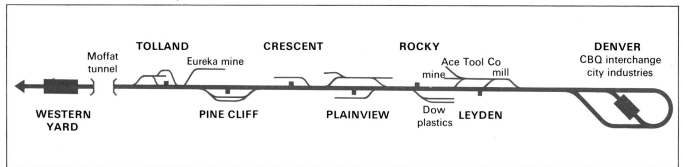

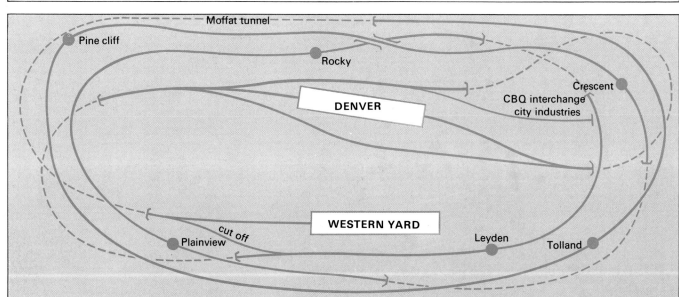

The existing layout portrays the 80km (50 mile) climb from Denver to the Moffat Tunnel, through which the trains run off-stage to Western Yard, a fictitious place which represents any destination west of Moffat Tunnel. Western Yard is rather like a fiddle yard, with the difference that all trains are switched (shunted) correctly by locos. There the freight cars are redistributed into new eastbound trains according to the card system.

Between Denver and the Moffat Tunnel, the modelled line makes three circuits of the room, gaining height on some stretches with two per cent grades like those of the prototype. It may be thought that this spiralling would create a very unrealistic impression, but by crossing one lap over another in places and putting some track in short tunnels, the busy operators are made to forget the circular nature of the layout and they automatically visualize it as one long main line.

Denver is very fully modelled, with a large freight yard, passenger station, loco yard, balloon loop to turn locomotives and trains, and in addition, a downtown industrial area and interchange tracks with the Burlington Northern to Chicago.

The intermediate points on the climb to the Moffat Tunnel are Leyden, Rocky (and the short branch to Dow Chemical Plant), Plainview, Crescent, Pine Cliff (and a branch to the ore mine at Eureka), Tolland and East

Portal. With the exception of Crescent, at all these locations there is either a passing track or a long siding (which can be used to allow trains to meet or overtake each other), and a few industrial spurs where freight cars can be set out or picked up. Within reason, as many as possible of these traffic-generating industries and spurs could be added to increase the scope of the card system, but it is not necessary actually to model the industries. Setting out and picking up cars at spots marked only by labels pinned to the baseboard reading 'Pickle Factory', 'Stock Pen', 'Coal Mine', etc. can be just as enjoyable, but one needs a vivid imagination!

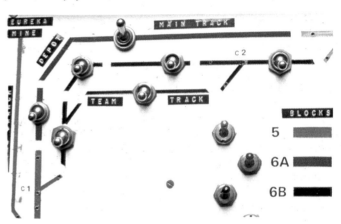

Track plans of the yards at Denver, Leyden and Western Yard

Part of the Pine Cliff control panel.

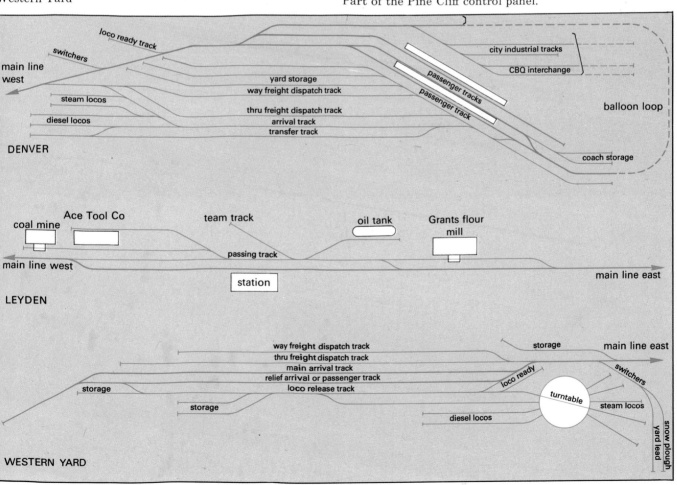

Cards and Waybills

The basic unit of Cliff Young's card and waybill system is a white card 100mm × 60mm (4″ × 2¼″) with a transparent pocket at the lower right-hand corner (made by fixing a rectangle of clear polythene to the card with adhesive tape). Before each pocket is made, details of its related freight car, e.g. 'BOX CAR, DRGW, 68340, Gold and Silver', are typed in the top left-hand corner of each card; then in the area to be covered by the pocket, either 'EMPTY CAR RETURN TO DENVER YARD' or 'EMPTY CAR RETURN TO WESTERN YARD' or 'SHUTTLE' is written, according to the way in which the car is intended to be used. Finally, in the top right-hand corner the code letter of the car category is typed. e.g. B for box car, S for stock car, G for gondola, H for hopper, T for tank car etc.

There are about 150 freight cars in service and each one has its own card – except in those cases where one card covers a group of cars which always travel together, such as the three ore cars which work between Eureka Mine and Garfield smelter (via Western Yard).

Car cards and waybills as used on the D&RGWRR. Bottom left is a typical Car card; one of these is made out for each freight car on the system, and incorporates a clear plastic pocket for the waybills. Top left are shown examples of 'Thru Freight' and 'Joker' waybills, and on the right are illustrated examples of standard waybills showing the front and reverse sides.

Above: Card racks in which the various waybills are held. On track the 'Caboose' cars at Denver.

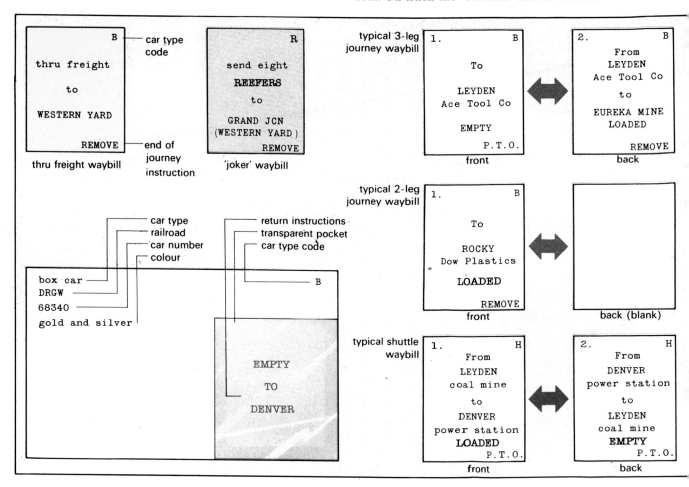

The next requirement for Cliff Young's layout was a stock of several hundred waybills 50mm high and 35mm wide ($2'' \times 1\frac{1}{2}''$) to slip into the transparent pockets. These were made of thin flexible card – white for way freights (local) and yellow for 'thru' freights (express). Brief instructions were then written on these waybills to cover every conceivable car movement within the scope of the layout. One such card might read 'To LEYDEN, Ace Tool Co., Empty' on the first side, with 'PTO' written at the bottom, and 'From LEYDEN, Ace Tool Co., To EUREKA MINE, Loaded' (with tools presumably) on the reverse side, and with 'REMOVE' written at the bottom. The two sides were numbered boldly (1) and (2) respectively.

In the top right-hand corner of each waybill was printed the code letter of the type of car needed for the assignment. Thus the waybill just quoted would have had 'B' for box car. When this car finally reached the mine, removing the waybill would reveal the typed instruction for the return of the empty car to one or other of the two main yards. Thus one waybill could send the car on a three-stage journey. Another waybill might direct a loaded car from Denver or Western Yard to an industry and with 'REMOVE' printed at the bottom of the first side, the car would later return empty to its home yard after a journey of only two legs. Every car with 'SHUTTLE' under the pocket had a permanent waybill with 'PTO' on both sides so as to make a car shuttle between two points – e.g. a coal hopper, loaded one way, empty the other, between the coal mine at Leyden and the Denver City power station.

The preparation of the cards and waybills involved much labour and thought at the time, but once the job was done, all that remained was to add further cards and waybills as additional freight cars were acquired. The waybills, when not in use, were stored in two boxes, divided into coded compartments: one at Denver and one at Western Yard. An empty compartment in each box was marked 'USED' and waybills once removed from the cards were dropped into this. Between sessions, these were shuffled and distributed to the backs of their respective packs.

To add some spice to operations, a few jokers were buried in the packs: emergency waybills ordering eight reefers to be sent at once to Grand Junction (Western Yard) to cope with a glut of fruit in the fall, or ten stock cars urgently needed at Tolland because of a cattle drive.

The overall movement of trains is under the control of the Chief Despatcher. While the passenger trains run to a timetable, all freight trains are run as extras and arrangements have to be made for them to cross other trains en route.

This story is about freight operation, but it should be mentioned that all the DRGW passenger trains which ran through the Moffat Tunnel in the 1950s are modelled and operated to a timetable using a fast clock. This adds to the problems of the freight train crews, who must avoid delaying the passenger trains.

A 0-8-0 Steam Switcher in the locomotive yard at Denver. Note the signal cabin in the background.

The Denver Yardmaster

The system is continuous and operations carry on from the point reached at the end of the previous session. However, let us start with the arrival of an eastbound freight at Denver Yard. The engineer (driver) runs the locomotive round the balloon loop to the loco depot. The Yardmaster examines the cards and gives new waybills to all the cars returning empty, except reefers. He then switches any reefers to the icing track, westbound cars with yellow waybills directly to the thru freight despatch track and westbound cars with white waybills to the yard for isolation in a way freight later.

Eastbound cars for the City industrial area and the Burlington (CBQ) yard for interchange are switched to the transfer track and later run as a new train round the Loop to the City area of Denver. Some cars in the arriving freight may have waybills for local delivery, such as a coal hopper to the loco depot or a tank car of fuel for the diesel track; the Yardmaster must switch these also. He has seven racks where cards are placed according to their destinations; they are arranged as follows:

1. DISPATCH: Way Freight
2. DISPATCH: Thru Freight
3. ICE TRACK: Reefers
4. HOLD: In Yard
5. TRANSFER: to City and CBQ
6. CITY: Industries
7. CBQ: Interchange

The waybills are drawn from the front of the packs in order and are not pre-selected by the Yardmaster. His only discretionary powers are to choose from the yard the maximum eight cars which make up every way freight, to run transfer freights to and from the City area as required, and to vary the consist of a thru freight from the normal maximum of twelve cars and caboose.

The Way Freight Engineer

When a way freight leaves Denver, it is driven on one of the two main-line cab controllers to Leyden and into the passing siding. The engineer then uses the local cab there for switching. There are five spurs at Leyden, three of which serve a coal mine, a flour mill and the Ace Tool Co. respectively. The other two are a team track (for road vehicles) and an oil tank spur.

At the front of the baseboard at Leyden, two adjacent racks marked 'SET OUT' and 'PICK UP' hold cards. If the engineer has to set out three cars, for example, he can pick up three westbound cars if available. If not, he will leave with a shorter train and may load up to the maximum of eight cars further on. The relevant cards are taken from the 'PICK UP' rack, all the cards in 'SET OUT' are moved into 'PICK UP' and the cards of the cars dropped at Leyden go into the now empty 'SET OUT' rack after their waybills have been removed or turned over as indicated at the bottom of each.

The way freight plods on, repeating the same procedure at each station, being delayed en route by passenger trains, fast freights and probably by another way freight in the opposite direction. At Pine Cliff there are three racks marked 'SET OUT', 'HOLD' and 'PICK UP'; the cards are moved one step from left to right every time a way freight calls. At Crescent with its single spur, there is only one rack marked 'PICK UP'.

On arrival at Western Yard, our freight is dealt with as follows. Empty cars without waybills are given new ones (marked 'XW' for Ex Western) from the Western Yard store, the assumption being that these cars are now returning eastwards. Other waybills in the card pockets are either removed or turned over. The cars are then made up into eastbound way or thru freights according to whether they now have white or yellow waybills. Their cards are placed in the two despatch racks. Excess cars are switched to storage tracks and their cards placed in the 'HOLD' rack.

Mr. Young can always run the layout on his own if he wishes – perhaps working a way freight from one end of the line to the other – but to run the full passenger and freight service properly requires a team of four keen and experienced operators. Such an evening's entertainment is not only most enjoyable, but those who take part have the added satisfaction of knowing that they are faithfully reproducing, albeit in miniature, the working of one of North America's major railroads.

Opposite: This diagram illustrates the progress of a typical boxcar on a journey from Denver to Western Yard, via Leyden, showing how the car cards and waybills are dealt with at each stage of the journey.

Left: Just arriving at the Denver freight yard is a 2-8-2 steam engine acquired by the Denver Rio Grande Western from the Denver and Salt Lake railroad.

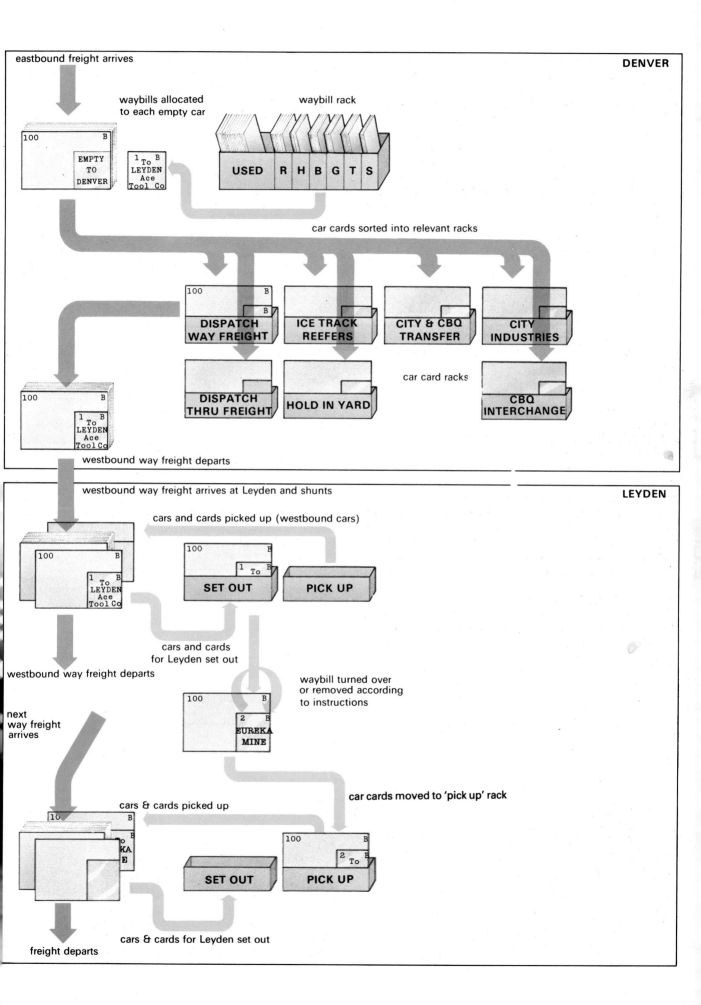

eastbound freight arrives

DENVER

waybills allocated
to each empty car

waybill rack

100   B

EMPTY
TO
DENVER

1 To B
LEYDEN
Ace
Tool Co

USED   R H B G T S

car cards sorted into relevant racks

100   B
            B
DISPATCH
WAY FREIGHT

ICE TRACK
REEFERS

CITY & CBQ
TRANSFER

CITY
INDUSTRIES

100   B
1 To B
LEYDEN
Ace
Tool Co

DISPATCH
THRU FREIGHT

HOLD IN YARD

car card racks

CBQ
INTERCHANGE

westbound way freight departs

westbound way freight arrives at Leyden and shunts

LEYDEN

cars and cards picked up (westbound cars)

100   B

1 To B
LEYDEN
Ace
Tool Co

100   B
1 To B
SET OUT

PICK UP

cars and cards
for Leyden set out

waybill turned over
or removed according
to instructions

100   B
2 B
EUREKA
MINE

westbound way freight departs

next
way freight
arrives

car cards moved to 'pick up' rack

cars & cards picked up

10   B
B
KA
E

100   B
2 To B
SET OUT

PICK UP

cars & cards for Leyden set out

freight departs

The Sherwood Section of the LMS

The first thing that will strike the visitor to the Sherwood Section is its sheer scale. On arriving at Norman Eagles' thatched cottage deep in the Buckinghamshire countryside he will be taken, not into the house, but to an enormous shed at the bottom of the garden. Through the windows he will see nine men, hard at work, each intent on operating the part of the line for which they are on that day responsible.

The Sherwood Section can trace its origins back to 1921, and the oldest locomotive running dates from November 1931. Sherwood has already lasted more than twice as long as the London Midland and Scottish Railway upon which it is based. New locomotives and rolling stock have been added over the years, all of them handbuilt. There are now over 54 locomotives on the roster, with three more under construction.

Although the entire railway is owned by Mr. Eagles, the Sherwood Section is very much a group effort. The Sherwood 'gang' numbers 14, and one member has been in service now for over 40 years. The present layout is the fifth to be built and was commissioned in 1968. It is housed in a prefabricated cedarwood building approximately 10m × 7.3m (33' × 24').

For the track and rolling stock to have lasted so well, withstanding intensive operation over a very long period, they needed to have been solidly constructed. While the Sherwood Section cannot aspire to the fine-scale standards that are currently *de rigeur*, it has seen a steady improvement in the level of accuracy achieved over the years.

Two important characteristics, however, have not changed. The first is that the track is deliberately left unballasted. Although this does detract somewhat from the otherwise realistic impression of the line it makes maintenance easier and makes a much higher standard of reliability possible. The reaction of the Sherwood gang to any pedantic individual who criticizes the line in this respect is to invite him to come and ballast the line himself. With over 300m (1,000') of O gauge track to cover, he would find he had let himself in for a Herculean task.

Clockwork versus Electric

The other unusual aspect of the Sherwood Section is that it is entirely worked by clockwork propulsion. This again is partly an historical matter, for in the inter-war years, clockwork was the rule rather than the exception. While the change to electric operation has obviously been considered very seriously, it has been consistently rejected – not so much on grounds of expense, but because of the greater flexibility, and, in a certain sense also, the greater realism that clockwork can offer. Furthermore, the excessively high speed running traditionally associated with clockwork is largely avoided on the Sherwood Section as most of the clockwork mechanisms are fitted with governors.

Clockwork operation gives complete freedom from all the technical limitations of electricity. Double-heading, reversing loops, and stabling of locomotives wherever required, present no problems, while there is no wiring nor control equipment for faults to occur in. One particular train movement, the running of three light engines coupled together, would formerly have been difficult without independently powered locomotives, although in point of fact it could now be achieved electrically with the help of silicone chips.

The key to the realism of clockwork is precisely this – that each locomotive is independently powered. Rather than all drawing power from a common source, every one of the 54 Sherwood locomotives has its own performance characteristics and these are known to the people who operate the line. On the real railway it was an established fact that steam locomotives of the same class could handle very differently, and this is just as true on the model. For example, there are two 'Royal Scots' shedded at Nottingham Castle, both fitted with similar mechanisms. Yet No. 6113 is noticeably more powerful than No. 6119, and is used in preference for hauling the heavier trains.

Inertia is another important factor, since full-size freight and passenger trains are difficult to get under way, but once rolling are also difficult to stop. With electric operation, unless some kind of inertia is built into the control system electronically, trains will respond instantly. With clockwork, the opposite is the case. Trains pull away slowly from stations under the watchful eyes of the operators, but once they are out on the main line in full cry, nothing can stop them, barring accidents. Assuming that the operator has judged the weight of the train accurately in relation to the power of the locomotive and the distance to the next stop, then the train should slow to a halt alongside the platform at the end of its run. It must be admitted, however, that there are occasions when either a little banking assistance or a little brake force has to be applied.

The History of Sherwood

The imaginary railway system upon which Sherwood Section is based has a completely fictitious but equally plausible history. The line runs through a part of England which in the time of Robin Hood was well known for its densely wooded character, and according to Norman Eagles it was built in the 1890s to provide Nottingham with an outlet to the East Coast.

The Midland and Humber Railway, as it was then known, ran from a terminus station at Nottingham Castle to its own docks at Port Trent, at the confluence of the Rivers Trent and Humber. However, shortage of capital brought about the commercial failure of the company, and in 1911 it was absorbed by the Midland Railway, which in turn was merged into the new London Midland and Scottish Railway at the grouping of 1923.

The model shows the Sherwood Section as it might have been in the first fortnight of August 1937 and is historically correct down to such details as the wording of advertisements and the prices in the shops. As can be seen from the map, the Sherwood Section has an elaborate route network, serving a total of 12 stations. In essence it comprises a main line, with suburban loop, a rural branch line (which can be reached by two routes), a light railway and a short colliery branch.

Since no actual timetable ever existed for the line, one had to be built up from scratch. Timetabling comes naturally to 'the governor' however, as in his other life he was responsible for scheduling the bus services of London Transport – indeed there are many people who say that the buses have not been the same since Mr. Eagles retired!

Opposite: Nottingham Castle at 8.32 pm: A Royal Scot Class departs for Trent town.

Left: Map showing the route of the Sherwood Section of the LMS. The stations actually modelled are shown in capital letters.

Above: Deeley tender for Midland Compound 4-4-0 awaiting entry to the paint shops.

Operating

Freight Trains and Pigeon Specials

With freight trains, the operator must work well in advance if he is to be sure that the requisite train of the correct type is marshalled and ready to leave on time. As well as stating the type of freight train, the timetable specifies the number of vehicles so that the accommodation at any yard is not exceeded. Besides the master timetable, a list for each yard and siding is maintained, showing the arrival and departure of every vehicle during the 24 hours. This ensures that the capacity of that yard or siding is at no time exceeded.

One of the gang acts as Goods Agent and supplies each operator with a card detailing the freight loads which require to be transported from point to point. There is in addition a regular coal traffic from Gretley Colliery to Port Trent, while once every day a loco coal train runs direct from the colliery to the various loco depots along the line. Secondly, for each of the 20 parcel vans and other similar stock, a working list is kept showing the particular trains to which the vehicle must be attached.

Over and above the normal timetable trains, the operators also have to run various special workings. These include excursions, permanent way workings, and pigeon specials. Excursions, for instance, are run for the Nottingham Goose Fair, FA Cup Ties, Women's Institute outings, cruises on the River Humber, educational rambles and so on. Permanent way workings can, on the other hand, involve the repair of a bridge girder, with the consequent occupation of one track for, say, three hours. Such an operation requires the operators to exercise their ingenuity in rerouting the affected traffic as required. Today, pigeon specials are no longer run, but in the 1930s it was a common occurrence for racing pigeons to be carried in special trains of parcels vans (being released at the destination to fly home).

Movement of trains is controlled by over 100 signal arms from 11 signal boxes. Trains are passed from box to box, and cannot be despatched until the next man down the line has set his home signal at clear. Bell codes between boxes are only used selectively, otherwise the cumulative ringing would be almost deafening, but by one means or another the relevant person is usually made aware of the imminent arrival of a train.

Life on the Sherwood Section may seem rather complex, as indeed it is; a certain amount of training is required before a new member of the gang can be initiated. But the supply of willing volunteers is unlikely to run short, since the very complexity of the Sherwood Section is what makes it such a rewarding and enjoyable line to work on.

Track plan of Nottingham Castle station.

Above: Fowler class OF 0-4-0 saddle tank 7002, one of the Trent yard shunters.

Table showing the principal passenger services operated on the Sherwood Section during peak and off-peak periods.

APPROXIMATE SERVICE FREQUENCIES		
Service	Peak periods	Normal
Nottingham Castle – Trent Town	30 min.	60 min.
Nottingham Castle – Port Trent (Boat Express)	1 journey	1 journey
Nottingham Castle – Bradcaster	60 min.	120 min.
Trent Town – Bradcaster (a)	Irregular,	Irregular,
Port Trent – Bradcaster	120 min. approx.	120 min. approx.
Nottingham Castle – Blidworth Dale – Friars Hollow	24 min.	60 min.
Nottingham Castle – Oxton – Monksgate – Friars Hollow	24 min.	60 min.
Rufford Market – Bradcaster	—	Journeys (b)
Oxton – Gretley Colliery (Push-pull train)	48 min. (c)	60 min. (c)
Port Trent – Lincoln North	3 journeys per day	

a   Augmented by push-pull journeys
b   Connects with Main Line trains at Rufford Market
c   Connects with Local trains at Oxton

The Timetable

As might be expected, the Sherwood timetable is a work of some considerable complexity, particularly since one of the main reasons for expanding the layout was to give more scope for Mr. Eagles' genius in this sphere. The result is that the line runs very much like a real railway, with the nine operators in the role of district controllers. They can only afford to be vaguely aware of what is happening on the rest of the line as their responsibility begins and ends with their own specific district or station.

Some concessions had to be made to time and distance since, despite the length of the line, trains only take a short time to travel between stations; and similarly, the marshalling of a train can take place more quickly on the model than it could on the prototype. All trains are run strictly to time, but time itself is speeded up – the clock on the wall running at 83 shortened minutes to the real hour. This means that while the timetabled frequencies of the trains are realistic, the operators are not kept waiting unduly between trains, their workload varying between quieter and busier periods of operation.

Approximate service frequencies for all passenger routes are shown in diagrammatic form, but two examples will help to illustrate the diversity of operation. At one extreme is the light railway from Port Trent to Lincoln North, which runs three times per day in a suitably leisurely manner. At the other extreme is the evening rush-hour service from Nottingham Castle, with suburban trains departing for Friar's Hollow every

12 minutes by alternate routes.

In contrast with more recent trends in the timetabling of suburban services, trains do not run at fixed intervals. This is not only true to period, but is also one factor making it more difficult for the operators to memorize the timetable, and thus perhaps become bored. There is, however, little chance of that happening. It takes four operating sessions to run the full 24-hour timetable and the operators are moved around between the nine different districts, so all in all there are 36 different combinations of time and place for each operator to come to terms with. Since there are less than a dozen operating sessions each year, this should take some time.

Besides passenger services, there are many parcels, newspaper, fish, milk, milk tank and horsebox trains operated every 24 hours, together with more than 90 freight trains. It would not be practicable for the operators to work from a copy of the whole timetable, so station books are compiled for each station.

Right: Trent yard at 4 am with ex-Midland LMS 0-6-0 3049 standing with a freight train for Friars Hollow.

Table showing the various vehicles occupying the bay platform and track 3A at Nottingham Castle Station during a 24-hour period. Similar tables are made out for each platform and siding on the Sherwood Section.

NOTTINGHAM CASTLE – TRACK OCCUPATION			
Time	Track 3A	Time	Bay Platform
4.00 am	PV(GE), GT, PV, MV(GN)	4.00 am	3C
4.08	PV(GE), GT, PV, MV(GN), 2HB	5.44	empty
5.46	PV(GE), GT, PV, MV(GN)	5.46	2HB, MT
6.13	PV(GE), GT, 4PV, MV(GN)	6.13	4HB, MT, PV, MCV
6.22	PV(GE), 4PV, MV(GN)	9.55	4HB, MT, MCV
6.54	2PV	10.37	4HB
7.03	6PV, CV	10.48	4HB, OW, GB
9.16	PV, CV	11.24	4HB
9.20	PV, CV, C	11.38	7HB
9.45	PV, CV, 2C	11.53	8HB
10.22	PV, CV	1.40 pm	empty
11.32	2PV, CV	2.46	2FV, C
11.38	2PV, CV, MV, PV(GE)	3.32	2FV
11.53	2PV, CV, MV, PV(GE), 2FV	3.46	2FV, 3MT
12.40 pm	3PV, MV, PV(GE), 2FV	3.56	3MT
2.45	PV	5.59	3MT, C
3.38	PV, CW	6.48	2C
4.24	2PV, CW, PV(GE)	7.22	empty
6.03	2PV, CW, PV(GE), C	7.55	3C
7.22	2PV, CW, PV(GE)	8.35	empty
8.49	PV(GE)	9.46	PV
9.46	PV(GE), PV, 3RM	10.44	PV, 3C
12.08 am	3RM	12.17 am	3C
12.17	empty		
12.30	2PV, NV		
1.24	empty		
2.41	PV(GE), 3PV, NV		
3.04	PV(GE), GT, PV, MV(GN)		

C	Carriage	GB	Goods brake van	MV(GN)	MilkVan (Great Northern)	PV	Parcels Van		
CV	Cream Van	GT	Gas Tank	MCV	Motor Car Van	PV(GE)	Parcels Van (Great Eastern)		
CW	Carriage Wagon	HB	Horse Box	MT	Milk Tank	OW	Open Wagon		
FV	Fish Van	MV	Milk Van	NV	Newspaper Van	RM	Royal Mail Carriage		

LAYOUT REVIEW

The ultimate in model railway building is to create a large and fully operational system which is either a miniature version of an existing railway, or an imaginary one based on a particular place or period. It is the dream of many modellers to build such a layout with enough realism that those who operate it or view it in action can very easily believe that it is the real thing.

There are many ways of achieving that goal, as this review of several outstanding layouts demonstrates. They are all quite spectacular, yet the approach and philosophy of their builders is sometimes very different.

There are enthusiasts like Bob Hegge, who built his Crooked Mountain Lines layout alone, for his own enjoyment, though fellow enthusiasts often help with the operations. Other modellers work as teams, like the three British enthusiasts who have designed their layout for public display only. What is more, when it has been viewed by the public six or seven times, the Wyandotte model is dismantled and a new, equally fictitious railway is constructed.

The Sunset Valley system, on the other hand, could never go on public display because it runs through three rooms of its owner's house. Nor will it be changed because, after 25 years, it is still evolving and is far from complete.

Some layouts are entirely scratchbuilt; others use manufactured or kit-built rolling stock or accessories. Many depict an era in railway history that has long passed, but utilise sophisticated new methods of control, such as computers.

The permutations are endless, but as this review shows, the results can be astonishingly realistic. The layouts shown here also have one other thing in common: they have given their creators tremendous enjoyment and satisfaction . . . which is what model railways are all about.

Rio Grande 2-8-8-2 Mallet passes through Highfield
on John Porter's North American Lines system,
among the best of American layouts.

Altenbeken

Proceeding eastwards out of Paderborn the Deutsches Bundesbahn main line to Hannover and Kassel winds its way around a mountainside in a most model-like manner in that it describes a spiral to gain height and passes over quite a high viaduct, shortly afterwards reaching Altenbeken. This place, 'Alk' in railway parlance, is occupied mainly by employees of DB and is a fascinating junction with the main line splitting to Hannover in the east and Kassel to the south. On the north side is a marshalling yard with a hump siding having a dead end, while on the south side is a loco depot, plus holding sidings for passenger trains. To the south of the approach roads to the station are goods storage sidings.

Day and night there is constant movement in all parts of the station, with locomotive changes, re-marshalling of some passenger trains and many goods trains, passenger train reversals from the terminal roads and movement to and from the storage sidings.

The prototype signal box at Altenbeken takes a minimum of three men to operate it, But Rolf Ertmer is fully capable of operating a prototype service on his layout single handed. In consequence during an operating session there is one golden rule – do not talk!

The Layout Plan

The aim from the outset was to have as prototypical a scene as possible from a train-service point of view, and therefore the design had to cater for a station which could be completely emptied of full-length trains into a total of 26 train storage sidings (some of which could accept more than one train). These sidings could obviously not be accommodated on the same level as the basic layout and therefore had to be placed underneath. Use is therefore made of a double-track spiral at one end of the layout, which also leads to a branch line terminal station called Kasselhohe.

The baseboard is built on three levels, starting from the low-level storage sidings. The spiral has a total of $5\frac{1}{2}$ turns and is open in the centre so that one can pop up and view the layout. The track plan also includes a reversing loop underneath so that trains return in a different direction – continuous running is possible, but hardly ever done. The track was constructed by Rolf Ertmer from components supplied by the German company Fritz Nemec. There are about 144 turnouts – all solenoid operated – and as Rolf could not find a commercially available motor which satisfied his needs he developed his own.

The era chosen for the layout is in the period prior to electrification, so there is no overhead traction wire. In this period the turnouts on the prototype had position-indicating lanterns, and the motors are developed to allow these to be used and illuminated. Double slips, scissors crossings and three-way turnouts were also still in vogue – from the early 1960s onwards DB ripped these out wholesale. A noteworthy feature is that the entire layout is fully signalled – having semaphore, colour light signals, and also dwarf light signals.

After spending much time searching for the coupling to best suit his needs, Rolf eventually settled for the Piko I coupling, which is extremely gentle in action, and once unlatched will permit stock to be loose shunted. Coupling of two wagons on the other hand can take place without any movement. It is thus possible to operate the entire layout from a comfortable armchair in front of the control panel.

Below: Rolf Ertmer's attention to the minutest detail gives a high degree of realism to the freight yard scene.

Right: Track plan of the Altenbeken line.

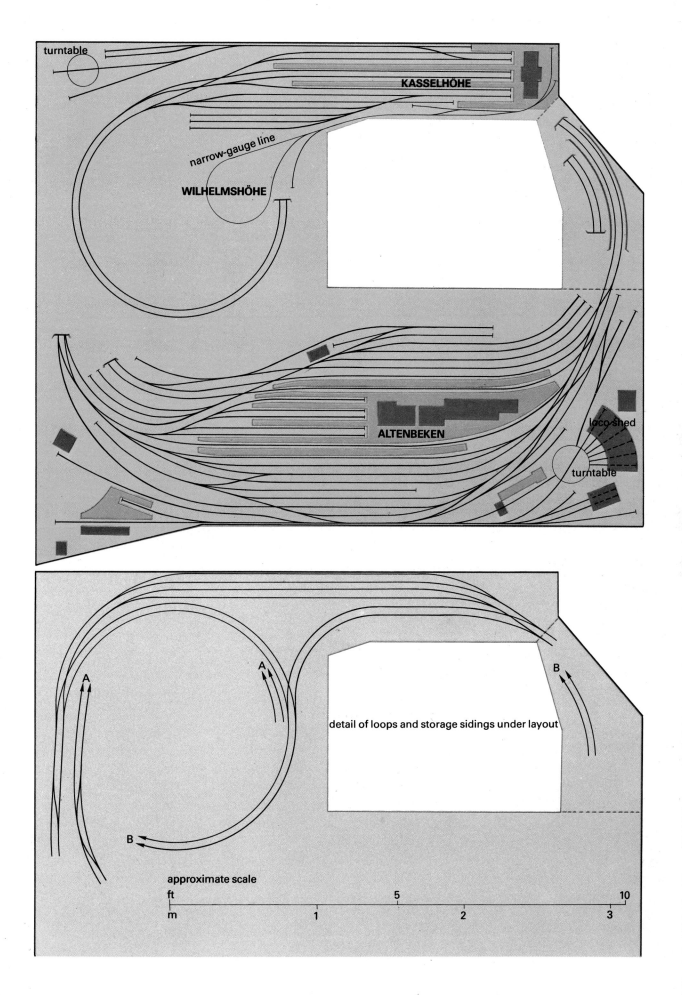

turntable

KASSELHÖHE

narrow-gauge line

WILHELMSHÖHE

ALTENBEKEN

loco shed

turntable

A

A

B

detail of loops and storage sidings under layout

B

approximate scale

ft 5 10

m 1 2 3

Control

The control panel incorporates a form of cab control for the three transistorized controllers which give out a boost voltage for overcoming armature lock or inertia. In addition there are section switches on the track diagram and home-made turnout switches of metal strip. These are turned against simple stops to show the position of turnouts.

There is a separate control panel on the visitors side, from which the hump marshalling yard can be controlled. Even those uninitiated in the operation of the layout can take over a goods train and shunt it out, without involving the working of the layout as a whole. They thus become part of the organisation very quickly and their success encourages them to tackle more complex operations.

One thing for the visitor to learn is the numbering of the tracks – a characteristic feature of DB practice. The marshalling roads for goods trains on the north side are numbered 1–9, the passenger train roads on the north side are numbered in the 10s, the passenger train roads on the south side are numbered in the 20s and the terminal roads are numbered in the 30s. Then there are the turnout numbers and the signals for each road – even marshalling movements being protected by signals – so one does have to be a bit of a walking computer at times!

It is to be expected that a professional photographer like Rolf Ertmer would have an eye for detail and colouring. The buildings, scenery and rolling stock are painted to look as if they had been exposed to the elements. The general atmosphere is very much that of a railway where steam traction predominates. The station building of Altenbeken is modelled exactly as the prototype, except that Rolf forgot the level crossing across the southern tracks for the restaurant owner's van and the postal vehicles. The loco depot has a six-road roundhouse, in front of which is a Fleischmann turntable modified with additional spurs and solenoid position latching.

Below: A part of the intricate control panel.

Opposite: An 'early morning' view from the churchtower towards the station.

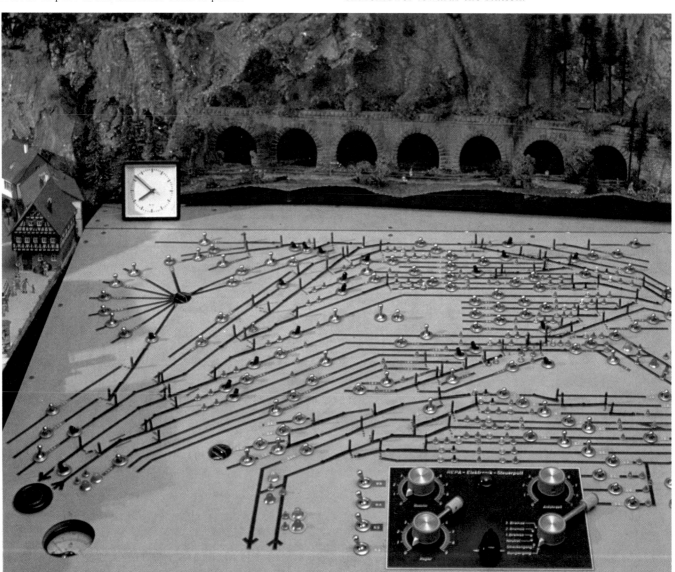

Rolling Stock
This brings us to the stock on the layout, which has been chosen to represent that seen in the appropriate era on the prototype. All Rolf's coaches are of scale length, having been made so in many instances by making two coaches out of three with judicious cutting and joining. All goods stock has been modified with Piko I couplings and with pin-point axle wheels. Locos mostly originate from German commercial sources, except one Japanese tank loco. The locos have been weathered and/or super-detailed with fitments from Merker and Fischer or Gunther, and in some instances the drives have been rebuilt to give better slow-speed performance and lower sound levels. Locos are also re-numbered and re-lettered in accordance with the prototype, which is important when there is more than one of the same class. Some locos have been modified so that the smoke-box doors open and the fire tubes and blast pipes are visible. If any loco does not run exactly to requirements – i.e. slowly, quietly and with sufficient tractive effort for its correct duty – out it goes! In consequence there is a wall cabinet in the railway room the contents of which would make many a modeller happy.

Gerry Veit

Below: Kasselhöhe station throat with the locomotive depot in the background, and the narrow-gauge line at bottom left.

Opposite: The atmosphere of a busy motive power depot is captured in this view of Altenbeken locomotive shed.

The Buckingham Branch

As a child I developed a Hornby O gauge layout, which was fixed on the bedroom floor and subsequently on shelving around a garage. There I began to build up a scenic layout making most of the lineside features myself. An account of this layout appeared in the Meccano Magazine of April 1932. It was not until 1945 that I took up railway modelling in 4mm scale and the first Buckingham Branch was constructed and exhibited at the Model Railway Club Exhibition in April 1948. Two of the stations on that line won bronze medals at the 1947 and 1948 Model Engineers Exhibitions.

I wanted a hobby that would provide an outlet for my ability of being able to create things with my hands. As a student of history I was interested in making a picture of the railway scene at the turn of the century and at the same time making a model railway that could be operated on similar principles to the real thing, namely a movement of trains serving a particular area and working to a predetermined timetable. The Great Central Railway was chosen since it was one not being extensively modelled by others and I wanted the challenge of carrying out the historical research.

The year 1907 was selected because it was the last year that the Great Central retained its two colour coach livery of brown and cream. I was also attracted by the Robinson Great Central locomotives which were simple in external detail and since I was setting out to build everything from scratch they appeared to present less problems than many others. My first priority is that a model railway must work effectively, then secondly that it should look like the real thing so that when the line is in operation it is possible to imagine you are watching an actual railway scene back in 1907.

The locomotives, rolling stock and signals are built as accurately to scale as the prototype information allows, much dependence being placed upon photographs of originals. Buildings and other structures within the company fence are based on buildings on the Great Central or one of its associated companies. Buildings and scenic effects outside the fence are mainly taken from actual buildings I feel make an attractive model, but some are completely free-lance. No attempt has been made to reproduce an actual railway scene.

Below: Buckingham Central Station with Pollitt 4-4-0 No. 269 about to leave platform 1 for Marylebone.

Right: Track plan of the Buckingham branch and a map showing the fictitious location of the railway.

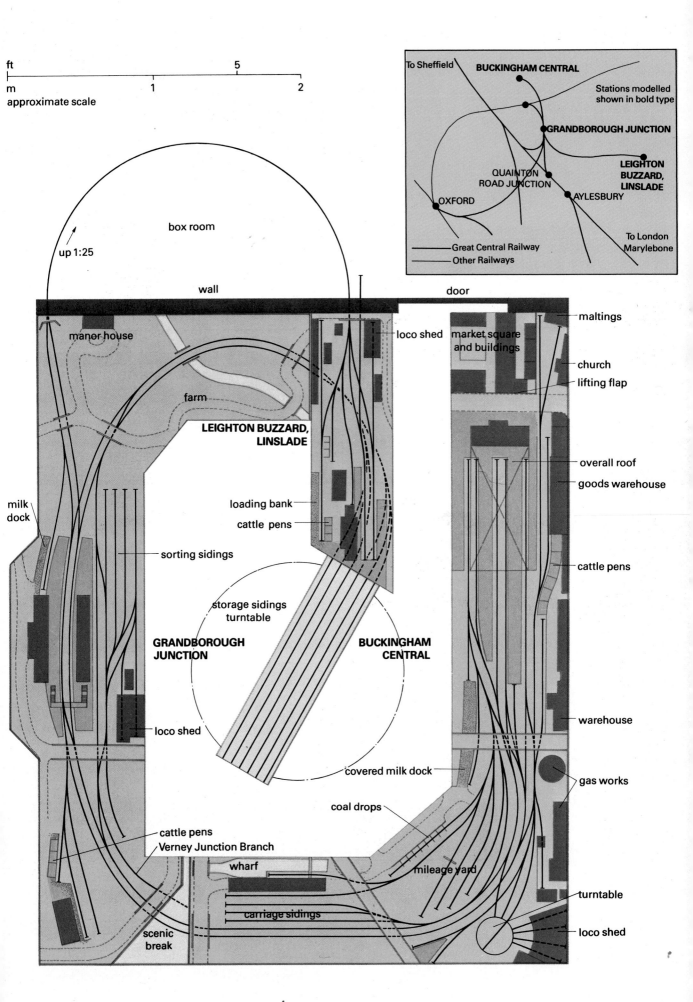

The techniques I have used are largely those for creating a picture in three dimensions. The layout is visually divided into sections by the insertion of road bridges, while it is balanced by the height of background buildings. I build in order to look at the railway from a distance of 500mm (1′ 6″) – anything that is not obviously seen, such as the underframe details of wagons is often represented by a mere suggestion that there is something there, while great attention is paid to prominent details, such as roofs, chimney pots and the tops of coaches and wagons. My tools are the simplest, i.e. a portable workbench often on the kitchen table, a fret machine plus the belief that there is a simple way of doing everything.

The challenge is to create models from basic raw materials in wood, metal and plastic. The present line as far as the baseboard and track plan is concerned was commenced in 1949, but over the years each section has been replaced stage by stage. It has also been adapted to meet various domestic circumstances, being in turn semi-portable, completely portable and finally permanent, as it has grown and shrunk and grown again to fit in the space available as I have moved from house to house. The locomotives and rolling stock have increased considerably over the years and all that was constructed for the first layout in 1948 is still in use, including many of the buildings and other lineside structures.

Left: Grandborough Junction with LD&ECR 0-4-4 T No. 17.

Below: Leighton Buzzard Linslade Station showing end of Great Central Steam rail car.

Operation by Computer

Being a permanent layout, Buckingham is not available for exhibition. It is designed to be operated by one or more people and up to five can be fully occupied. There is, however, always one other operator, a machine that looks after that part of the railway which is off scene, i.e. the hidden sidings. This machine is a computer which I built myself – it is programmed for a day's working through a sequence of train movements. It is controlled by a clock which every ten minutes moves a punched paper progressively forward to feed information to various pieces of electrical equipment.

Right: The market square captures the early 1900 period of the railway.

Below: G.C. Class 13 No. 971, a model built in 1965, seen on shed in the Buckingham yard.

Opposite: The Roundhouse at Buckingham.

When a train is due to arrive at Grandborough Junction a bell rings at that station. On receiving an answering ring, the computer rings the code for a particular class of train and at the same time sets up the track for that train in the storage sidings. On being told the line is clear it switches the current through to the train which then proceeds on its journey. In the same way when a train is due to depart for the storage sidings the computer responds with the correct bell code and sends the train into a predetermined siding. If a train is overdue in either direction the clock stops and will only restart when the correct train is run. The computer also gives warning when the storage sidings need to be turned round, indicates which lines are in use and passes reminders when trains are due to leave or arrive at any of the stations. All the stations are linked by bells and when there are two or more operators the trains are despatched through the block system using the bells according to normal practice. This computer and the revolving storage sidings are two of the contributions I like to think I have made to the hobby.

Buckingham is distinctive in that nearly everything has been scratchbuilt including track, locomotives and rolling stock. In this it represents the approach to railway modelling of the late 1940s when there were very few finished models available commercially and no kits at all. Consequently it is a very individualistic model railway.

I think Buckingham has gone far beyond its original expectations. Judging by the many visitors I have who come to see it each year and the little group of friends who come for regular running sessions, it has resulted in giving much pleasure to many people. I personally find it a great relaxation to enter my railway room, switch on and run the next train on the time table. Over the years my railway activities have led me into an ever widening circle of friends, even from overseas, and as one comes to face retirement it is good to have a hobby that one can continue to pursue and even find time to make the things for which there was no time in busy working days.

The Reverend Peter Denny

Below: A detail of the Buckingham Goods Yard with overhead crane. The wagons in the foreground are standing at the coal drops.

Right: One of the superb Great Central Railway coaches with the LD&ECR 0-4-4 T No. 17 in the foreground.

GRANDBOROUGH JUNCTION

The Crooked Mountain Lines

The Crooked Mountain Lines began in H0 gauge in the early 1950s. Built in the basement of my home in Hazelwood, Missouri, it was born as a steam railway, but in 1955 it went under the overhead catenary as a full electric operation. Power is delivered through two rails and, like the prototype, a pantograph pickup through the catenary. This layout was all in H0 gauge with scratchbuilt catenary and rails put down on wooden sleepers glued into place.

In 1956, I converted the Crooked Mountain Lines to 0 gauge using code 172 rail gauge. This layout was also built in the basement and catenary again took care of the power supply. In 1962 the Crooked Mountain Lines was rebuilt using commercial H0 equipment. However, in 1965, I sold all the H0 gear and decided to build and work in $\frac{1}{4}''$ scale using fine-scale wheels and code 100 rail. This type of building would make for a far more prototypical appearance.

The Crooked Mountain Lines is built and operated in a large basement which it fills entirely. The operation of the railway takes place on three levels in a 'U' design with a yard in the centre. Although the yard was an afterthought, it gives me more space for operating and running the equipment.

Right: Like all the other equipment on the Crooked Mountain Lines, this electric combine was scratch-built by Robert Hegge. It is constructed of wood and brass, has flywheel drive and sprung trucks. It is seen emerging from the car barn at the centre of the layout.

Below: A Class B Illinois Traction System locomotive built of brass by Robert Wade of St Louis, Missouri, is seen running on Robert Hegge's Crooked Mountain Lines $\frac{1}{4}$-inch scale layout.

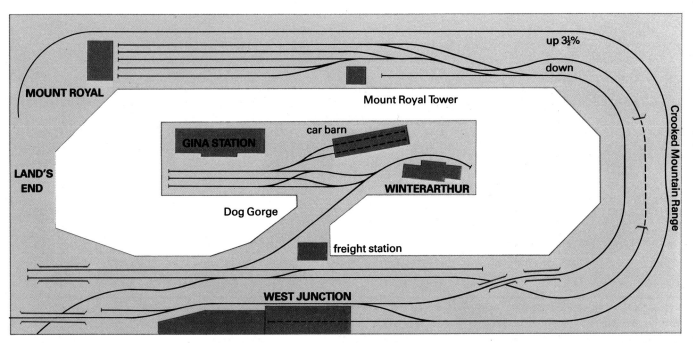

MOUNT ROYAL

up 3½%

down

Mount Royal Tower

Crooked Mountain Range

GINA STATION

car barn

LAND'S
END

WINTERARTHUR

Dog Gorge

freight station

WEST JUNCTION

Left and below: A typical example of the rugged
mountainside and detail of scratch-built perfection.

Above: Track plan of the Crooked Mountain Lines.

In the building of the Crooked Mountain Lines, I tried to make the model as prototypical in appearance as possible. This was to be a miniature version of the real thing, not just a model railway. All structures are weathered and old in appearance as well as in design. The rolling stock has also been weathered to represent a sort of run-down railway, that has seen better days.

The period of operation of the Crooked Mountain Lines is in the early 1930s and the United States is deep in its depression. The railway is not operating in the red but the profit is not all that great. The company has neither the time nor money to keep the equipment in an immaculate appearance. They are far more concerned with the fine running condition of the rolling stock and electric locomotives.

As the railroad is set in the extremely rugged Northwestern part of the United States, mountain scenery is built from the ceiling of the basement almost

down to the floor level. Over 200 kilos (450 lbs) of plaster was used in the construction of this scenery, and both oil and dry powder paint are used. Before painting is carried out a final coat of cheap white paint mixed with sand, to give an earth-like appearance, is applied. Colouring of the rocks and earth comes next. Most of the trees are made by hand using a variety of materials first made by Mother Nature. All structures on the layout are scratch-built from wood, but with commercial windows and doors.

All equipment is built by hand using only motors, transmissions and brass flywheels from commercial sources. The flywheel operation in the locomotives allows for prototype starting and stopping of the equipment. The large locomotives even seem to have a prototypical growl as they climb the steep $3\frac{1}{2}\%$ gradients in the Crooked Mountains.

Code 100 steel rail is mounted on wooden sleepers

Below: The York electric combine comes into view on the low level track. Rock scenery and greenery were all hand-built by the owner.

Right: Maintenance work being carried out on the Crooked Mountain Lines. The Caboose was scratch-built by Robert Hegge.

glued to the wooden roadbed. Each sleeper contains four spikes holding the rail in place. Sand is used for road ballast and is glued in place. The complete rail and roadbed is then painted a ballast grey. Once dry, the sleepers then receive four coats of paint giving them an old and stained appearance. In the yards the sleepers are sunk into the earth as if they have been there for years. The steel rail is also painted in various stages of rust or oil appearance.

The Crooked Mountain Lines is built up on regular wooden bench work, then on a wooden base. The roadbed is cut from plywood to the correct radius and glued in place. Crumpled up newspapers were used as a mould for plaster-shell type of scenery. Once the plaster was dry the newspapers were pulled away. In some places on the railroad, aluminium window screen was used for the scenery base. In many cases this was a much quicker form of construction. The scenery was formed by dipping many small pieces of cloth into the plaster, then laying them in place on the wire or paper moulds. Some rock castings were also used on the layout.

Right: Several metal kits were used in this structure combine with fine track work in the foreground.

Below: Switch motor at work on the Crooked Mountain Lines. Hard shell type plaster is shown coloured in oils and spray bombs. Code 100 steel rail is used for proper prototype appearance.

Below right: This imposing station is the headquarters of the Crooked Mountain Lines. It is of wood construction and has been weathered.

One attraction that visitors often call to my attention is the use of earthworks carried below the level of the trackwork. This gives a more attractive overall design with the mountains running almost to the floor and creating deep canyons or gorges—and achieves a better prototypical appearance.

An interesting fact about the running of the Crooked Mountain Lines is that no two pieces of locomotive equipment is the same, nor are the paint colours alike. While most of the box, switch or freight locomotives might be painted in red, they are not all in the same shade of red! One of the locomotives is orange while another has been sprayed yellow. Why doesn't this railroad have all the equipment painted in the same colours? Because the various power equipment was purchased from other lines throughout the United States that had gone out of business. And at this moment in time, the paint shops just haven't gotten around to painting all the equipment the same colour—and probably they never will!

As a rule the Crooked Mountain Lines is run by one person and was specifically built for the enjoyment of its owner. I run the equipment from a small control unit that I can carry about on my belt or hold in my hand. Thus I am able to walk about the layout working all turnouts by hand and am close to the equipment at all times. Performing the operation by hand requires more time, rather than a large control panel, but is more fun. One-hand control is used for the main line and a second unit works the small island yard. The Crooked Mountain Lines works on point-to-point operation, and it is built on three levels from chest height to just above eye level. A more prototypical appearance is given by the added height of the layout.

The Crooked Mountain Lines has been shown on television and has been featured extensively in the model railroad press. It has been seen by countless model railway enthusiasts from all over the United States and several other countries. Since the Crooked Mountain Lines is the only fully operational catenary-run layout in this part of the United States, I am often called on to display its method of operation.

The overhead catenary is constructed of phosphor-bronze wire. Small springs are used at the ends of the

Above: Proper use of detailed components give correct prototype appearance to the cars.

Below: The sun sets in the mid-west behind a wood combine of the Crooked Mountain Lines.

Left: End of the main yard on the Crooked Mountain Lines with a variety of scratch-built flywheel mounted locomotives, mostly built by owner Robert Hegge.

tracks to keep the wire tight for the best possible electrical contact and operation. Because no commercial types can withstand continuous use, the tall pantographs mounted on top of the locomotives have been hand built by myself.

Short trains are the rule on the Crooked Mountain Lines. This is because placement of the turnouts allows trains of only five cars or less. In this electric operation, freight is the main source of income with some passengers being carried now and then. Each locomotive has room to carry a small amount of baggage, so even a single unit running alone can make a run pay with various small loads of freight carried in the interior. I find it's more fun to operate in this manner.

A model railroad is never really complete. After all, one can always build another structure, or add a tree or two. My future plans call for more telegraph poles and wires being strung about the landscape. Some are already in place. More trees will be planted with more greenery added in various places. On the whole the construction of the layout has been carried out according to my original ideas. I visualized the complete layout in my head before it was built and it has turned out very much as I first planned.

Bob Hegge

Right: Two-car train of wood and brass crosses a wooden trestle constructed from scratch by Robert Hegge for his Crooked Mountain Lines.

Below: View in the Mount Royal yards of the Crooked Mountain Lines, showing scratchbuilt tower and baggage motor car. Equipment and rails give used appearance.

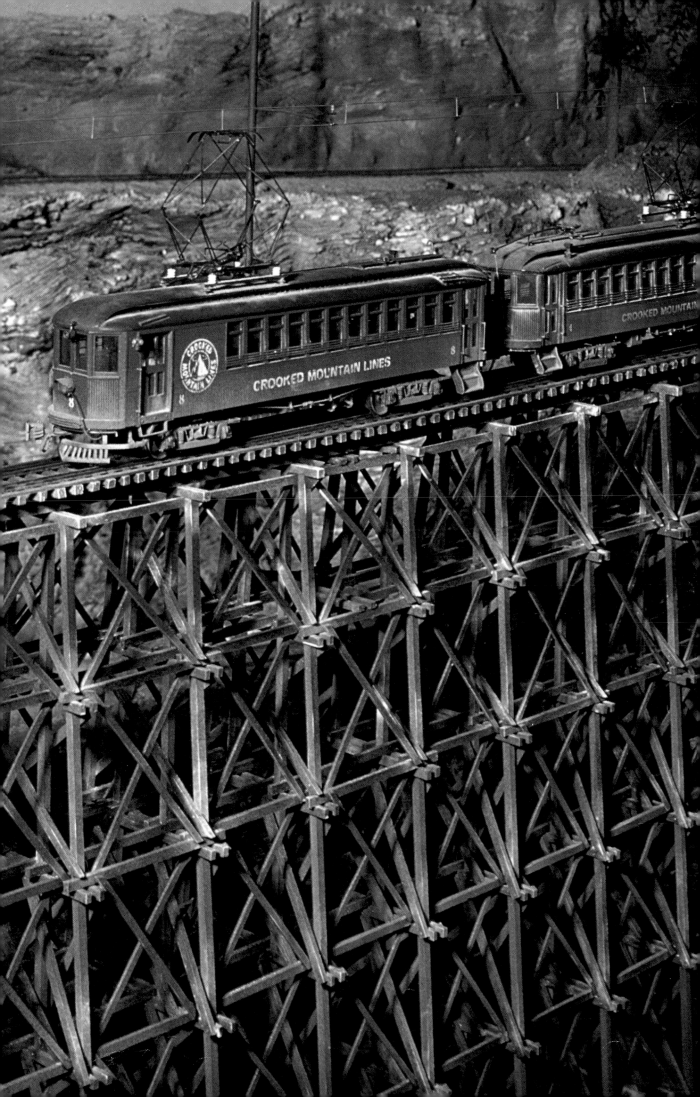

Heckmondwike

In order to fully understand and appreciate Heckmondwike it is necessary to have an understanding of the British 4mm scale section of the hobby and its evolution since the early 1920s. At first sight this may seem a rather sweeping statement but closer examination of the facts will reveal that the roots of Heckmondwike lie in a period of model railway history which existed before any of its builders were born!

In the early 1920s the hobby in the UK saw the introduction of HO which is 3.5mm scale, 16.5mm track gauge and OO, which is 4mm scale, also using 16.5mm track gauge. Readers will of course quickly note that HO is much closer 'to scale' than OO gauge which is equivalent to an actual 4′ 1½″. With the passage of time since OO was introduced so many years ago, modellers may well wonder why the reasons given – which were that it would help to get electric motors into the small boilered British outline models and allow more space for outside valve gear, etc. – are still valid. By 1939, OO was gaining strength rapidly, at the expense of HO, due mainly to support from the trade.

It was the availability of commercial parts for OO, plus the fact that in those days only three-rail track was widely available, that led to the next development. More realistic, two-rail track could be made by soldering brass or nickel-silver rail to punched brass sleepers, and so while making the track oneself it was just as easy to place the rails slightly wider apart. The most popular dimension for this new, 'scale' track was a gauge of 18mm, or *EM gauge*, representing 4′ 6″ on the prototype – still slightly narrower than the full 4′ 8½″. So by the outbreak of World War II, HO as the scale modeller's gauge was on the way out, being replaced by EM gauge, a system to which OO rolling stock could be converted.

Track plan of the Heckmondwike layout.

The Origins of Protofour

With the resumption of the hobby at the end of the war, one might have expected EM to have made considerable strides but this was not so and in fact some years elapsed before EM gathered momentum. However, no sooner had EM become established than the pace setters in the hobby became restless again and began to advocate still finer wheel standards. But then in the late 1960s 'Protofour' arrived, proudly proclaimed as the ultimate in fine scale modelling, 18.83mm track gauge (equal to 4′ 8½″) with 4mm scale.

It is easy to see how all this happened. Apart from track, all OO parts could be used for EM and so the adoption of another scale was pointless. Then the use of existing wheels on 18mm gauge track led to the desire for more accurate wheel profiles and tighter clearances through turnouts, and so the stage was set for the principle of 'exact scale'. Protofour does have an extra (10 thou.) 0.25mm clearance through some of the pointwork, but to all intents and purposes it is an exact scale system. The problem was that in the late 1960s it was still mostly theory and while its supporters claimed it would work, many of them remained unconvinced.

It was the old problem of the chicken and the egg. Until it could be proved a workable system the trade wouldn't support Protofour and until the trade supported it, modellers could not obtain the parts they needed to prove that the system was workable – and so matters rested until late 1972. By then some small layouts had been built, and one company had even begun to market a comprehensive range of parts. However, what was needed to really prove the point was a fairly large layout, capable of display at exhibitions, and this was the challenge that the newly-formed North London Group took up.

An ex-Midland railway 2P 4-4-0 brings a cattle train into the storage sidings.

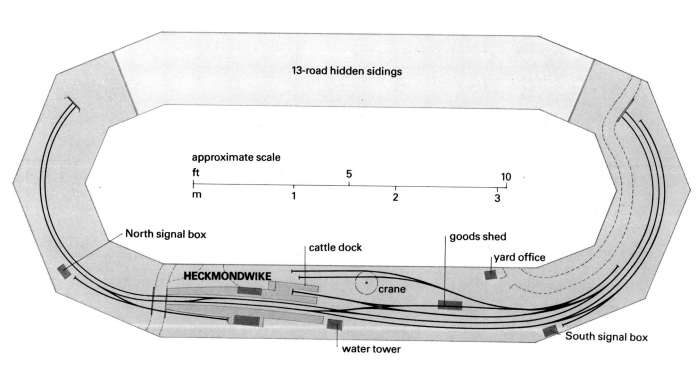

Only our ignorance of exactly what lay before us could possibly have led to such a decision, particularly as most of us were new to the hobby. On the other hand the fact that so much was achieved by inexperienced modellers was ample evidence of the viability of Protofour techniques. In a sense too, this inexperience was a positive advantage as there were fewer old ideas to *unlearn* and more scope for finding new and better solutions to modelling problems.

All being said and done, work at last began on the layout early in 1973. Following correspondence with magazine editor, Cyril Freezer, the following criteria were laid down for 'Heckmondwike' as it was to become known. . . .

1. To function at least as well as the best OO layouts
2. To create and sustain interest in the model press
3. To be a full double-track main line
4. To be fully and correctly signalled
5. Trains to be run at scale speeds
6. To appear authentic, even without rolling stock.

Never ones to do things by halves, we also committed outselves to making Heckmondwike 'Run better than any other 4mm scale layout previously exhibited'. The prototype to be followed was that of the LMS (Midland Section) in the 1930s.

Only once we had begun work did the magnitude of the task really begin to dawn on us. It was not simply a question of building a layout – everything had to be worked out from first principles. In theory this idea was fine – simply reduce everything to the exact scale dimensions. Due to shortage of space, model railway curves are nearly always sharper than scale to enable layouts to fit inside people's houses, but in prototype terms, attempting to run trains around such sharp curves would inevitably result in derailments and so there had to be a compromise somewhere. The answer was to make the locomotive chassis bend. Similarly a novel form of suspension for coach bogies and four-wheeled wagons was developed. Known as 'compensation', it effectively ensured that all four wheels remained firmly on the rails. This elegantly simple suspension consists basically of pivoting one axle around a fixed central point so that the wheels can move vertically. Thus the wagon chassis, instead of being rigid, has

An ex-Midland railway 3F 0-6-0 hauling a train of ballast wagons. Note the realistic appearance and super elevation of the track, although the chairs have not yet been added in this photograph.

enough flexibility to ride smoothly over any bumps in the track rather than bouncing along as do most models.

The development of the four and six-wheel bogie compensated system took time, as indeed did the compensated tender drive, double bogie 4-4-0 and 0-4-4T chassis. Similarly we could have used commercial turnout motors, but preferred to design our own.

For motive power, all the various commercial motors available were rigourously tested and finally two were adopted as standard for use in all Heckmondwike locomotives. The problems came when we decided to design and build our own controllers.

Operation and Signalling

The chosen method of operation decreed that every train movement should be correctly signalled before current passed to the track. This meant first of all that we had to build working models of Midland Railway signals to fit the selected prototype. Then we had also to cope with the shunting moves which on a real railway would have been controlled by hand or flag. This led to further electrical complications which had to be re-

solved by a group member whose previous experience of electronics was virtually nil.

The group decided at the time to use a flat-topped baseboard, but in retrospect an open-topped baseboard would have been preferable as part of the line could perhaps have been built upon an embankment.

At exhibitions, Heckmondwike is presented in 'bookstall fashion', with the storage sidings hidden from view. The use of subdued colours on the layout for reasons of authenticity was made up for by the very powerful 'light curtain' with which the display was illuminated and the finished result was a tremendous crowd-puller.

Since the virtual completion of Heckmondwike, and its successful showing at a number of model railway exhibitions, the North London Group has now gone on to its next pioneering project in fine scale modelling – 'Bodmin'. This is an attempt to apply Protofour techniques to that most typical of British layouts, the Great Western Railway branch line.

Bob Essery

An aerial view of Heckmondwike Station. The uncluttered layout of the buildings adds to the realism of the scene.

Golden Gate Model Railroaders

The Golden Gate Model Railroaders is located in the basement of the Josephine D. Randall Junior Museum, San Francisco, California. The museum is run by the San Francisco City and County Recreation and Park Department and in its day-by-day operation it houses exhibits of paleological, primitive Indian and early San Francisco artefacts. There is a modest zoo and a sizeable workroom for instruction in wood, metalwork and mechanics. The museum is oriented toward children of elementary school or early high school age.

The reason for the railway's rather unusual location is that the museum's authorities felt a model railway with scenic and operational emphasis on the terrain and economics of Northern California would be interesting and instructive to both young and old alike. Student groups visit the museum regularly from many different schools, and the model railway club co-operates with the museum by holding open house during museum-sponsored activities.

The club also has regular monthly operation nights for the pleasure of its members. The public is always welcome, but the nature and amount of rolling stock is not assured. These are also fun nights. As far as possible, a schedule of quarterly open houses or shows is maintained for the public, and the twice-a-week club work nights are open to public observation.

The Golden Gate Lines has for all its years been essentially an HO gauge layout. In recent years a small relating narrow gauge (HOn3) operation has been added, but this is at the moment a simple double loop arrangement which is to be extended to relate to other parts of the HO layout. All operations are electrically controlled.

The club room is roughly 17m × 11.5m (58′ × 38′) – the layout covering a U-shaped area of 15m × 10m (50′ × 33′). The centre of the U-shape provides a public viewing area of about 5m × 2.5m (16′ × 8′). There is a 11.5m × 3.6m (38″ × 12′) storage and work area and an approach room for the public leading to the layout which houses exhibits during major shows.

The club was incorporated in 1950 with its layout then in a small rehabilitated house. When the house was sold in about 1960, the club was invited to begin a layout at the museum. Initially the club's layout was an elongated loop occupying about one-third of the present display room with the freight and passenger yards much as they are now. In 1964 the room was cleared and the club extended the railway on a level basis to cover the area now occupied by the Valley Division. In 1967 the

Track-plan of the Golden Gate Railroad.

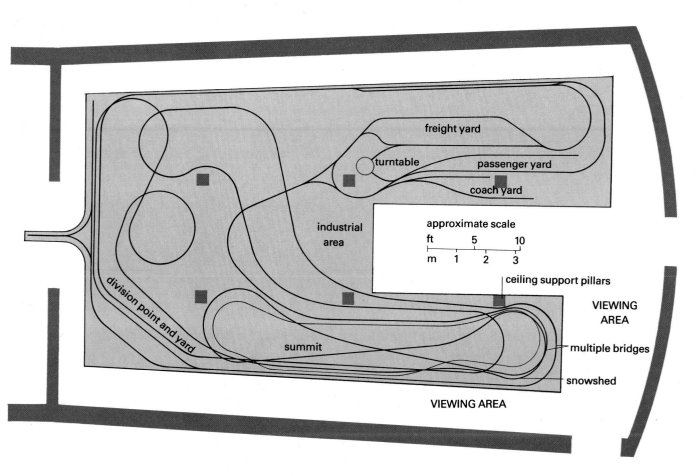

Mountain Division, which contains the major elevations to a summit area, was installed. The entire layout, substantially in its present form, was operating by 1968. The running and construction of the layout at the peak of its development called for the combined efforts of 15 or more workers on two or more nights a week over a period of about 11 years.

The club had originally been formed largely because many interested modellers, lacking space for home layouts (this was long before N gauge), felt the need for a place where they could operate on a regular basis. In moving to the museum it was understood that the members would endeavour to provide a layout which depicted the Northern California countryside – its deserts, valleys and mountain areas. The mountain area which was built stresses in a small way the rugged granite-faced rocks of the Sierras. It was felt that the trackwork should reflect scale accuracy, and all sleepers were hand laid and ballasted, and rails spiked individually. Mainline track on the Valley Division wad laid in code 100 rail; the Mountain Division was laid in code 83. Most of the sidings are in smaller code 70 rail.

As a club layout, it was necessary to provide for the operation of a variety of locomotives ranging in size from the largest Union Pacific 'Big Boy' to the small Shays and Heislers. In order to allow for interchange of cars, particularly in freight operation, NMRA weight standards and knuckle-type couplers were adopted. Like many other model railway clubs, the Golden Gate Lines owns very little motive power or rolling stock, most of the equipment being supplied by its members. Collectively the club can call upon up to 250 locomotives, 700 freight items, and 100 passenger carriages.

During the building of the Golden Gate Lines some electronic sophistication was injected, particularly in switch control on the passenger and freight yard ladders. However, we have found that too elaborate electrical or electronic devices installed by knowledgeable temporary members have proved difficult to maintain or repair when emergencies confront less experienced operators.

Many materials and techniques have been used to create the landscaped scenery, including most of the popular methods in use today. Trees and shrubs are constructed from local natural vegetation. Scenery construction is combined with benchwork and tracklaying so that even though there are areas where benchwork and tracklaying are still to be started, areas under construction have complete scenery.

Below: On the Golden Gate turntable in front of the Roundhouse are the Sante Fe SD 40 No. 5003 general freight engine, with an SD 45-2 which was one of five locomotives painted in red-white-and-blue to mark America's bi-centenary in 1976.

Sometimes this can cause frustration for the scene builders, especially when the track planners think up a brilliant concept which would need a new route through scenery that has already been completed.

Level trackwork in the yards and Valley Division is supported by heavy plywood covered with Celotex. Mountain Division trackwork is laid on bent wooden strips covered with matching Celotex. Much of the scenery considered 'temporary', even though some of it has been in place now for ten years or more, is of the hydrocal, hardshell, 'zip-textured' variety, covered by varied scenic techniques and coloured by both dry colours worked into the ground cover and by acrylic paints. More permanent rock scenes are built up from plaster castings out of moulds created from rocks found in the hillside immediately behind the museum. These castings are coloured by delicate wash tints using acrylic paints. The only area of the layout considered scenically permanent is the rockwork supporting the triple level bridges.

The Golden Gate Lines is used fundamentally for the personal pleasure of its members. Although they are rarely used in public operation (the purpose at these times being to keep as many trains operating in view as possible), they are equipped with clocks for model railway 'fast time', and this concept is used by the members in private operating sessions. When sufficient members are on hand to provide both operators and dispatchers, the dispatchers organize and direct the operation. With four mainline cabs, two freight yard cabs, roundhouse cabs, passenger cab, ultimately a diesel yard cab, an operator at the Division Point between Valley and Mountain Divisions, narrow gauge operator and 'train chasers' manning an intercommunication system, optimum operation calls for from a dozen to 15 people. In emergency situations four men can produce a passable semblance of mainline operation, including passage through yard areas. There is a telephonic intercab communications system which permits contact between operators with a minimum of personal conversation or across-the-layout gesturing.

Initially the concept of the Golden Gate Lines was to depict a railway system in the quarter of a century from 1930 to 1955 – during the changeover from steam to diesel power. The original older members of the club were devoted to the locomotives, freight and passenger trains of the steam era. However, in its effort to make itself available to younger members, and with the older

members gradually fading from club activity, the original historical concept has been modified by the preferences of the younger generation of enthusiasts.

With the advent of more diesel operation, we have received complaints from the older steam railway enthusiasts. No doubt more steam will show up in the future, but we must always face the fact that the younger modellers and their approach to extensive diesel operation will probably ultimately dominate.

Those who have been working on the layout since the days of the original single loop have the feeling that the Golden Gate Lines has fulfilled its original expectations for many years, and the museum found in the model railway lure for 'customers'. But with publicity there came huge crowds to view the train operations. And although we were pleased that we were fostering a very real interest in our hobby, whether from the viewpoint of the casual visitor or the dyed-in-the-wool model enthusiast, we reached a stage where we could not accommodate the crowds that came. So these days we restrict our publicity mainly to model railway magazines and hobby stores, so that those most truly interested will know of our events, and on arrival will have time and space to enjoy the layout.   *Robert F. Vaughn*

Opposite: The Sierra articulated 2-6-6-2 locomotive No. 6 was built for hauling lumber.

Below: Southern Pacific's 2-8-2 Mikado No. 744 pulling freight through a mountainous section of the Golden Gate Model Railroaders' layout.

Sunset Valley

First let me say that we do not think of the Sunset Valley as a layout. We think of it as a transportation system modelled in miniature with all the possible authenticity we can incorporate to follow the prototype. The Fillmore division, based on a location near Los Angeles, California, is the section of the Sunset Valley that is modelled in my basement—the remaining portions are simply imagined. It is a freelance design in that it is not copied after any specific prototype. However, even in freelance modelling it is essential to study the prototype and follow prototype practices.

The Sunset Valley as modelled in my basement is H0 scale at 3.5mm to one foot. All track is standard gauge, i.e. simulating a 4′ 8½″ track spacing, and 12 volt DC is used for propulsion. The total system is divided up into electrical blocks and any one of the eight control cabs, simulating controls in a real locomotive, can be connected to any one of the blocks. We can thus operate up to eight different locomotives simultaneously on the system with each one under independent control.

The Sunset Valley Railroad is located in the very spacious basement of my home and it occupies about three-quarters of the total basement area with running rights through the basement bathroom, through the clothes chute, over the work-bench, the laundry tubs and behind the washer and dryer. It occupies three main rooms plus adjoining hallway space.

The Sunset Valley is a private home layout and although I frequently invite in a group of enthusiasts to operate the system as they would a real railway, my long-range goal is eventually to have the whole system transported – it is portable – and set up permanently in a public museum.

I have been modelling the Sunset Valley since I was five years old, which makes very nearly 40 years on the one layout. It started as a Lionel 0–27 system with two-cab operation, about 17m (57′) of track and six turnouts. However, even on this system my main theme was to emulate prototypical railway operation, and to ensure this we used, among other things, a fast clock, timetables, waybills, signals and dispatching.

When I was about 16 I changed to 0 gauge, again setting up for a system specifically designed to carry out a transportation concept with prototypical fidelity. This stage, however, lasted for two years only, due to impending matrimony. A year later the present Sunset Valley system was started.

About seven years was spent in building up rolling stock and structure kits. We had no room for a layout during those early years but everything was built to fit into the planned system once space became available. Finally I could wait no longer and three portable modules were constructed in my in-laws' basement, my father-in-law during this period becoming an active H0 kit-building hobbyist. The portable modules turned out to be of great advantage to the Sunset Valley, because

Below: The engine facilities at the Fillmore service area, at one end of the Sunset Valley layout.

Right: The Merchant Prince passes through Snake Creek, a typical eastern coal mining town.

when in 1961 we bought our first present home, they were easily transported from my father-in-law's house to ours. Additional modules were constructed until now there are about 26 for the completely functional system.

I have always thought of the Sunset Valley as a well-rounded, balanced system with a 'something for everyone' concept. The first priority in planning was to support realistic prototypical operations with as long a main line as possible, without having too much track and no scenery. Numerous towns along the line (14 were built) were needed to provide a purpose for the movement of goods and people from one point to another. Plenty of industries along the line were the key to realistic work for the local freights. Efficient yard operation was a necessity to keep train makeup and classification up with the heavy main line traffic demands.

I also wanted a system in which a number of operators could be employed to duplicate the roles of real railway employees. Cab control was considered essential so that each engineer could stay with his train, simulating its road crew over the total run. Tower operators would route the trains but they would have no control over their speed and direction.

Bottom: 2-8-0 No. 109 switching a local freight at Walnut Hill.

Top: 4-6-2 No. 601 passes over one of the bridges in the San Janet mountain range with a special train, whilst a diesel-hauled coal train passes below.

We are continually striving to operate the railway in a manner ever closer to the prototype. To us, railway operation is a science: the goal is to transport goods and people, and the procedure employed must be as safe as humanly possible. Every operation is guided by a book of rules published by the operation department. We find the more we operate the railway like the prototype, the more fascinating it becomes.

There are 16 separate operating positions on the Sunset Valley. We typically operate with between 8 and 14 people, with the more experienced operators covering two or more posts. Everything is done as closely as possible to prototypical techniques. A telephone system connects all the operating positions via a regular telephone switchboard at the dispatcher's office, and all the traffic movements are recorded on a graphical train sheet. A typical timetable schedule session will move approximately 40 trains over the system with a classification of about 300 freight car movements. Full passenger traffic is provided including ten commuter trains into and out of the Fillmore terminal area.

Accuracy and quality are also continually strived for commodities in all areas on the Sunset Valley as it is the total rail transportation system concept that we are

Top: A circus train hauled by a 'Big Boy' articulated locomotive arriving at East Fork.

Bottom: Dual FT diesel units haul a freight train in the San Janet mountains.

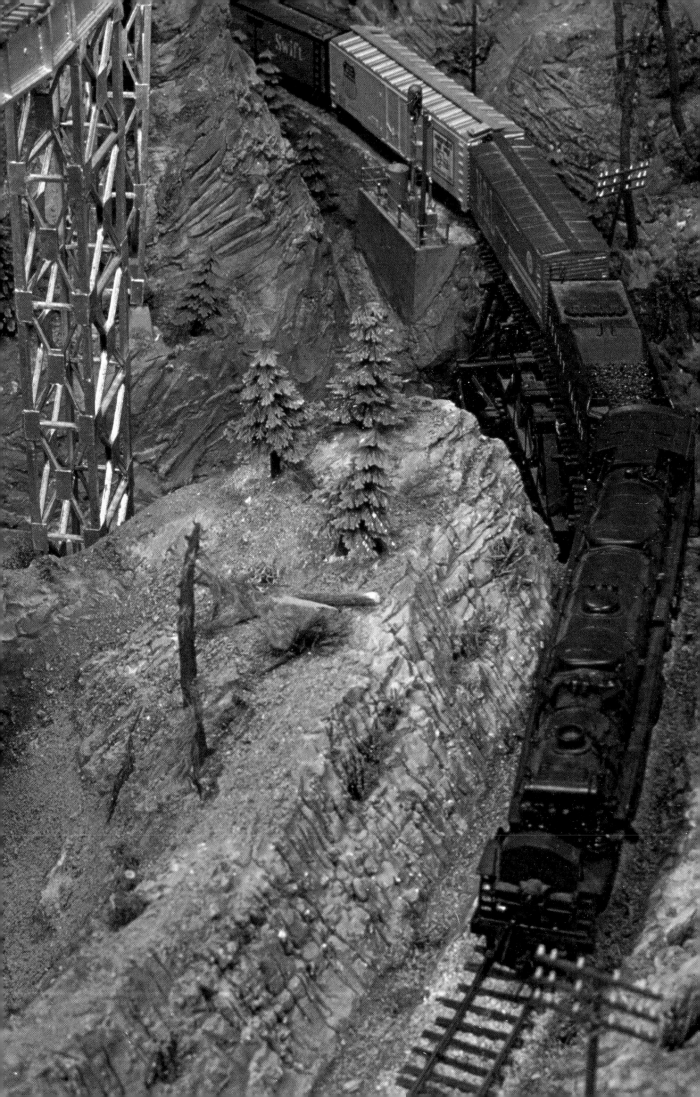

trying to emulate in overall approach as well as in infinite detail. Realistic scenery with great amounts of detail is important, but its role is supportive only as it relates to the justification of the transportation system as a whole. The Sunset Valley is the system and the scenery is merely providing the landscape upon which the railway operates.

Likewise the electrical system, although quite complex—with over 20,000m (65,000ft) of wire, 3,000 terminal strip connections, 288 relays, 264 panel switches, 394 diodes, 218 transistors, 1,029 panel and signal lamps, to name only a few of the components—is obviously important but is not the end result and like the scenery merely plays a supportive role.

Essentially having fun is the primary goal and I enjoy all the various facets of model railway construction. I find that the more realistic I make the railroad, in terms of both its construction and in the realism in which the operation is carried out, the more fun it becomes.

No really special techniques were used in the construction of the Sunset Valley. My main philosophy is to work very carefully, with lots of thought put into each project, and to do it the best way possible—however long it takes. Any problems, be it kinks in trackwork, either vertical or horizontal, or whatever can and must be worked out, with some rebuilding if necessary, but my main principle is to build the layout in modular sections so that it can be moved. There is no way I could justify the blood, sweat and tears, and also the loving care, that I have put into its construction without knowing that it is built in portable modules and if the need arises can be moved.

Left: A rock cutting in the San Janet range, note the attention given to the positioning of the shrubs and trees, and the realistic track.

Above: Kleinman's Dock & Timber Transfer Company's wharf at Edsport. Careful detailing adds realism and atmosphere to the model.

Below: Small industrial buildings and sidings, such as the Sunkist citrus fruit growers exchange at San Clemente, provide opportunities for interesting freight operation.

The Sunset Valley has had a relatively long history, with the present layout already 25 years under construction and still far from complete. In terms of specific changes during this period, there have been very few. Mainly we have been and are still striving to carry out the original plan. The basic track plan has remained unchanged, although some new industry spurs, interchange tracks, set-out tracks have been added, much as a real railroad does as it makes modifications to adapt to

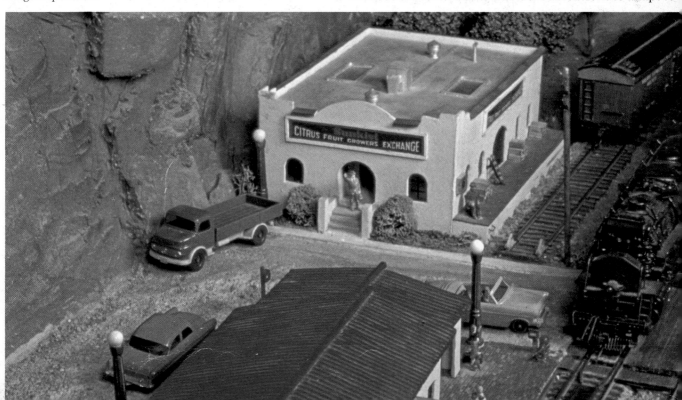

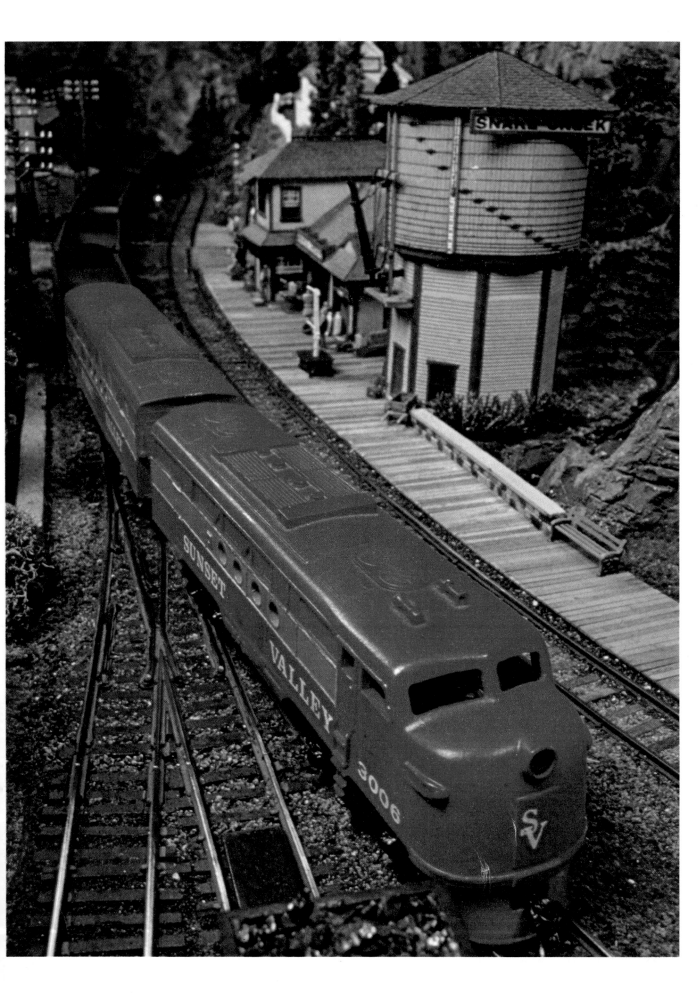

new requirements. The ideals of interchange with other rail systems and with the Fillmore division joining other (as yet unmodelled) portions of the system have become an increasing and very important part of Sunset Valley thinking over the last few years. Such concepts, even in their most basic form, add dimension to our system, as our rolling stock is envisaged travelling to points far outside the confines of our own railway room. All however is designed and carried out to add specific operational interest and realism to the basic concept of emulating a real live rail transportation system.

The addition of walkaround cabs is also a recent change that has done much to enhance operation. In fact there is now so much detail that I want to include, and so much of it far beyond what was conceived many years ago, that I often get the feeling that I now have more work ahead of me to finish the Sunset Valley than I had when I started. The progress of the hobby in terms of improved mechanisms, electronics, superdetail, etc., simply means that there is more that can be done today and much more to do it with. Technological advances

Left: Dual FT diesel locomotive passing Snake Creek with a coal train. The circular water tower lends typical American flavour to the scene.

Bottom: The diesel repair shops at Fillmore, with two locomotives inside for servicing.

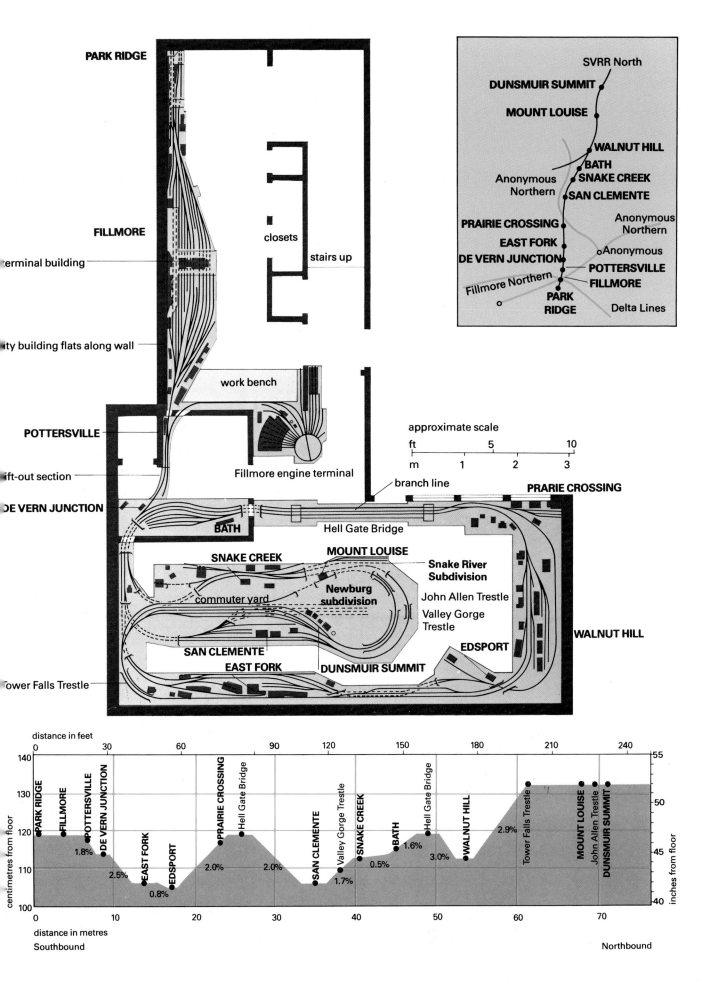

PARK RIDGE

FILLMORE

terminal building

city building flats along wall

POTTERSVILLE

lift-out section

DE VERN JUNCTION

Tower Falls Trestle

closets

stairs up

work bench

Fillmore engine terminal

BATH

Hell Gate Bridge

branch line

approximate scale

ft		5		10
m	1	2	3

PRARIE CROSSING

SNAKE CREEK

MOUNT LOUISE

commuter yard

Newburg subdivision

Snake River Subdivision

John Allen Trestle

Valley Gorge Trestle

EDSPORT

SAN CLEMENTE

EAST FORK

DUNSMUIR SUMMIT

WALNUT HILL

SVRR North

DUNSMUIR SUMMIT

MOUNT LOUISE

WALNUT HILL

BATH

SNAKE CREEK

Anonymous Northern

SAN CLEMENTE

Anonymous Northern

PRAIRIE CROSSING

Anonymous

EAST FORK

DE VERN JUNCTION

POTTERSVILLE

FILLMORE

Fillmore Northern

PARK RIDGE

Delta Lines

distance in feet

centimetres from floor

inches from floor

PARK RIDGE · FILLMORE · POTTERSVILLE · DE VERN JUNCTION — 1.8% — 2.5% — EAST FORK — 0.8% — EDSPORT · PRAIRIE CROSSING · Hell Gate Bridge — 2.0% — 2.0% — SAN CLEMENTE · Valley Gorge Trestle — 1.7% — SNAKE CREEK — 0.5% — BATH — 1.6% — Hell Gate Bridge — 3.0% — WALNUT HILL — 2.9% — Tower Falls Trestle · MOUNT LOUISE · John Allen Trestle · DUNSMUIR SUMMIT

distance in metres

Southbound

Northbound

have played a great part in model railway building and provide us with reliable equipment that enables us to concentrate more on the operational aspects—for as with real railways, our models are meant to operate efficiently. And when we carry our operation out with prototypical fidelity, our fun is further enriched.

The building and operation of the Sunset Valley has more than fulfilled my original expectations. Building a system with operational realism in mind and then operating it in a realistic manner close to the prototype provides everlasting interest and challenge. Even more important it provides a great deal of personal enjoyment. If you can get just one-tenth the fun out of running a model railway that I have on the Sunset Valley, your reward will be great.   *Bruce Chubb*

Left: Track-Plan of the Sunset Valley Railroad with gradient diagram and map of the system.

Below: Thoughtful positioning of miniature figures and vehicles is shown to advantage in this view of the level crossing at Walnut Hill.

Wyandotte Transfer

Wyandotte Transfer is an American $\frac{1}{4}''$ (48:1 scale) layout built by a group of three British modellers—Alan Day, Paul Stapleton and Steve Dennison. Whilst Wyandotte Transfer is fictitious, Wyandotte itself is a real town in Michigan and visitors from the US have confirmed that the layout well captures the atmosphere of that area. As the builders were totally reliant on commercially available equipment, 12 volt DC, 2-rail operation was adopted as standard. The layout was never designed to be used in a domestic situation as its size, 65m × 0.5m (21′ × 1′10″), whilst small for 0 Gauge, is too large for the average British semi-detached house. Therefore the layout was constructed on five easily transportable baseboards, 1.25m × 0.5m (4′3″ × 1′10″) and, except for testing purposes, the layout is only operated at public displays. When not being exhibited the layout is stored in a ground floor work-room in my London home.

All three partners in this project have other model-ling interests, running concurrently with Wyandotte Transfer; these include British N, German H0 and American Narrow Gauge. Moreover, before they became interested in American modelling, the three had tried their hand at most forms of modelling in most scales. All three, collectively known as the Wyandotte Group, derive a tremendous amount of pleasure from exhibiting layouts at the many model railway exhibitions that have become such a common feature of British modelling. Therefore in the Spring of 1976, with an invitation to an exhibition in early 1977 already accepted, but with no layout to take, the three put their minds to producing a new layout in just nine months. A British 0 gauge layout was considered but the extra challenge of American modelling, combined with the availability of cheap ready-to-run equipment, proved decisive factors in their final choice. Unfortunately much of the equipment used on Wyandotte is now discontinued, such as Atlas, and can only be picked up secondhand.

Left and right: Typical 'factory units' which characterise the Wyandotte Transfer background scenery.

At no time was a highly accurate model planned, as scale fidelity often means delicate parts that are easily damaged during transportation to and from exhibitions. The limited space available ruled out extensive scenery, so low-relief factories were used as a backscene, with various focal points, such as an oil terminal in the foreground. These factory units, that give the layout so much of its character, were kit-bashed from Con-Cor brewery kits—seven such kits being used to make all the various buildings seen on the layout. This industrial setting has greatly increased operational potential, as there is scope for traffic from one factory unit to another, e.g. wood from the timber yard to the furniture factory at the other end of the layout. Early in the life of the layout it was decided that a logical pattern was required in order to maximize operational interest. Therefore Alan worked out a sequence of operation that keeps the layout's three operators fully occupied for three hours.

Many American layouts use track work that is, to British eyes, considerably overscale. And so when the trackwork was built, code 100 rail was chosen to give improved appearance. All trackwork uses standard 'copper clad' techniques.

Walk-around controllers were built for Wyandotte Transfer with the actual control knobs in a small hand-held module on a flex some 5m (15') long attached to the main control panel. This means that the operator can follow his train to either end of the layout and be well positioned to oversee the uncoupling. Another feature of the layout is the weathering of both the rolling stock and the buildings and this adds considerably to the layout's industrial atmosphere.

It is part of the group's underlying philosophy that once a layout has been exhibited six or seven times it is scrapped and a replacement is made. Therefore by the time this book is published Wyandotte will no longer be in existence. Thus although some parts may survive—in modified form—a new layout, of concept as yet undecided, will be in course of preparation. Wyandotte has served its purpose, not only as a layout in its own right, but, more importantly, as a test bed for several new ideas.

It is a maxim in model railways that there is no substitute for practical experience, and the experience gained in this project will ensure that Wyandotte's successor, a more ambitious project. However, it is also true that as one problem is solved so another one appears and it is this that makes railway modelling so fascinating and challenging.   *Paul Stapleton*

Zero 1

The development of solid-state circuitry for radios, tape recorders and televisions, both decreasing their real prices while increasing their quality and reliability, has passed by with little or no effect on the electrics of the model railway. The introduction of the silicon chip into domestic products has helped to bring automatic control into washing machines and cookers. Infra-red remote control of televisions has been with us since 1975 and at least this technology has been used for an elementary system of train control enabling the user to control more than one train on one track simultaneously by switching the motor independently of the current in the track. This system however, has limitations in terms of the number of locos which can be controlled as well as being limited by line-of-sight (i.e. no control in tunnels).

To state the obvious, on conventional model railway systems locomotives are controlled on sections of track by controlling the current in the track which is interpreted by the motor in the loco. This means that if there are two locos on the same track section not only do they share the current and therefore run at lower speeds but they also accelerate and decelerate together—they cannot be independently controlled. In order to reproduce anything like true prototypical train operation, complicated block wiring needs to be introduced with probably some sort of cab control for optimum operational flexibility. The amount of wiring involved is a daunting prospect for the budding modeller thinking of

Below: Tiny locomotive modules ('chips') can be fitted to almost all OO and HO locomotives and can be coded by the user.

Below right: Computerised Master Control Unit contains 'the brain' behind the system, sending coded messages down the track to individual locomotives.

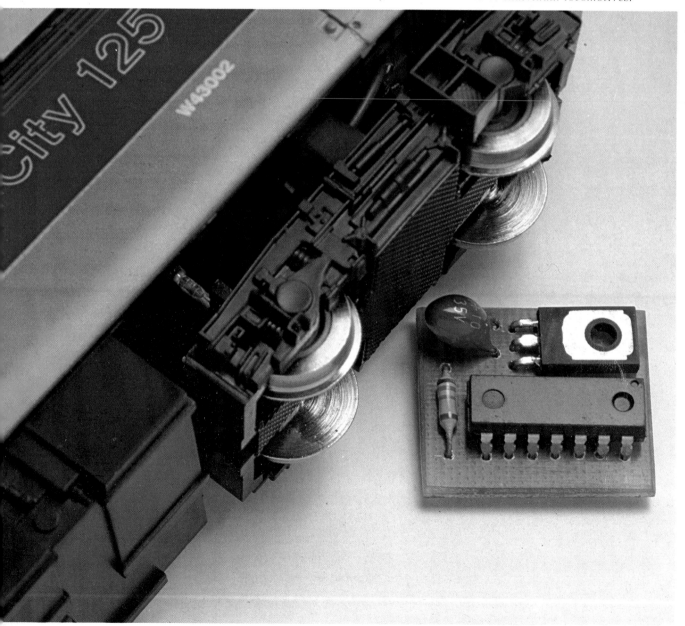

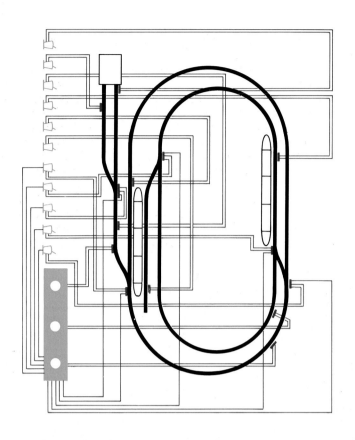

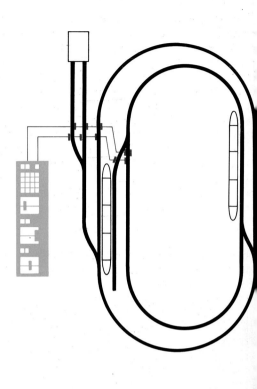

expanding his layout from a simple oval track to something offering a little more in terms of play value. In the opinion of some industry personnel the wiring problem has been the greatest single factor restraining the expansion of the model railway market.

A number of model railway manufacturers have begun to develop new electronic control systems for model railways. Hornby's 'Zero 1' is based on micro-electronic technology and enables the user to control not only locos but also to operate turnouts and other electrical accessories. This with just two wires from the controller to the track.

The big change with Zero 1 is that control takes place in the locomotive and not in the track which means that locos can be independently controlled even when they are in the same track section. This eliminates the need for isolating sections and switches with all their associated wiring which even with a small layout can represent a considerable amount of effort in planning, execution and expense. However, Zero 1 cannot overcome electrical laws and an isolated section will still be needed in a layout which incorporates a reverse loop! The problem of common return, however, is completely eliminated.

The Zero 1 system is made up of four separate elements, the master control unit, the slave control unit and two types of control module—one for locos and the other for operating accessories.

The master controller incorporates everything needed for the complete control system. The 4 amp transformer has two power outputs—one at 16 volts AC, the other 20 volts AC. The system control panel of the master consists of a calculator style keyboard with 17 keys and 3 indicator lights. The loco control section contains separate speed and direction controls and a manually operated cursor scale which reminds the user which loco is under control. The master also contains the 'micro-processor'—a miniature computer which has been specially designed and programmed to enable the operator to control his complete system from the keyboard and operate his locomotives in a truly realistic manner. Four levels of 'inertia' are programmed into the master controller. The slave control units are designed for use with the master controller and give the user simultaneous and independent control of additional locos.

The two types of module contain the same electronic 'chip' but have different external connections and coding switches. The loco module has 3 wires and can be coded 16 ways, whereas the accessory module has 5 wires and can be coded 69 different ways. The loco modules can be added to almost all makes of locomotive providing there is space somewhere in the loco or tender. If space is not available, as in most N-gauge locos for example, then the module can be located in a permanently coupled wagon or coach.

Zero 1 allows the user 16 uniquely coded locos on the layout at one time but the judicious use of isolating points or a turntable and roundhouse can also allow the possibility of storing more locos with duplicated codes for use as alternatives in the operating diagram.

Any of the locos can be called up via the control keyboard and operated using the speed and direction controls on the master. The addition of up to 3 slave control units permits the user to control 4 trains simultaneously. The total power consumption of the loco motors plus any coach lights etc., determines the number of trains which can be run at any one time using the 4 amps output of the 4 amp system transformer located in the master. With efficient modern motors it is perfectly feasible to run more than 4 trains and control them with the appropriate number of slaves. The total power drain is the only limiting factor (apart from the human brain and manual dexterity!).

The master control unit has the ability to run at least 4 trains simultaneously without the user needing any slave units at all. A simple keyboard operation allows the operator to call up 3 locos in turn, set them running, and leave them running at constant speeds whilst controlling the 4th loco with the master's speed and direction controls. This facility is particularly useful for the user with a twin track oval, for example, with a shunting yard complex and who wants to leave a couple of expresses moving whilst marshalling another train in the sidings.

The loco control modules can be coded by the user himself. The small printed circuit board which carries the 'chip' and the other components of the module has 4 copper 'tracks' printed on its edge. By using the 4-digit switching finger provided with the module any one of 16 codes can be allocated to the module. The user simply breaks off the appropriate combination of digits and clips the remaining fingers on to the edge of the module. The module with its coded switching finger attached is then fixed into the loco between the pickups and the motor. The connections are clip-fit and no soldering is required. The device is rated at 1 amp and can take 3 amps surge so it is capable of addition to some of the more efficient 0-gauge locos as well as the 00 and H0 products for which it was principally designed.

The coded loco module receives the pulse messages sent from the keyboard and speed controls via the micro-processor and reacts only when its own unique

Below and right: Slave Control Unit. Up to three of these can be added to the Master Control, allowing for operation of up to four trains at a time.

code is transmitted down the track. The module itself rectifies the 20 volts AC in the track and passes the appropriate amount of current to the standard 12 volt DC motor in the loco which then moves as instructed. The chip in the module has a memory which ensures then the loco obeys the last command given to it. Any interference caused by dirty track or poor contacts is therefore totally overcome.

The fact that the control takes place in the loco and not through variations in the current in the track has two implications. The first is that loco and coach lights can be kept permanently illuminated even when the trains are stationary because there is a constant voltage in the track. The second and major implication is that real shunting, marshalling and double heading of trains are possible without the isolation problems associated with conventional systems. In fact with Zero 1 you can even reproduce full speed head-on collisions! Zero 1 enhances the potential enjoyment which can be derived from the operating side of model railways' without reducing any of the fun of construction. For those enthusiasts whose particular bent is building different track systems Zero 1 has the added advantage that only one track connection is necessary so that the track layout can be changed almost at will without any worry about rewiring.

Additional operational realism is provided with the inclusion of 4 levels of inertia in the master control unit. The choice of an inertia level for a particular loco is completely up to the user and he can change the level as desired using the control keyboard. The level allocated to a loco depends on the type of loco, weight and length of train and layout configuration but with 4 levels, from a slow increase in the rate of acceleration and deceleration to a rapid increase, the user should be able to find an appropriate level for each train. Using inertia, as in real full size railways, the 'driver' has to judge when to start slowing down in order to bring the train to a halt in the platform and to avoid an embarrassing overshoot and consequent reversal.

The conversion of a layout for Zero 1 locomotive control must be total. Any loco without a Zero 1 loco module will not operate on the 20 volts AC of the Zero 1 system. For turnout and accessory control however, the enthusiast can operate his traditional turnout control system until the introduction on the Phase 2 modules and even then he can retain his traditional system in part or in total using separate 16 volt AC output of the master controller. The accessory module takes its power and instructions directly from the track and its coding finger and module allows for 69 different codes all addressable from the master control unit keyboard.

Glossary

Abutment supporting structure on each side of an arch or bridge.

Adhesion maintenance of contact between wheel and rail; the frictional grip of wheel to rail.

Alternating Current (AC) standard household current. A current that reverses its direction of flow at regular intervals. Each move from zero to maximum strength and back to zero is known as a cycle.

Ampere or **Amp** unit used to measure electrical strength.

Articulation steam locomotive having two sets of cylinders each driving an independent group of wheels supporting two sets of frames joined by a pivot or hinged joint.

Articulated locomotive applies to any locomotive featuring two or more sets of wheels and cylinders mounted on separate or hinged frames. Permits loco to pass over curves more easily.

ATC (Automatic Trail Control) term covering various systems designed to assist the driver and provide against his mishandling of the misinterpretation of signals. Range from simple cab warning systems to fully automatic control.

Automatic Coupler couplers which will couple and uncouple automatically through the use of uncoupling ramps, permanent or electro-magnets; permits remote operation as opposed to manual or hand methods.

Baggage car American term for luggage van.

Ballast material placed between the sleepers and formation of railway track to distribute the load of passing traffic, prevent lateral and longitudinal movement of the track, provide effective drainage and a convenient medium for maintaining level and gradient.

Ballast bed the layer of material spread over the formation on which the sleepers and track are laid.

Ballast materials crushed granite, whinstone, slag, limestone flints and ash are all materials in common use.

Banking assisting the working of a train, usually when ascending a gradient, by attaching one or more locomotives to the rear.

Baseboard. The baseboard is the structure carrying the model railway.

Bay platform. A bay platform (or bay road) is a short terminal platform let into a longer one, normally for terminating branch or local trains.

Bellows American term for corridor connections:— flexible connection or corridor providing access from the end of one carriage to another.

Big Boy popular name for largest steam locomotive, the 4–8–8–4 Union Pacific.

Body shell basic body section of vehicle without internal fittings.

Bogie (American truck) independent short wheel base truck with four or six wheels, capable of pivoting about the centre at which it is attached to the underframe of long vehicles.

Boiler steam producing unit. Locomotive type consists essentially of a fire box surrounded by a water space in which the combustion of fuel takes place, and barrel containing the flue tubes surrounded by water.

Bolster transverse floating beam member of bogie suspension system supporting the weight of vehicle body.

Box car American term for van or covered freight vehicle.

Branch-line minor line acting as a feeder to main trunk lines.

Cab enclosure on locomotive to shelter engineer, fireman, etc.

Cab Control means of operating and controlling one or more trains singly or simultaneously within model railroad (trains operating independent of one another's actions).

Caboose car (American term) for breakmen and other crew; office for conductor at rear of freight train; often used for temporary living quarters on long hauls.

Cant amount by which one rail of a curved track is raised above the other. Cant is 'positive' when the outer rail is higher than the inner rail and 'negative' when the inner rail is higher than the outer.

Car American term for carriage or wagon.

Catenary supporting cable for the contact or conductor wire of an overhead electrification system.

Chipboard:— Panel board made of wooden particles bonded together, American: Particle Board.

Clear signal fixed signal displaying a green, or proceed without restriction, aspect.

COFC (American term) container on flat car.

Converter machine for converting electric power from alternating current to direct current or vice versa.

Coupling (American, Coupler) device for connecting vehicles together. Many types in common use, ranging from simple three link to automatic which may also provide electrical and air services connections.

Crossing means by which a train on one line of track crosses another on same level.

Crossing loop additional line or loop on single line sections of railway to enable trains to cross or pass one another.

Crossover junction between two parallel railway tracks.

Current rate of flow of electricity round a circuit.

Curve classified as
1. simple—one of radious throughout
2. Compound—two or more simple curves of similar flexure
3. Reverse—a compound curve of contrary flexure.

Cutout Circuit Breaker a switch or fuse that automatically opens the circuit in the event of a current over-load.

Dead-end short section of running line terminating at buffer stops.

Dead man's handle device for cutting off power and applying the brakes in the event of the driver becoming incapacitated whilst driving.

Deck American term for cab floor or footplate.

Diagram display in diagrammatic form of track-work and signals controlled by a signalbox. The display may provide illuminated indications of signal and point operation, train positions, and descriptions.

Diesel compression ignition, internal combustion engine.

Direct current electrical current which flows in one direction continuously.

Distant Signal. Signal in British practice which provides a warning to approaching trains of the state of stop signals ahead.

Down-grade American term for falling gradient—down-hill.

Drawbar (American, Draft iron) device for connecting locomotive to tender or to train.

Drive transmission of power.

Drop side type of wagon where the vertical side is hinged horizontally and can be lowered to facilitate loading and unloading.

Dual gauge track able to accommodate vehicles of two different wheel gauges. Usually achieved by the laying of a third length of rail, one being common to both gauges.

Dumb Bell:— Model layout arrangement consisting of two reversing loops connected together, American:— 'Dog Bone'.

Earth Electrical connection to complete a circuit.

Embankment ridge of earth or rock to raise the natural ground level.

End-to-End Model layout consisting of a length of track with a terminal at each end, American:— 'Point-to-point'.

Engine commonly referred to as the locomotive.

Fiddle Yard a British modelling term for a set of sidings where trains are terminated and stored.

Firebox part of a steam locomotive boiler where combustion of the fuel takes place.

Fishplates pieces of metal for joining rail lengths together. Fitted on either side of the web of adjacent rails and held together by fish plates and rail webs.

Flange projecting edge or rim on the periphery of a wheel or rail.

Footplate (American, Deck) cab floor or operating platform of steam locomotive.

Free-lance modelling implies a model which is not directly based on an actual prototype. Good free-lance modelling does, however, owe allegiance to prototype practice, and can be justified by reference to actual examples.

Freight Yard a track arrangement used for the storage of freight cars.

Gauge standard measure; the distance between running edges or inner faces of the rails of railway track.

Goods British term for general freight.

Governor device for maintaining as closely as possible a constant engine crankshaft speed over long periods during which the load on the engine may vary.

Grade/gradient slope or inclination to the horizontal, as a percentage, or unit rise or fall to the horizontal or slope length.

Gravity shunting American gravity yard wagon sorting or train marshalling undertaken on a falling gradient without the aid of a shunting locomotive or switcher.

Grouping amalgamation of the major railway companies in England, Scotland & Wales to form the LMS, LNE, GW and S railways on 1st January, 1923.

Halt stopping place, without normal station facilities, for local train services.

Headshunt. A headshunt, or shunting neck, is a road running parallel with the main line, facing the goods yards. It is so arranged that shunting can take place along it, without interference with running on the main line.

Home signal semaphore stop signal, located close to signal box controlling entrance to next block section, station or junction area. In complicated track layouts there may also be outer and inner home signals.

Hooper freight vehicle with facility for discharging load through floor.

Horsebox: American term Wagon for the conveyance of horses.

Horsecar. American term.

Horse power a unit of power equal to 75kg metres per sec, 33,ooo ft per lb per min, or 746 watts.

Hot box an overheated vehicle axlebox bearing resulting from breakdown of lubricating film between bearing and journal.

Hump yard marshalling yard with artificial mound or hump over which wagons are propelled and then gravitate to correct siding and position in the yard.

Inspection car self propelled service vehicle used for inspecting track.

Interchange point, or the exchange, of passengers or freight between trains or modes of transport.

Island Platform an island platform is one with tracks on both faces.

Jacket American term for outer covering of thin sheet steel over the lagging material of a locomotive boiler, cylinder or other insulated heat radiating surface.

Journal log compiled by the guard of the make-up and events of train/movement.

Key wedge of hard wood or spring steel inserted between rail and chair to hold rail firmly in position at correct gauge.

Ladder American term for marshalling yard or siding layout where a series of points on switches follow each other giving leads off a straight line to one side.

Ladder term sometimes given to rack rail of mountain railway system.

Level crossing of two railways, or a railway and road, on the same level.

Light engine locomotive running without a train.

Limit of shunt board marking the point beyond which vehicles must not pass during shunting operations.

Lint Surgical bandage useful in model railway scenic work, American Cast Gauge.

Load gauge the limiting dimensions of height and width of rolling stock and loads carried to ensure adequate clearance with lineside structures.

Local line line of track normally exclusively used by suburban or stopping passenger trains.

Loop continuous circular connection between up and down lines at terminal station or yard enabling trains to reverse direction without releasing locomotive.

Loose coupled vehicles of a train loosely coupled together with three link couplings.

Lubricating oil viscous liquid introduced between moving surfaces to reduce friction.

Mail train express train including mail carrying vehicles which may have provision for letter sorting en route.

Main line primary trunk route running line used by fastest or most important trains.

Main track American term for 'Main Line'.

Marshalling yard area where wagons are sorted, assembled and marshalled into trains.

MBSO motorbrake second open carriage/car.

Motor bogie bogie having driving wheels or motored axles.

Motorman driver of an electric tram, railcar or multiple unit train.

Mountain railway specialized form of railway for ascending mountains.

Multiple-aspect signalling (MAS) a system of colour light signalling, that could be provided either by multi-lens, or searchlight signals in which each signal unit can display more than two aspects.

Multiple track a section of railway track having more than just one up line and one down line.

Multiple unit two or more locomotives or powered vehicles coupled together, or in a train, operated by only one driver.

Narrow gauge railway track of less than the standard gauge.

Normal usual position of points or signals before action initiated by signalman to allow a train movement.

Observation far passenger-carrying vehicle, usually at rear of train, with windows and seating arranged to give maximum view of passing scenery.

Overhead catenary and contact wire of a suspended electrical distribution system.

Packing maintaining the correct level of sleepers by adjustments in the amount of ballast beneath.

Panel desk or board on which operating switches for points and signals are mounted.

Pantograph link between overhead contact system and power circuit of an electric locomotive or multiple unit through which the power required is transmitted. Simplest form is spring loaded pivoted diamond frame with copper or carbon contact strip.

Parlor car American term for luxuriously fitted railway carriage.

Permanent Way Term for track-bed and tracks in position.

Pick-up electric current collector.

Pick-up freight train which stops at intermediate points to pick up or put off freight vehicles on an as required basis.

Piggy-back system for conveying road vehicles on railway flat cars or wagons.

Pilot American term for cowcatcher.

Pilot additional locomotive coupled to the front of the train locomotive to provide assistance over a heavy graded section of line.

Platelayer Track maintenance man.

Platelayer's hut small shed for use of platelayers, American section house.

Point assembly of trackwork including a tapered movable rail by which a train is directed from one line to another.

Power Unit a device which converts high-voltage mains current into low voltage currents, often with several outputs.

Pulse Power a system whereby the locomotive is fed intermittent pulses of current.

Pullman car railway carriage providing a high standard of comfort and service for which a supplementary fare must be paid.

Rail car self-propelled passenger carrying vehicle.

Reefer American term for regulating the speed of freight vehicles running down a hump in mechanised marshalling yards. Another name for rail brake.

Reversing station point where train reverses direction of travel during course of journey. May be at normal dead end or terminal station layout or on zig-zag section of steeply graded line.

Right of way precedence given to one train to proceed before another.

Rolling stock carriages and wagons; railway vehicles.

Round house engine shed in which the locomotive stabling berths radiate from a turntable.

Scenic Break a scenic break is a deliberate block introduced to disguise the fact that the main line links two sections of a scenic layout which either clash or should, in practice, be widely separated.

Scissor crossing junction between two parallel railway tracks enabling trains to cross over from one to the other in either direction.

Semaphore type of fixed signal with a pivoted arm which can be raised or lowered as required. Of two general types 'upper' and 'lower' quadrant. In both, the arm in horizontal position denotes 'on', 'stop' or 'danger'.

Semi-conductor material used in electric traction rectifiers, whose electrical resistance depends on the direction of the applied voltage. Germanium and Silicon are typical examples.

Siding line used for temporary stabling or accommodation of vehicles or trains, American: Spur.

Starter Signal Signal in British practice which gives authority to a train to proceed into a block section.

Shunt American term switch direct onto a minor track; marshal vehicles into a particular order.

Shuttle train which gives a frequent return service over a short route.

Siding line used for temporary stabling or accommodation of vehicles or trains.

Signal means of controlling the movement of trains by warning or advising the driver of the occupational state of the line ahead or intention to divert to another route or line.

Signal box (American, Tower) building housing equipment for operation of points and signals in a particular area or section of route.

Silo American term for sand storage tower for filling locomotive sand boxes.

Six-footway area between parallel railway tracks.

Skew bridge spans obliquely and is therefore longer than the square gap.

Slab track rails laid on a continuous concrete or asphalt base instead of conventional sleepers and ballast, to minimize settlement and changes in alignment, thus reducing maintenance costs.

Sleeper steel, wood or precast concrete beam for holding the rails to correct gauge and distributing to the ballast the load imposed by passing trains.

Snow plough special vehicle propelled by, or attachment to, front of locomotive to remove snow from railway. The snow plough may be of simple wedge shape or rotary type.

Snow shed substantially built shed with sloping roof erected over the railway to provide a path for avalanches without blocking the line.

Solebar longitudinal main frame outer member of carriage or wagon under-frame, usually of channel section.

Soleplate longitudinal main frame member of fabricated or built up carriage bogie, usually of standard rolled steel section of pressings. Also a plate inserted between the chairs and the sleeper at a pair of points to maintain the correct gauge and prevent any spreading of the gauge that might occur from the gradual enlargement of the spike holes in the wooden sleepers.

Spark arrester device, usually in the form of a mesh or baffle plate fitted in the smoke box to prevent the emission of live coals and sparks from the chimney or smoke stack.

Special train one not shown in the working time table or pre-planned.

Spike square section heavy steel nail driven into wooden sleeper to affix flanged rail in position.

Spot American term—to marshall or shunt.

Stabling accommodating for a short period of time.

Staff wooden staff which must be carried by each train travelling on single line section of railway branch line to maintain absolute block working and prevent possibility of head-on collision.

Stagger interlacing of sleepers at switches and crossing or, making rail joints in one running rail not to coincide with those in other rail.

Standard gauge most common distance between rails in a country.

Stock car American term for vehicle used for the conveyance of cattle.

Stub American term for short dead end siding.

Stub axle short non-revolving axle which supports only one wheel.

Stud Contact. Similar to 3-rail, but the conductor rail is replaced by a row of energised stus along the centre of the track. A long collector skate on the locomotive picks up current. Used by Märklin and in O gauge. Some old OO-gauge 3-rail systems have been converted to this system.

Superelevation see Cant.

Suspension connecting system, including springs, between vehicle wheel and body, designed to give best possible riding qualities by keeping unsprung weights to a minimum and reducing shock loadings on track. Switch device for opening and closing electrical circuit.

Switch American term for points.

Synchronous electric motor whose speed varies in direct proportion to the frequency of the supply.

Tank locomotive one which carries its fuel and water supplies on its own main frames.

Tank wagon freight vehicle designed to carry liquids or gases in a tank like container.

Tender locomotive one which carries its fuel and/or water supplies in a separate semi-permanently coupled vehicle.

Tender first tender locomotive running with tender leading in direction of travel.

Terminal—the end of the line (or departure point); includes the station, switches, associated buildings, towers and other equipment.

Three-way point or switch making connections to three alternative routes.

Three-rail, Current is fed from a centre or side conductor rail, return is through the uninsulated wheels and track: now obsolete.

Tie American term for sleeper.

Tin Plate—Commonly associated with toy trains that do not conform to scale or gauge standards. The name 'tin plate' originated during the last century when many an early model, crude or otherwise, was fashioned out of tin.

Tipping wagon freight vehicle with facility for unloading contents by tilting body.

Toe tip of switch rail at the end which fits against the stock rail.

Token authority for train to enter single line section. Of different forms including wooden staff, electric staff, tablet, key token. Each unique and engraved with names of stations at each end of single line section to which they apply.

Tongue switch blade or rail.

Tower American term for signal box. Control centre of mechanized marshalling yard.

Trace graphical record of track alignment produced by recording instruments located in a vehicle travelling over the line.

Tail lamp lamp affixed to, or illuminated if an integral part of, the rear end of the last vehicle, to indicate the train is complete.

Trailing points switches which connect converging lines in direction of travel.

Trailer Truck—A rear locomotive truck with two or four small wheels.

Tramway light railway or rails for tram-cars.

Tramcar (American, Streetcar) electrically operated public service passenger vehicle on rails in the street.

Transformer device which by electro-magnetic induction converts one voltage of alternating current to another.

Trolley pole mounted on a roof of electric vehicle with wheel attached to outer end to pick up electric current from overhead contact wire.

Truck—The assembly that supports a car of locomotive and houses the wheels and axles.

Turnout—A section of track that turns out from the mainline, often referred to as a switch.

Turntable—A rotating device that enables you to turn locomotives completely around, or to spot them for roundhouse stalls.

Two-rail. Current is fed along both rails of the track, the rails and wheels being insulated from one another. The normal method of supply.

Tyre (American, Tire) steel band forming the periphery of a wheel on which the flange and tread profile is formed.

Underbridge underline bridge carrying the railway over a gap, road, river or whatever.

Underframe framework or structure which supports the body of a carriage or wagon.

Underpass—A roadway going beneath an overpass, scenic effect, bridge, overhang, etc.

Up-line line over which trains normally travel towards the headquarters of the railway company concerned.

Up-train one which travels on or in the direction of the up line.

Van covered vehicle for conveyance of luggage, goods or use of guard.

Vanderbilt Tender—A cylindrical-shaped tender featuring a partially squared-off front; used for either coal or oil and especially popular among model rails.

Vestibule covered gangway giving access between vehicles.

Voltage electromotive force (analogous to a pressure) measured in volts.

Wagon railway vehicle for the conveyance of goods.

Wheel set pair of wheels secured to an axle.

White Spirit:— Mineral Spring used for thinning oil-based paint, American Napthan.

Wing rail continuous running rail forming the obtuse angle of a diamond crossing. Also running rail from switch heel towards nose which is then set to form check rail past nose of common crossing.

Worm Gear—A gear with slightly slanted or dished teeth to mesh with the worm. In model railroading the worm gear is usually mounted on the driving axle.

Wye—A triangular shaped track arrangement used as a junction, and for turning trains and engines.

Yard—A group of tracks, generally within an enclosed area where switching chores are performed for storage, classification.

Zamac—Trade name for zinc-aluminium alloy die-casting metal used widely for pressure die-casting in model trains.

Index

Acknowledgements

The Publishers would like to thank the following companies for their assistance and loan of models for the photography in this book.

MEGA Models Ltd.
26 Rathbone Place
London W1P 1DJ.

Ted's Engine House
6307 Westfield Avenue
Pennsauken, N.J. 08108
U.S.A.

Victors (Model Railways) Ltd.
166 Pentonville Road
London N1 9JL.

Illustrations and artwork by

Lyn. D. Brooks
Roger Courthold
Bob Stoneman
Nigel Waller

L. D. Brooks 129, 130; Bruce Chubb 77, 86 below, 198, 199, 200, 201, 202, 203, 204, 205, 207; Colourviews Picture Library 97 Patrick Whitehouse; Harry Drummond 116, 117, 118, 119; Mike Dyers Associates 4, 5, 8, 9, 13, 14, 15, 16, 19, 21, 23, 24, 27, 32, 34, 35, 36, 37, 43, 51, 58, 75, 81, 82, 83, 98, 99, 100, 101, 102, 103, 104, 105, 107, 108, 109, 110, 111, 112, 113, 114, 115, 120, 121, 122, 123, 126, 127 left, 128, 133, 139, 140, 141, 143, 144, 148, 151, 152, 153, 154, 156, 157, 159, 160, 161, 170, 172, 173, 174, 175, 176, 177, 208, 209; Rolf Ertmen 41, 67, 135, 166, 167, 168, 169; Laurie Franklyn 38, 39, 63, 195, 196, 197; Phillip Godfrey 68, 69, 84, 86 above, 190, 191, 192, 193; Phillip Gray 11; Bob Hegge 125, 178, 179, 180, 181, 182, 183, 184, 185, 186, 187, 188, 189; Hornby 18, 22, 212, 213; W. Allen McClelland 30; Brian Monaghan Back endpapers, front endpapers, 2, 3, 12, 25, 26, 29, 33, 40, 57, 61, 64, 71, 89, 91, 95, 163; Don Santel 4, 5; John Van Reimsdijk 2